Rough Consensus

Rough Consensus

How Engineers, Hackers, and Spies
Built the Internet

Michael J Bommarito II

First Edition

2026

Rough Consensus:
How Engineers, Hackers, and Spies Built the Internet

Cover design and typesetting by the author. Printed in the United States of America.

Book Website: `builttheinternet.com`

Author Website: `michaelbommarito.com`

ISBN 979-8-9947460-0-4 (paperback)

ISBN 979-8-9947460-1-1 (ebook)

Publisher's Cataloging-in-Publication Data
Names: Bommarito, Michael J., II, author.
Title: Rough consensus :
how engineers, hackers, and spies built the internet / Michael J Bommarito II.
Description: First edition. | Michigan : 2026. | Includes bibliographical references.
Identifiers: ISBN 979-8-9947460-0-4 (paperback) | ISBN 979-8-9947460-1-1 (ebook)
Subjects: LCSH:
Internet—History.
Computer network protocols—History.
Internet—Security measures.
Computer security.
Data protection.

Classification: LCC TK5105.875.I57 B66 2026 | DDC 004.678—dc23

For the engineers who built a network on trust,
and for those who keep it running despite everything.

For Steve Crocker, who asked the first question.

But most especially,
in memory of Jon Postel (1943–1998) and Dan Kaminsky (1979–2021),
who trusted the network and gave it their lives.

CONTENTS

====================================

PROLOGUE

I grew up on the internet in the 1990s, when logging on felt like heading west on a trail full of new friends and strange stories.

Back then, the internet felt like it belonged to us—the ones who showed up, learned the protocols, contributed. No algorithms decided what we should see. No platforms constrained what we could build. No advertisements followed us across sites. No paid influencers drowned out the genuine chatter on `comp.lang.lisp`. And nothing stopped you from port scanning half the internet.

The system wasn't watching back. For better or worse, neither was anyone else.

We didn't know then that these were the last years of something magical. The network we loved ran on assumptions it could not prove, and those assumptions were about to meet the world it was swallowing.

This book is about those assumptions.

The engineers who built the internet assumed trust. They were colleagues, a few hundred people who often knew each other by first name. When they wrote protocols for sending mail or resolving addresses or routing packets, they did not add authentication. Who needs authentication when you work with the person, when you bike past their house every day, when you'll see them next month? The authentication layer was external, because the entire network fit inside a single small social circle.

Today it's different. It's been decades since the internet lived within two degrees of social connection. Now it carries the banking system, the power grid, the hospitals, and the elections. More than five billion people—some of them adversarial—rely on infrastructure built for a few thousand friends and acquaintances.

But despite how much has changed, the protocols still trust.

This book is an apology to the people and the assumptions that got us here. The evidence they left behind (the RFCs, starting with the one that apologized for existing; the decades of decisions made by people who couldn't see the cliff and built anyway; the hope, in every one of them, that someone on the next network would be a friend) is still with us. It is the whole archive, and this book is built from it.

Most of the time, they were right. Some of the time, they were wrong.

This is the story of what they built, what broke, and what still works. It begins, prophetically, with a crash and an apology.

PART I

THE NETWORK

CHAPTER 1

THE REQUEST FOR COMMENTS

Very little of what is here is firm and reactions are expected.

— Steve Crocker, RFC 1, April 7, 1969

It's late on the night of October 29, 1969, and Room 3420 of Boelter Hall is lit by fluorescent tubes and the glow of a teletype terminal. Charley Kline, a twenty-one-year-old student programmer at UCLA, sits at the keyboard of an SDS Sigma 7, a hulking mainframe that costs more than most houses. Beside him a telephone receiver lies off its hook, the line open to Stanford Research Institute, three hundred fifty miles north.

On the other end, Bill Duvall waits at his own terminal, an SDS 940. Between them runs something new: a fifty-kilobit leased line connecting two Interface Message Processors—refrigerator-sized computers that will route messages across this experimental network. Four machines in total. Two universities. One idea about to be tested.

Kline types "L."

"Got the L," Duvall confirms through the telephone handset.

Kline types "O."

"Got the O."

Kline types "G"—and the host-to-IMP software crashes. The connection dies. The first message ever sent across the network that will become the internet is two letters long: `LO`.

Leonard Kleinrock, the professor supervising from across the room, would later say their "lo" "could not have been a more succinct, a more powerful or a more prophetic message."[1] Lo and behold. As if the network knew what it was becoming and announced itself with accidental poetry. Decades later, the filmmaker Werner Herzog named his documentary about the internet *Lo and Behold* in tribute to those two letters.

Within an hour, Kline and Duvall got the full `LOGIN` working. The bug was fixed; the connection held. But the crash came first. Before the network carried its first complete word, it had already failed and recovered. That pattern—break, fix, keep running—would repeat for the next fifty years.

No one in Room 3420 imagined five billion users. They couldn't imagine email, the web, ransomware, online banking. They imagined researchers at four universities sharing files. The world they built for was the world they knew—a few hundred people, a handful of nodes, problems measured in kilobytes.

Six months earlier, another graduate student had set this moment in motion—though he had no idea what he was starting.

1.1. THE FIRST NOTE

Steve Crocker was twenty-four years old, a graduate student at UCLA, and he had a problem no one was solving.

The Advanced Research Projects Agency had funded four universities to connect their computers. UCLA would be the first node, followed by Stanford Research Institute, UC Santa Barbara, and the University of Utah. Bolt, Beranek and Newman was building the IMPs in Cambridge. The hardware would handle routing. But no one had specified what the computers themselves should say to each other once connected.

Crocker and his fellow students had been waiting for the protocol documents to arrive from the East Coast. MIT, Harvard, BBN—someone there would surely take the lead. Weeks passed. The first IMP was scheduled for delivery in September. Nothing came from the East.[2]

So Crocker decided to write something himself.

The problem was authority. He had none. "We were just a bunch of graduate students," Crocker would later explain, "and we didn't have the authority to issue specifications or standards."[3] If he published something that sounded too official, the established researchers might dismiss it. Or worse, take offense that a student had presumed to dictate terms.

Crocker wrote late at night in his apartment, away from the computer lab and its distractions, terrified of getting it wrong. The document he was drafting would end up shaping how the internet developed. He had no way of knowing that; what he knew was the fear.

His solution was linguistic. Rather than call his document a specification or a standard, Crocker chose a title that disclaimed authority: Request for Comments. Not a proclamation but an invitation. The title signaled he expected pushback, that nothing was settled, that the document was provisional by design.[4]

The opening words reinforced this humility:

> RFC 1 --- April 7, 1969 --- Steve Crocker
>
> Very little of what is here is firm and reactions are expected.

The message was clear: argue with me. Tell me where I'm wrong. We'll figure this out together.

He numbered the document "1" and sent it to the other sites on April 7, 1969.

Two weeks later, Crocker published RFC 3, which codified the humility into formal policy. "The content of a NWG note may be any thought, suggestion, etc. related to the HOST software or other aspect of the network," he wrote. "Notes are encouraged to be timely rather than polished." The minimum length for a contribution was one sentence. There would be no gatekeeping, no peer review, no committee approval. If you had an idea, you wrote it down and sent it out.[5]

The humility did real work. In Crocker's system, nobody had to tell anyone they were wrong; you published an alternative instead. RFC 4 could contradict RFC 3, and both stayed in the archive. Ideas competed, and the ones that won were the ones somebody actually implemented.

But there was an assumption buried in the process, one so obvious that nobody bothered to state it. Crocker was writing for colleagues. The Network Working Group that would review his documents numbered perhaps two dozen people scattered across four universities. Trust was built into the system because trust already existed in the room.

No one asked what would happen when the room got bigger.

The Network Working Group had no charter and no budget. Crocker led it because he was willing to do the work. It was a frontier settlement, a few people in unmapped territory making up the rules as they went, and meetings happened wherever people could gather: a conference room at UCLA, a borrowed office at Stanford, the margins of academic conferences. Invitations did not exist. If you cared about the problem, you showed up.

At the time, Jon Postel was a quiet, bearded man surrounded by creeping stacks of paper. The stacks weren't clutter—they were the original RFC filing system, and they would migrate with him from his UCLA office to USC's Information Sciences Institute. Jon assigned numbers, caught typos, and made sure anyone who wanted to contribute could find what had come before. It wasn't a formal position. No one had appointed him; he just did it because it had to be done.

For nearly thirty years, until his death in 1998, Postel would remain the RFC Editor, giving the system an institutional memory that would prove critical to its success.

Vint Cerf faced his own obstacle: he had been hard of hearing since boyhood, leaning on hearing aids to follow the conversation in crowded meeting rooms. He attended when his schedule allowed—a student like the others, working on the networking protocols that would one day become `TCP/IP`. Years later, he and his wife Sigrid—who had been deaf since early childhood—would become well-known advocates for the technology they relied on at home, email chief among the tools that let them communicate.

This cast of characters, largely graduate students in their mid-twenties, was betting on an idea that most telephone engineers considered absurd. The entire Bell System ran on circuit switching: when you dialed a number, the network reserved a dedicated wire between your phone and the other person's. The line was yours for the duration of the call. If you paused to think, the circuit sat idle. If the wire was cut, the call dropped. Wasteful, but predictable—and it had worked for a century.

Packet switching dispensed with the dedicated line. A message was chopped into small pieces called packets, each stamped with a destination and released into the network to find its own way; different pieces might travel different routes and reassemble at the far end. Nothing was reserved and nothing sat idle. When a path failed, the packets simply went around it. What the scheme required instead of a plan was cooperation between the machines at each end, and that cooperation was exactly what Crocker's group had to define.

So they worked the way the network did: in small pieces, routed by need. Crocker published an RFC proposing how hosts should begin a conversation. Someone at SRI found a flaw. Crocker published a revision. Postel assigned it a number and filed the original alongside it—nothing was deleted, nothing overwritten. The cycle repeated, each round producing something slightly more refined. Someone would sketch an idea on a chalkboard. Then someone else would try to implement it. If the code worked, the idea stuck. If it broke, someone wrote another RFC proposing a fix.

By the end of 1969, the network Kline and Duvall had tested that October night connected four nodes. By 1971, fifteen.[6] By 1973, thirty-seven. Each new node made the network more useful and the community slightly larger—but still small enough that everyone knew everyone.

The norms grew out of shared work and mutual dependence rather than any charter. "Rough consensus and running code," the motto David Clark would finally put into words at a 1992 IETF meeting, described a culture that had been in practice for more than two decades by then.[7] You earned your reputation by contributing, you registered disagreement by publishing an alternative, and what kept people honest was shame rather than enforcement—in a community that small, a bad reputation outran you.

These are frontier norms. They work beautifully when the group fits in a room. And still the protocols assumed it always would.

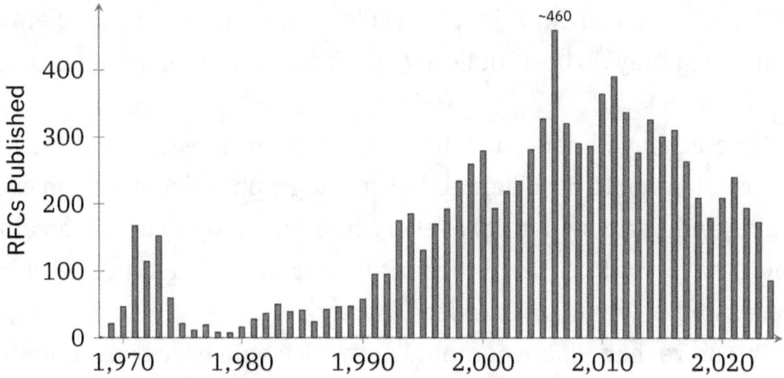

Figure 1.1: RFC publications by year, 1968–2024. From a single document in 1968 to nearly ten thousand today, the RFC archive traces the internet's growth. Peak production occurred in 2006 with approximately 460 RFCs.

1.2. THE BET

RFC 1 contains an assumption so fundamental that Crocker never wrote it down. He didn't need to. Everyone reading the document already knew.

The assumption is trust.

Crocker was writing for a club with fewer than a hundred members. They met in conference rooms and shared hotel bars at workshops. If someone misbehaved—sent junk traffic, ignored a specification, acted in bad faith—everyone would know by the next meeting. Social consequences enforced cooperation more effectively than any authentication mechanism could.

So the protocols inherited this DNA. Messages came from who they claimed to come from. Software would be used as its authors intended. Mistakes were honest. Malice was unthinkable—not globally, not in the world at large, but here, in this room, among these colleagues.

Some might call this naive. It wasn't—it was engineers and scientists doing what they do best: building an efficient solution to the problem *they* faced.

It could have been built the other way. A network designed for adversaries would have demanded cryptographic signatures on every packet and proof of identity at every hop. In 1969 the overhead alone would have sunk it: the entire internet ran on machines with less processing power than a modern thermostat.

But more than that: a paranoid network would have been a slow network. A complex network. A network that graduate students couldn't build in their spare time, that couldn't grow through informal collaboration, that couldn't accumulate protocols through rough consensus and running code.

So the engineers chose simplicity over paranoia and speed over verification, and they bet that the frontier would stay a frontier—that the people using the network would remain the kind of people building it.

The bet paid off for nineteen years. The network grew from four nodes to sixty thousand hosts. Email spread. File transfer worked. Remote login connected researchers across continents. The protocols did exactly what they were designed to do, in exactly the environment they were built for.

The cost of the bet came due on a single evening in November 1988.

1.3. NOVEMBER 2, 1988

1.3.1. THE RELEASE

How big was the internet in 1988?

No one actually knew. The network that had connected four universities in 1969 now linked roughly sixty thousand hosts—universities, government labs, defense contractors, research hospitals.[8] But there was no central registry, no master list. The network had grown the way the protocols had: organically, node by node, with nobody keeping count. The number sixty thousand was an estimate, and not a confident one.

Robert Tappan Morris wanted a real answer. He was twenty-two, a first-year graduate student at Cornell, and the son of a cryptographer.[9] His father had helped build Unix's password encryption at Bell Labs with Ken Thompson and would later become chief scientist at the NSA's National Computer Security Center. The younger Morris had grown up debugging code with his father. He understood how computers worked, and how they failed.

Counting every machine on a network with no central directory was its own problem. You could ask system administrators, but there were thousands of them and no list that reached them all. You could scan for addresses, but the address space was vast and mostly empty. Or you could write a program that counted for you—one that copied itself from machine to machine, hopping along the connections the network was built on, tallying hosts as it went. A census taker that traveled the network on its own.

Morris wrote the program. It would slip quietly from host to host, check whether it had already visited, and move on. When it finished, he'd have his number.

On the evening of November 2, he logged into a machine at MIT.[10] Not Cornell—he didn't want the program traced back to his home institution. Sometime after 8:30 PM Eastern, he released it.

It worked. It worked too well.

1.3.2. THE SPREAD

The worm exploited four vulnerabilities, and each one reflected the trust assumptions that had shaped the ARPANET from the beginning.[11]

To understand how, start with what these machines were. The computers on the 1988 internet weren't personal—they were shared. A university might have one or two big Unix systems, and dozens of researchers would log into the same machine at the same time, each running their own terminal session. Behind the scenes, programs called **daemons** ran constantly in the background, handling requests. The name comes from Maxwell's demon—the thought experiment about a creature that sorts molecules without being told to. A mail daemon accepted incoming messages. A print daemon managed the queue for the printer down the hall. Each daemon listened and waited, trusting that the requests it received were legitimate.

`sendmail` was the mail daemon on most Unix systems. It had a debug mode—a testing backdoor that allowed remote administration. The mode should have been disabled on production machines. Often it wasn't. Morris's worm sent commands through the debug interface that made `sendmail` download and execute the worm code. The program assumed administrators would configure it safely. They hadn't.

`fingerd`—the finger daemon—answered a simpler question: who's logged in right now? On a shared machine with thirty users, this mattered. If you wanted to know whether a colleague was at her desk before walking across campus, you could type `finger sue@stanford` and find out. The `fingerd` daemon would accept the query, look up the answer, and send it back. But the program trusted its input without checking how much data was arriving. Morris sent far more data than `fingerd` expected, and the excess spilled past the program's memory boundaries, overwriting the machine's own instructions with new ones—instructions that told the computer to execute the worm. This technique, stuffing more data into a program than it has room for, would later be named a **buffer overflow**. It remains among the most common vulnerabilities in software today.

The third vulnerability was a feature, not a bug. Unix machines could trust one another through files called `.rhosts`—if you'd authenticated on machine A, machine B would let you in without a password. Researchers used it constantly. Who wants to type credentials every time they switch between the machines in their own lab? Morris's worm exploited this chain: once it compromised one machine, it could walk through the network as that machine's trusted guest.

The fourth vector was the most elemental. The worm carried a dictionary of 432 common words and tried them as passwords against the Unix `/etc/passwd` file. It also tried the username itself, the username reversed, and the username doubled. The system trusted users to choose strong passwords. Many hadn't. A researcher who chose "password" or their own name handed Morris's worm the keys.

Morris had intended a slow, invisible propagation. His worm would check whether a machine was already infected before copying itself, but he worried administrators might fake infection to inoculate their systems. So he added an override: one time in seven, the worm would reinstall anyway.

The one-in-seven ratio was wrong. A machine did not get infected once; it got reinfected, again and again, every new copy of the worm claiming its own share of memory and processing power. Machines meant to run a few dozen programs were running hundreds. They froze, rebooted, and were immediately reinfected.

By morning, roughly six thousand machines were compromised—about ten percent of the internet.[8]

1.3.3. THE RESPONSE

There was no playbook. No incident response teams. No security mailing lists. The network had no procedure for surviving a graduate student.

System administrators discovered the problem when their machines slowed, then froze. They called each other on telephones—the same telephones the network was supposed to replace. Comparing symptoms, pulling cables from walls, powering down servers. The most primitive defense imaginable: if the worm spreads through the network, cut the network.

Morris realized his mistake that night. He called Andrew Sudduth, a computer manager at Harvard, and asked him to distribute instructions for killing the worm. Sudduth sent the message anonymously—but the network was already too clogged to carry it. The cure couldn't reach the patients.[12]

Morris also called a friend—Paul Graham, a graduate student at Harvard. Graham suggested writing a second program to kill the first. Morris refused. "I had messed up with the first one," he later testified, "and it didn't appear that I would be able to do any better the second time."[12]

Graham, testifying as a prosecution witness, would later defend Morris's intentions while faulting his execution. "I said, 'You idiot,' " Graham told the jury. "It was such a good idea and he just blew it. I was so mad."[12]

In the worm's aftermath, DARPA asked Carnegie Mellon's Software Engineering Institute to establish a computer emergency response team.[13,14] CERT/CC would coordinate responses to future incidents, publish advisories, serve as a clearinghouse. The internet needed a fire department. Now it had one.

Before the week was out, an anonymous tip to the *New York Times* revealed Morris's identity. Investigators traced the worm back to him.

In 1990, Morris became the first person convicted under the Computer Fraud and Abuse Act of 1986.[15] The sentence: three years probation, four hundred hours of community service, $10,050 in fines.

1.3.4. THE AFTERMATH

Morris did not go to prison. He became a tenured professor at MIT. And in 2005, he co-founded a company with the friend he had called that November night. The company was Y Combinator.

Y Combinator became Silicon Valley's most influential startup accelerator, funding Airbnb, Dropbox, Stripe, Reddit, and thousands of other companies. Anyone who had written an early RFC would have recognized the philosophy: launch fast, fix problems when they find you, trust that your users will behave. Morris had stress-tested that bet by accident in 1988. His own institution went on to teach it to a generation of founders, many of whom repeated it at enormous scale, collecting user data with the same breezy confidence in good faith that had shaped the protocols themselves.

Graham had called it "such a good idea." Y Combinator would make a business of such good ideas.

The conviction didn't end Morris's career. It barely interrupted it. But it did end something else.

None of the vulnerabilities the worm exploited were new. `sendmail`'s debug mode was in the manual. Buffer overflows were a known class of bug. The `.rhosts` trust chain was a feature that administrators relied on every day. Everyone knew these things were there. Nobody had thought to ask what happened when someone used them all at once.

After the worm, they started asking. System administrators disabled debug modes, tightened password policies, reconsidered which machines should trust which. CERT published advisories. Firewalls went up. Intrusion detection systems appeared on networks that had never needed monitoring.

The protocols underneath didn't change. IP still delivered packets without checking who sent them. TCP still opened connections on faith. The trust was still there, woven into every layer. The new defenses went on top, and they have been going on top ever since.

Crocker is still at it. More than fifty years after he numbered that first document and sent it to three other universities, he still shows up to working group meetings, still contributes to standards. When interviewers ask whether he regrets building protocols without security, he says what he has always said: the network would never have grown if they had designed it for adversaries.[3]

He's right, and that's the hard part. The trust was never a mistake. That trust was why any of it worked—the reason four nodes could become four million, the reason a handful of graduate students could build something that five billion people would one day depend on. A system that demanded cryptographic proof before every connection would have been a smaller system, a slower one, and almost certainly not the one that ended up carrying the world's banking, medical records, and elections. The vulnerability and the miracle were the same thing.

The RFCs kept accumulating—more than nine thousand by 2025, each one a quiet act of faith that strangers would implement it honestly. The trust was broken on a November night in 1988, and the trust held anyway. The packets kept flowing. They still are.

But the worm was only the beginning. Nobody turned off the trust. Passwords went on crossing the wire in plain text, any machine could still claim any address, and the packets kept getting routed on faith, the way they always had.

The next test wouldn't come from a graduate student with a census program. It would come from a spy.

CHAPTER 2

THE REMOTE LOGIN

The function of the Telnet process
is to make a terminal at a user site
appear over the network as logically equivalent
to a terminal "directly" connected to the server site.

— RFC 97, February 1971[16]

2.1. THE VERY LONG CORD

John Melvin sat in front of a Teletype at Stanford Research Institute in early 1971, typing commands that would travel three hundred fifty miles. The machine in front of him was a hulking beige rectangle—its keyboard mechanical, its printhead clacking with each character. Anyone walking past would think he was using a local computer.

He wasn't. The machine he was talking to was at UCLA. And that was the whole point—making the network disappear, making the terminal lie so convincingly that the distance between two cities collapsed into the click of a key.

In 1971, computing resources were precious. A single mainframe might cost a million dollars. If you needed software that existed only at another institution, your options were limited: fly there, ship data on tape, or beg for an account. The ARPANET promised something better. Connect the computers, and researchers could share them.

Terminals were the obstacle.

Every computer manufacturer had invented its own way of talking to humans. An IBM terminal sent different codes than a DEC terminal. The control characters that moved a cursor, cleared a screen, or signaled the end of a line varied from system to system. If you connected a UCLA terminal to a machine at MIT, nothing worked right. The cursor would jump. The backspace key might print garbage. Even the concept of a "line" meant different things to different machines.

Melvin and his colleague Richard Watson were trying to solve this at SRI. Their solution was published in February 1971 as RFC 97: "A First Cut at a Proposed Telnet Protocol."[16]

The core idea was elegant. Instead of requiring every terminal type to understand every computer type, they invented a fictional terminal: the **Network Virtual Terminal**, the `NVT`. Your terminal speaks its own dialect; the `NVT` speaks a common language; the remote computer speaks yet another. The `NVT` sits in the middle, converting between them. It had a keyboard that could generate all 128 ASCII character codes and a printer that understood a standard set of control characters. The `NVT` was deliberately simple: no graphics, no color, just text.

The protocol worked like this: the user's `Telnet` client translated their local terminal's quirks into `NVT` format. The `NVT` data traveled over the wire. At the server side, another `Telnet` process translated from `NVT` into whatever the local machine expected. The user saw their familiar terminal; the server saw its familiar input.

"The user should be able to cause generation of all codes which a server system terminal can generate," Melvin and Watson wrote.

Remote access was useless if it felt foreign. The point was to create an illusion: you were there, even though you weren't.

The protocol evolved over the next twelve years, and by May 1983, when Postel and Joyce Reynolds published RFC 854, `Telnet` had matured into a proper standard.[17] The `NVT` was carefully specified, the option negotiation system—DO, DON'T, WILL, and WON'T commands—was formalized, and remote login finally had a complete specification.

Reynolds was Postel's closest collaborator at ISI, and together they authored dozens of RFCs. RFC 854 was one of many—methodical, thorough, precise.

The specification Postel and Reynolds wrote assumed something that seemed obvious in 1983: the network was private. They focused on mechanics: how characters were transmitted, how options were negotiated, how the `NVT` translated between systems. They never discussed encryption. Authentication beyond a login prompt went unmentioned.

In their world, it was a trusted wire between friends.

2.2. THE ILLUSION

2.2.1. HOW TELNET WORKS

Think of `Telnet` as a very long cord plugging your keyboard into a distant computer.

When you type, your keystrokes travel over the wire. When the computer responds, its output travels back. If the connection is fast enough, you feel like you're sitting at the remote machine. The network becomes invisible.

That invisibility cuts both ways—when the wire disappears, so does everyone else who might be on it.

A `Telnet` client opens a `TCP` connection to port 23 on the server. A port is like an apartment number. The `IP` address gets you to the right building; the number on the door tells you where to knock once you are inside, and `Telnet` answers at door 23 the way the web answers at 80 and mail at 25. `TCP` keeps the packets flowing in order underneath, and `Telnet` rides on top of it, carrying your keystrokes exactly as you typed them.

The connection starts with option negotiation. Both sides agree on ground rules: echo, binary mode, terminal type. The server sends "DO ECHO"; the client responds "WILL" or "WON'T." None of this is encrypted, so an eavesdropper sees the setup and watches everything that follows.

RFC 854 describes this negotiation:

```
RFC 854 --- May 1983 --- Postel & Reynolds

The basic strategy for setting up the use of options is
to have either party (or both) initiate a request that
some option take effect. The other party may then either
accept or reject the request. If the request is accepted
the option immediately takes effect; if it is rejected the
associated aspect of the connection remains as specified
for an NVT.
```

Once the options are settled, the connection becomes a bidirectional stream of characters. You type; the characters go to the server. The server runs your commands; the output comes back. Every keystroke crosses the network. The illusion depends on low latency.

The Network Virtual Terminal sits at the heart of this. Both ends pretend they're talking to an `NVT`, translating to and from their local conventions. The NVT uses seven-bit ASCII. Carriage return followed by line feed means "new line." Specific control codes signal interrupts and aborts. A VT100 terminal in California can talk to an IBM mainframe in Massachusetts because both sides speak NVT.

That universality is the problem. Any terminal can talk to any machine—and anyone watching the wire can read what they're saying. The characters that cross the network are human-readable. Your password looks like your password.

2.2.2. THE INVISIBLE WIRE

`Telnet`'s weakness lies elsewhere: not who belongs on the network, but what anyone on it can see.

Every keystroke travels in plain text—the password no better protected than the command that follows it. The protocol has no encryption, because Postel and Reynolds were writing for the ARPANET, which ran over dedicated leased lines to terminals in locked computer rooms. To eavesdrop, you had to get physical access to a cable inside a secure facility.

RFC 854 devotes pages to option negotiation and terminal emulation, but the words "security" and "encryption" never appear at all. The premise was environmental: controlled infrastructure meant controlled access.

This wasn't written in any RFC. It didn't need to be. Trust was the water the fish swam in.

`Telnet` cannot verify that the server is who it claims to be. No certificates, no cryptographic proofs. If someone redirects your connection to their machine instead of the real server, you type your password into their login prompt and never know the difference.

The danger extended past `Telnet`. The Berkeley "r-commands" like `rlogin` and `rsh` let an administrator create a file named `.rhosts` telling the system to trust anyone who connected from the hosts it listed. Convenience was the whole idea—a researcher with accounts on several machines could stop typing the same password over and over.

But trust propagates: compromise one machine in a trusted relationship, and you gain access to all its partners.

Trust the machine, trust the network, trust that everyone with access belongs—this made sense in a world of locked computer rooms and leased lines. It became dangerous when that world changed.

2.3. SEVENTY-FIVE CENTS

The discrepancy was 75 cents.

Clifford Stoll didn't care about 75 cents. He was an astronomer, not an accountant. But this was August 1986, he had just taken a job as a systems administrator at Lawrence Berkeley Laboratory, and someone had asked him to figure out why the computer accounting system didn't balance.[18,19] Nine seconds of computer time—worth 75 cents—had no matching account.

Stoll was curious, because nine seconds wasn't a rounding error. Someone had used the system without being charged, which meant an unauthorized account. He started digging.

The FBI wasn't interested. "How much money was lost?" the agent asked. "Um ...75 cents," Stoll replied. "Don't bother us with such trifles."[19]

Stoll kept at it anyway. The unbilled time belonged to an intruder who had broken into the Lawrence Berkeley systems and was using them to attack other computers. He was skilled, and he was in no hurry.

In the months that followed, Stoll tracked him across dozens of networks, through military systems and university computers, watching in real time as he pillaged sensitive databases.

The intruder's name was Markus Hess. He was a young German hacker operating from Hannover, selling what he found to the KGB.[20]

2.3.1. THE HUNT

Hess's technique relied on the trust that `Telnet` took for granted.

He would connect to a system over `Telnet`, log in with guessed or stolen credentials, and explore. Passwords traveled in cleartext, but Hess rarely needed to watch the wire. Once inside a machine, he copied its password file and cracked it offline, and planted Trojan-horse login programs that captured fresh passwords as unsuspecting users typed them. Then he used `Telnet` to hop to the next machine, collecting more credentials, building a chain of access that stretched from system to system.

The Unix trusted hosts mechanism was particularly useful. Many systems allowed passwordless login from certain machines. Once Hess broke into one machine, every system that trusted it fell open to him too. The network trusted him because he was coming from a trusted machine.

Stoll watched the intruder work. He hooked up printers to log every keystroke. He set traps, creating fake files with tempting names. He tracked the attacker's movements across a maze of systems, through military contractors and research labs, watching the commands scroll by.

Hess would connect to Lawrence Berkeley, then hop to a military contractor, then to a Navy system, then to an Army database. Each connection was plaintext. Each system trusted the one before it. The chain of trust became a highway for espionage.

No one wanted responsibility: the FBI saw only a 75-cent theft, the CIA said the intrusions were domestic, and the NSA said the intruder was foreign but the crimes were American.

Stoll kept investigating and built a honeypot: a fake "SDI" database filled with invented documents about Reagan's missile defense program. The file names were irresistible, and when Hess downloaded them, Stoll had proof that the intrusions were espionage, not idle curiosity.

The investigation took ten months. Stoll traced the connections across the Atlantic to Germany and worked with German authorities, who searched Hess's Hannover apartment in June 1987. Then the case stalled—the trace on the phone line had been set up without proper judicial authorization, and the evidence against Hess lapsed. He was not arrested until March 1989, and was finally convicted of espionage on February 15, 1990.[20,21] He had sold what he found to the KGB for cash and cocaine.

2.3.2. WHAT TELNET REVEALED

The Cuckoo's Egg—Stoll's 1989 book about the investigation—became the first popular account of computer espionage.[19] It demonstrated something the protocol designers had never imagined: their private network had become public.

Hess used `Telnet` exactly as designed. Cleartext passwords came with it, and in 1983 that was a reasonable way to build a protocol.

But the community had changed. The ARPANET had been absorbed into the larger internet, the leased lines had become a global mesh, and the locked computer room was now anyone's home.

Stoll's 75-cent discrepancy revealed how easily strangers could watch your passwords flow by.

After Stoll's book was published, security researchers began to take password protection more seriously, but `Telnet` remained in use for years because the convenience was hard to give up. Encryption was expensive, complicated, and often subject to export controls.

It would take another decade before `Telnet` began to fade. In 1995, Tatu Ylönen at Helsinki University of Technology released `SSH`, the Secure Shell, after his university's network was compromised by a password-sniffing attack.[22] `SSH` looked like `Telnet` to users but encrypted everything—passwords were protected and sessions were authenticated.

In January 2006, the IETF published the core `SSH` protocol suite as RFCs 4251 through 4254.[23–26] By then, most security-conscious organizations had already switched, and `Telnet` retreated to legacy systems.

The attack lived in the gap between the network the protocol expected and the network it got. Protocols outlive their creators—and these had been built for friends, not for the world.

But `Telnet` never died. It just faded from view.

From December 1, 2025, through January 14, 2026, GreyNoise's Global Observation Grid recorded an average of approximately 914,000 non-spoofable `Telnet` sessions per day.[27] This was sensor-grid visibility into unsolicited traffic, not a measurement of all `Telnet` traffic crossing the internet. Even so, it showed that the protocol Postel and Reynolds had designed for trusted networks—the one that sent every password in cleartext—remained an active target forty years later.

Then, on January 14, 2026, at 21:00 UTC, the traffic visible to those sensors collapsed. In a single hour, observed `Telnet` sessions dropped 65 percent. By the next hour, they were down 83 percent from baseline. Eighteen autonomous systems that had each produced significant pre-drop volume went completely silent in GreyNoise's data, including networks operated by Vultr, Cox, Charter, and British Telecom.

Six days later, security researchers disclosed CVE-2026-24061: a critical authentication bypass in GNU Inetutils `telnetd`.[28] An attacker could inject arguments through the USER environment variable during option negotiation—the same negotiation system that RFC 854 had specified in 1983. By sending `-f root` as a username, an attacker received an unauthenticated root shell. The vulnerability was eleven years old.

GreyNoise proposed one explanation: a transit provider may have received advance warning and filtered port 23 before the announcement went public. But the researchers were explicit that they could not prove the connection; the timing could have been coincidental. The borrowed time had almost run out.

And yet `Telnet` persists. As of February 10, 2026, GreyNoise was still observing roughly 373,000 sessions per day—about two-fifths of the pre-collapse baseline, but not zero.[27] The protocol written for a network of colleagues continues to attract traffic on a network of strangers.

`Telnet` gave you a window into a distant machine. But a window only lets you look and type. Sometimes you wanted to reach through it and take something home—a file, maybe, or a dataset or a program someone wrote three thousand miles away—and that took a different protocol, built in the same era, resting on the same assumptions.

CHAPTER 3

THE FILE TRANSFER

The objectives of FTP are
1) to promote sharing of files
(computer programs and/or data),
2) to encourage indirect or implicit
(via programs) use of remote computers,
3) to shield a user from variations
in file storage systems among hosts.

— RFC 959, October 1985

3.1. THE YELLOW LEGAL PAD

April 1971. Abhay Bhushan needed to move a file between two computers at MIT, machines a few minutes' walk apart. Both sat on the ARPANET, which now linked a few dozen computers at universities and research labs across the country. The network worked, messages traveled, but the computers spoke different languages, stored data differently, organized filesystems according to competing philosophies. Bhushan's GE 645 ran Multics, an operating system treating files like library books—organized, cataloged, protected. The machine across campus ran ITS, the Incompatible Time-sharing System, which provided no access controls at all. The file was just text, but it might as well have been written in cuneiform.

Elsewhere on the network, the usual solution was the mail. Researchers wrote data to magnetic tape, packaged it, and handed the parcel to the postal service. Days later somebody at the other end mounted it on a compatible drive and hoped the encoding matched. The joke in computer science departments held that a station wagon full of tapes had better bandwidth than any network—just terrible latency.

For collaborative work, shipping tapes was absurd. A network connected these machines. Why couldn't they just send files?

The ARPANET in 1971 connected machines with almost nothing in common. A PDP-10 at Harvard, an IBM 360 at UCLA, a GE 645 at MIT: each stored text differently, at seven bits per character or eight or nine packed into larger words. Line endings differed, and so did directory structures. So did the idea of what a file was—a byte stream on some machines, a stack of fixed-length records on others. An IBM mainframe's text file would be incomprehensible to a DEC minicomputer.

Bhushan was twenty-six, a researcher at MIT's Project MAC. He had arrived from India six years earlier, an engineering graduate of IIT Kanpur. Project MAC—"Machine-Aided Cognition," or "Man and Computer," depending on whom you asked—was a birthplace of time-sharing. The Multics system was experimental, ambitious, bristling with security features. Bhushan sat in perhaps the most advanced computing environment on Earth and couldn't share a document with the building next door, let alone across the country.

The problem wasn't the network. The Network Control Protocol already shipped data between machines, and `Telnet` already let users log in remotely. Files were harder. A file carries structure along with its bytes—line endings in text, sections and entry points in a program—and structure was what the machines disagreed about. Send a Multics text file to an ITS machine and you'd get gibberish: the bytes arrived, encoded wrong, broken in the wrong places, shaped for a filesystem that wasn't there.

The ARPANET community had been discussing file transfer since the network's earliest days. RFC 80, published in December 1970, proposed mechanisms for exchanging files. But those early proposals required users to understand the remote system's conventions. Bhushan wanted to hide the differences entirely.

He sketched a solution on a yellow legal pad, the same kind Steve Crocker had used drafting RFC 1. He called it a File Transfer Protocol.

His insight was to stop preserving the sender's format and translate it instead. The protocol would define neutral representations, a diplomatic language for data. A Multics system sending a text file would render it into that common tongue, and the ITS machine at the far end would render it back out. What traveled on the wire belonged to neither system: network ASCII, a standard representation any machine could speak.

The ARPANET itself used this logic. The Interface Message Processors translated at the boundaries, converting host-specific packets into network-standard messages and back. Bhushan applied the same principle one layer up, to files instead of packets. Let each system keep its internal representation. Just agree on what goes over the wire.

RFC 114 hit the ARPANET on April 16, 1971.[29] "A principal objective of the protocol," Bhushan wrote, "is to promote the indirect use of computers on the network." You could transfer a file without logging in, without learning a foreign operating system, without understanding how the receiving machine organized its storage. The protocol would handle the translation.

Bhushan tested on the hardest possible pair: "Since our implementation involves two dissimilar systems (Multics is a 'service' system, ITS is not) with different file systems (Multics provides elaborate access controls, ITS provides none), we feel that the file transfer mechanisms proposed are generalizable." If it worked between Multics and ITS, it would work anywhere.

Any computer on the ARPANET could now send files to any other, regardless of manufacturer, operating system, or internal storage format. The protocol defined transactions: retrieve, store, append, rename, delete. It defined data types: ASCII text, binary, EBCDIC for IBM mainframes. Two alien machines could negotiate a file transfer without knowing each other's internal architecture.

RFC 114 even reached toward remote program execution. Bhushan included an "execute" request—an early gesture at what we now call remote procedure calls. It never gained traction. File transfer was complicated enough.

The protocol changed fast. Engineers added features and fixed bugs, and within two months RFC 172 had revised the specification,[30] with more revisions to come. The file transfer problem had more wrinkles than anyone anticipated.

Some problems only surfaced once the protocol ran against real machines: what if the receiving machine runs out of disk space, or the connection drops mid-transfer?

The RFCs multiplied: 172, 265, 354, 542, 765. Engineers debated one connection or two, data compression, line-ending conventions. RFC 686, published in 1975, was titled "Leaving Well Enough Alone"—a plea from engineers tired of constant changes. The simple idea of "send a file" accumulated fourteen years of refinements.

In October 1985, Postel and Joyce Reynolds published RFC 959, the definitive specification.[31] Sixty pages describing data types, transfer modes, access controls, error handling. The objectives echoed

Bhushan's original vision: promote file sharing, encourage indirect use of remote computers, shield users from filesystem variations, transfer data reliably and efficiently.

RFC 959 codified the protocol's most distinctive feature, the separation of control and data. `Telnet` ran everything over a single connection. `FTP` used two. Commands and responses went over one and file content over the other, which meant a user could keep typing while a transfer ran. The split was practical. It also meant that, by default, the client told the server where to send the data.

In 1985, security meant access control—could the user read this file, or write to this directory? `FTP` handled authentication with username and password. The access control commands came first: `USER` to specify your identity, `PASS` for your password, optionally `ACCT` for billing. Only after authentication could you move files.

The protocol also permitted anonymous `FTP`: a server could accept the username "anonymous" and take the user's email address as the password. The convention grew out of practice. Administrators who wanted to share files publicly configured their servers to accept the special username, and the address went into the log the way a visitor signs a guest book. Nobody checked it against anything.

Anonymous `FTP` carried the ARPANET's culture forward. Research was meant to be shared and software was meant to be passed around. Universities ran public archives, government agencies published data, and developers left code on servers where anyone could take a copy. Trust by default now reached anyone who could open a connection to the machine. The protocol assumed those anonymous users would behave like colleagues, because for a long time they were.

The system worked—until it didn't.

3.2. TWO PHONE LINES

3.2.1. HOW FTP WORKS

Imagine a warehouse with two telephone lines. One line connects you to the warehouse manager. You call that line to give instructions: "Show me what's in aisle four. Ship the blue boxes to this address." The manager responds, confirms your requests, coordinates the work. The second line connects you to the loading dock. When the manager approves a shipment, workers use this line to describe what they're sending. Then the actual boxes appear at your door. You can keep talking to the manager even while shipments are in transit.

`FTP` works identically. One connection handles commands. Another handles data.

3.2.2. THE CONTROL CHANNEL

When you connect to an `FTP` server, your client opens a `TCP` connection to port 21. This control channel stays open for the entire session. Everything you type travels over this connection—and the remote host believes what you type without verification. You claim a username; it accepts. You claim an email address; it records it. The protocol believes you.

The conversation follows a simple pattern. You send `USER anonymous`, and the reply comes back `331 Please specify the password.` Your password is an email address, `PASS someone@example.com`, and the server answers `230 Login successful.` Three-digit codes carry the verdict—2xx for success, 5xx for failure, the rest in between.

```
$ ftp files.example.edu
Connected to files.example.edu.
220 Example FTP Server ready.
Name: anonymous
331 Please specify the password.
Password: user@domain.com
230 Login successful.
ftp> ls
200 PORT command successful.
150 Opening ASCII mode data connection.
pub/
incoming/
README
226 Transfer complete.
```

The server asked for a password and got an email address back. It compared that address to nothing at all, and answered "Login successful." The command vocabulary is small—authenticate, move around, move files, hang up—and the design assumed a human might type all of it by hand. Modern clients bury the conversation under graphical interfaces, but the words on the wire haven't changed.

3.2.3. THE DATA CHANNEL

File content travels over a separate connection. When you request a file, the server opens a new TCP connection for that data. When the transfer completes, this connection closes.

The separation solved a real problem. Bhushan's original 1971 design used a single connection for both commands and data, which meant that if you were sending a large file and needed to abort, you couldn't get a word in until the transfer stopped. Splitting the streams kept the session interactive, letting you issue an abort at any moment.

A sensible fix—but the second connection introduced a question that would haunt the protocol: where should the server send the data?

In **active mode**, the client tells the server where to send data. The client issues a `PORT` command with an `IP` address and port number. The server opens a connection to that address.

Here's what the server doesn't do: verify that the address belongs to the client. You could specify your own machine, or you could specify someone else's entirely—the server connects wherever you tell it.

In 1971, this seemed reasonable. Everyone connected was a colleague. No one would lie about their address.

In **passive mode**, the roles reverse. The client sends a `PASV` command, the server answers with its own `IP` address and port, and the client makes the connection. That fixed the firewall problem, since both connections now leave from the client's side. The trust underneath was untouched. Whatever arrived on the control channel—the username, the email address—the server still took at face value, no matter which end opened the data connection.

3.2.4. THE HONOR OF STRANGERS

`FTP` trusts clients to tell the truth about themselves. The pattern repeats: the unverified email address, the PORT command pointing anywhere the client chooses. The protocol asks questions and believes the answers.

Anonymous `FTP` made the trust explicit. RFC 959 calls the password "identification for access control" rather than authentication, and the wording is exact: what the field held was an email address offered as a courtesy. It was less a proof of identity than a promise to behave.

`Telnet` trusted the network path. `FTP` trusted the client's self-declarations. Both kinds of trust came from the same place: a network where reputation arrived ahead of you. In 1971 the ARPANET's researchers could fit in one conference room, and they knew each other's faces. Deception was not worth what it cost.

> RFC 959 --- October 1985 --- Postel & Reynolds
>
> Access controls define users' access privileges to the use of a system, and to the files in that system. Access controls are necessary to prevent unauthorized or accidental use of files. It is the prerogative of a server-FTP process to invoke access controls.

The weight is in one word: prerogative. The protocol defined mechanisms and required none of them, leaving each administrator to decide locally whether credentials got checked or uploads got restricted. The specification shrugged.

The open culture flourished on top of that shrug. If you wanted the GNU project's source code you fetched it from an anonymous FTP server, and the RFCs themselves went out the same way. University archives held BSD sources and Emacs and whatever papers a department had decided to make public. No one asked who you were, because the point was that knowledge should flow freely.

Then the internet opened to the world.

3.3. THE HIDDEN DIRECTORIES

By 1995 an underground network that called itself "the Scene" had been running for years, mostly out of sight, and its currency was stolen software. Release groups with names like Razor 1911, Fairlight, and

Drink or Die raced to crack new commercial software and put it into circulation within hours of the retail release. The hierarchy was rigid. Crackers who defeated copy protection sat at the top and couriers who moved the releases sat below them. At the bottom were leeches, who downloaded and gave nothing back.

The distribution ran on anonymous FTP servers, thousands of them, none belonging to the groups themselves. Participants hunted for misconfigured servers at universities and corporations, then built hidden directories inside them with names like `...` (three dots) or `.. ` (dot-dot-space). The trick worked because of how Unix printed a listing. A standard listing skips names that begin with a dot, so a directory called `...` never appears at all unless you ask for hidden files—and even then, sitting next to the ordinary `.` and `..` entries, it slides past unless you know to look for it. An administrator might find forty gigabytes of pirated software sitting in the physics department's file share. Universities made the best hosts, with bandwidth to spare and nobody watching.

Anonymous FTP made this trivial because many servers permitted anonymous uploads to `incoming` or `pub` directories. Couriers scanned networks for vulnerable servers—anonymous access enabled, write permissions available, fast connections, naive administrators—and called these "pubs," maintaining carefully guarded lists. The competition to find new pubs was as fierce as the competition to release software first.

Operation Buccaneer in 2001 led to prosecutions across six countries.[32] On a single December day, investigators executed roughly 70 search warrants in the United States, Britain, Australia, Finland, Norway, and Sweden. Defendants included corporate employees, government contractors, and a systems administrator at MIT. But for years, the protocol itself did nothing to stop them. FTP assumed that anonymous access meant public access. The Scene exploited that expectation without breaking the protocol.

The Scene's use of anonymous FTP was brazen, illegal, and eventually prosecuted, but a more subtle vulnerability lurked in the protocol itself. The Scene had abused the culture of anonymous access; the vulnerability Hobbit found lived in the protocol's fundamental architecture.

The PORT command let clients tell servers where to send data, and the connection opened without verification. In 1995, a security researcher who went by "Hobbit" realized what this meant.[33] The PORT command accepts any address, so you can direct traffic somewhere else entirely, and the request will be honored.

This became the FTP bounce attack. The attacker logs into an FTP server as anonymous and then, instead of asking for a file, issues a PORT command carrying some other machine's address. The server does what the specification says and opens a connection there. What the target sees is a connection from the FTP server. The attacker's own address never reaches it.

```
220 ftp.trusted-university.edu ready
USER anonymous
331 Please specify the password.
PASS attacker@fake.email
230 Login successful.
PORT 10,0,0,5,0,25
200 PORT command successful.
LIST
```

That PORT command told the server to connect to 10.0.0.5 on port 25—the SMTP mail port. The server dutifully opens a connection to an internal mail server and sends a directory listing. The listing isn't useful, but the connection is. The attacker has made the FTP server initiate a connection to an internal machine that might not be reachable from outside. If a firewall protects the target, it might trust connections from the FTP server's IP address. The attacker has bounced their probe through a legitimate server.

FTP bounce was particularly useful for reconnaissance, since port scanning normally left traces—the scanner's IP address appeared in every log. With the FTP bounce attack, those connections came from a legitimate university server instead.

The technique enabled port scanning through firewalls: an attacker could probe a target network by issuing PORT commands with different port numbers and observing the server's response. The attacker never made a direct connection—the FTP server did all the work.

More creatively, attackers could bypass access controls entirely. A firewall configured to trust a university's network would accept connections tunneled through that university's FTP server. The bounce attack turned trusted servers into unwitting proxies.

The FTP bounce attack wasn't a bug—the server was following the protocol correctly. The specification simply expected something no longer true: that users would only request connections to their own machines. RFC 959 had even anticipated third-party transfers. The specification explicitly described how "a user might wish to transfer files between two hosts, neither of which is a local host." This was a feature—back when every user could be trusted. Hobbit had used the feature for purposes its designers never imagined.

The fix seemed obvious: restrict where the PORT command could point, so most server implementations added this check within months. They would only accept PORT commands specifying the same IP address that the control connection came from.

The fix broke legitimate uses. Some organizations wanted data to move directly between two servers instead of through a client, and the three-way transfer RFC 959 documented became impossible. Passive mode helped, but it brought its own trouble with firewalls and NAT devices. Meanwhile the servers themselves were closing. An administrator would require authentication, then cut off anonymous uploads, then take the public directory down for good.

By the late 1990s the security model looked untenable. Passwords traveled in cleartext. The PORT command was a standing invitation, and anonymous access had come to mean liability. The Web was making FTP unnecessary anyway: HTTP served files over one connection, and a web server on port 80 passed through firewalls without special handling. FTP needed NAT helpers and stateful packet inspection to get through the same door.

Security-conscious organizations migrated to alternatives: SFTP encrypted everything and used a single connection, solving both the confidentiality problem and the firewall problem, while SCP provided secure copying over SSH. FTPS added TLS encryption to FTP, though the two-channel design made integration awkward.

The FTP bounce attack required no software bugs. Every command was valid. Every response was correct. The vulnerability was in the assumptions, not the code.

Bhushan, writing in 1971, wasn't naive—he explicitly noted the tension between Multics (which "provides elaborate access controls") and ITS (which "provides none"). But the ARPANET was small, the users were colleagues, and the risk of someone lying about their destination address was approximately zero.

No one in 1971 could imagine the warez scene. The protocol kept working, exactly as specified, in a world it was never designed to serve.

The archives are closed.

The RFC archive moved from anonymous FTP to HTTP long ago. The university servers that once held gigabytes of freely shared software have shut their public directories. The warez servers are gone. What remains is invisible: FTP running inside corporate networks, inside batch jobs scheduled years ago, inside mainframe workflows that nobody has touched since the Clinton administration. The protocol moves files between servers on a schedule nobody remembers setting, in directories nobody monitors, carrying data nobody watches arrive.

In 2021, Chrome and Firefox dropped native FTP support.[34] Browsers had treated FTP as a curiosity for years—something you could type into an address bar but almost never did. The browsers moved on. FTP didn't. It runs in the background of enterprise computing the way old pipes run behind new drywall: out of sight, past its design life, still carrying the load.

The open culture that anonymous FTP embodied didn't survive the internet's growth. Knowledge stopped flowing freely when the internet stopped being a collegial network. The protocol survived anyway—not as a statement of values, but as a ghost. The idealism is gone. The cron jobs remain.

`Telnet` carried keystrokes and FTP carried files, and both left the hardest problem to the layer beneath them: moving packets between machines at all. In 1973, that layer still spoke the ARPANET's private dialect, useless beyond its own borders. The engineers who set out to replace it would end up writing the language the whole world speaks.

CHAPTER 4

THE LANGUAGE OF PACKETS

TCP implementations will follow
a general principle of robustness:
be conservative in what you do,
be liberal in what you accept from others.

– RFC 793, Jon Postel, 1981

4.1. THE CABANA HYATT

Fall 1973. Vint Cerf sat in the lobby of the Cabana Hyatt in Palo Alto with Bob Kahn, the two of them filling pad after pad with scribbled notes.[35] They were trying to solve an impossible problem: how do you make networks that speak different languages communicate?

Cerf had been working on the ARPANET for years. He knew its protocol, NCP, intimately. Kahn had built the software that ran the IMPs. Between them, they understood the network better than anyone.

NCP was brilliant for what it did. It let ARPANET computers exchange messages reliably, efficiently, predictably. But NCP was married to the ARPANET's particular hardware. Try to connect to a satellite network or the packet radio systems the military was testing, and NCP fell apart.

DARPA wanted more: a network of networks—an "internetwork" tying together satellite links, radio connections, and whatever else the future might bring. The system had to survive pieces of it failing. The Cold War was not an abstraction.

So Cerf and Kahn sat in that hotel lobby and asked: what if the network didn't care what it was carrying?

The insight arrived in pieces over months of meetings. That June, on a break from a conference at a San Francisco hotel, Cerf had sketched the architecture on the back of an envelope—alone, between sessions, drawing clouds for the networks and boxes for the gateways that would join them. The Palo Alto sessions with Kahn turned the sketch into a design. The core idea was simple.

Split the problem in two.

One protocol would handle addressing and routing. It would wrap data in an envelope marked with a source and a destination, then trust the network to carry it. That was the Internet Protocol, IP, and it made no promises: packets might arrive out of order, or not at all. Trying was the whole job.

The other protocol would handle reliability. It would sit on top of IP and provide everything applications needed: guaranteed delivery, correct ordering, flow control. This was the Transmission Control Protocol—TCP.

Together, they became TCP/IP. Cerf and Kahn published their design in IEEE Transactions on Communications in May 1974.[36] The paper would be cited thousands of times. At the moment, it was just an idea. Rough consensus in a hotel lobby. Running code would follow.

Cerf had a personal stake in network communication. His wife Sigrid was deaf—spinal meningitis at age three had taken most of her hearing—and Cerf himself had worn hearing aids since he was thirteen. They met in 1965, in the waiting room of their hearing aid dealer in Los Angeles, and married the next year. In their world, communication for the deaf meant handwritten notes or face-to-face conversation. The teletype machines that preceded email were transforming it—text over wires, messages that didn't require hearing.

Cerf saw what networks could mean for people who couldn't pick up a phone. Email wasn't just a convenience; it was access.

He pushed the implementation forward. By 1978, multiple versions of `TCP/IP` were running at research sites. Postel was turning the informal designs into formal specifications. RFC 791 would define `IP`.[37] RFC 793 would define `TCP`.[38] September 1981.

But specifications are not deployment. The ARPANET still ran on `NCP`. Switching to `TCP/IP` meant rewriting everything, debugging everything, coordinating hundreds of sites across the country. The transition would require something unprecedented: a day when everyone switched at once.

They called it Flag Day.[39] January 1, 1983—New Year's Day—the entire ARPANET would cut over from `NCP` to `TCP/IP` in a single coordinated moment. Machines that weren't ready would simply stop working.

The planning took months. RFC 801, the transition plan, laid out the stakes in capital letters: "There are some very tempting shortcuts in the implementation of IP and TCP. DO NOT BE TEMPTED!"[39] Implementers took the shortcuts anyway—checksums ignored, inputs trusted—and those choices were still turning up as vulnerabilities decades later.

When the day came, Dan Lynch—who ran the computing facilities at USC's Information Sciences Institute—had 500 buttons made at his own expense.[40] "I survived the TCP transition," they read. He meant it as a joke, mostly.

The transition worked. Not perfectly—there were bugs, panics, sites that discovered their software wasn't quite ready. But it worked. The ARPANET had a new language.

The new language was also built to reach past the ARPANET. CSNET, which linked computer science departments outside it, was already exchanging traffic through gateways, and the NSF's networks would follow, with commercial carriers behind them. The "internet" had stopped being a theory. It was a network of networks, growing month by month.

Flag Day was the last time anyone could break everything at once. After January 1, 1983, backward compatibility became a permanent constraint. The internet had grown too large to reboot.

The protocols that Cerf and Kahn designed on envelopes and legal pads in 1973 became frozen in place. Their assumptions, their tradeoffs, their blind spots—all of it locked in by success.

And one of those assumptions would haunt the internet for decades.

4.2. THE HANDSHAKE

4.2.1. HOW TCP/IP WORKS

Think of the postal system. You write a letter, put it in an envelope, write an address on the front and a return address in the corner. You drop it in a mailbox. Postal workers sort it, route it, hand it from truck to truck until it reaches its destination.

`IP` works similarly.

Every piece of data gets wrapped in a packet with source and destination addresses. Routers examine the destination address and forward the packet toward its goal, one hop at a time. The packet might take different routes on different days. `IP` doesn't guarantee any particular path. It just tries to deliver.

The source address serves the same purpose as a return address. If something goes wrong, the source address tells routers where to send error messages.

Here is the first assumption: the source address is honest. When a packet arrives with source address 192.168.1.1, `IP` believes it. No verification. No proof. The address says what it says, and the network accepts it.

This made perfect sense in 1974. The ARPANET connected a few dozen sites. The researchers at each had met at conferences, collaborated on papers, shared the same professional circles. Lying about your address was pointless. Why would a Stanford researcher pretend to be at MIT?

The protocol encoded this expectation. RFC 791 describes how `IP` works.[37] Nowhere in its 45 pages does it mention authentication. The concept simply did not arise.

4.2.2. THE IP HEADER

Every `IP` packet begins with a header—metadata that routers use to move the packet through the network. Three fields do the real work: Source Address, Destination Address, and Time to Live. Notice what's conspicuously absent—no field that says "verified by" or "authenticated at." The addresses are claims, not proofs.

The Time to Live (TTL) starts at a number—typically 64 or 128. Each router that handles the packet subtracts one. When the counter reaches zero, the packet is discarded.

The Source and Destination fields are each 32 bits long. This is why `IPv4` addresses look like four numbers separated by dots: 192.168.1.1.

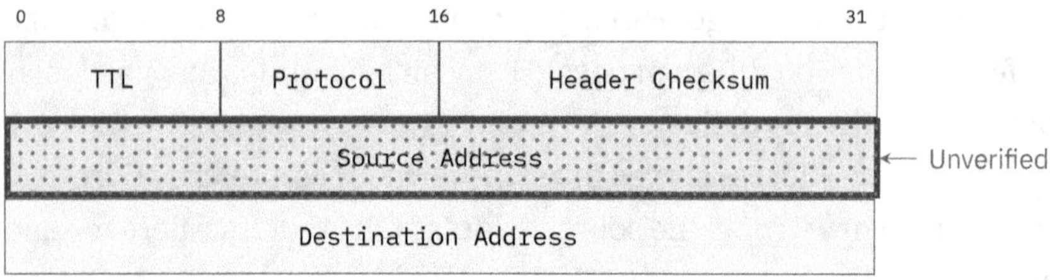

Figure 4.1: IPv4 header fields (simplified). The source address is accepted without verification.

Four billion addresses seemed infinite when the specification was finalized in 1981. That estimate proved insufficient.

The header has a checksum protecting against transmission errors. But a checksum only verifies the header wasn't damaged in transit. It says nothing about whether the source address is true.

4.2.3. BEST-EFFORT DELIVERY

What does IP actually promise? Almost nothing.

"Best-effort delivery" means the network tries to deliver packets but makes no guarantees. Packets might arrive out of order, might be duplicated, might vanish entirely—IP does not care. It just tries.

Why strip out all these guarantees? Because simplicity is power. By keeping IP minimal, Cerf and Kahn made it universal. Satellite links could carry IP packets. Radio networks could carry IP packets. Anything could, because IP asked so little.

The consequence: reliability had to come from somewhere else—enter TCP.

4.2.4. THE THREE-WAY HANDSHAKE

TCP supplies what IP leaves out: delivery you can count on, in the order you sent it, at a pace the receiving machine can keep up with (the protocol calls that flow control). All of it starts with the three-way handshake, a short opening exchange—two people shaking hands before they start talking.

The client goes first: "I want to connect." Its SYN packet carries a sequence number, a 32-bit value that will track every byte of the conversation to come. Back comes a SYN-ACK—two flags in one packet—agreeing to the connection and supplying a fresh sequence number for traffic in the other direction. The client acknowledges that number with an ACK, and the connection is open. Three packets, start to finish.

Notice what just happened. The server believed the client's address. The client believed the server's response came from the right place. Neither side proved who they were. The handshake completes based on an assumption: if you can finish it, you must be legitimate. Nobody checks further.

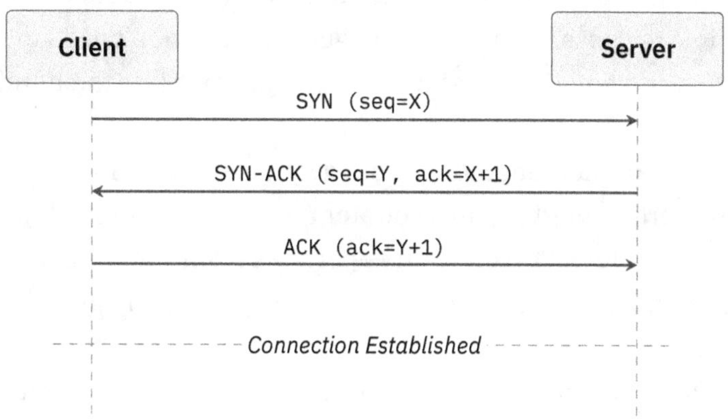

Figure 4.2: TCP three-way handshake. Both sides exchange sequence numbers to establish a connection.

Sequence numbers have two design purposes: reassembling out-of-order data and tracking what's been received. But systems came to rely on a third property: completing the handshake implied identity.

The assumption that emerged: if someone sends a SYN from address 192.168.1.1, receives the SYN-ACK, and successfully sends the ACK, then they must actually be at 192.168.1.1. After all, how else could they receive the SYN-ACK?

This reasoning was sound in 1974. It remained sound for two decades. Then someone realized it had a flaw.

4.2.5. SEQUENCE NUMBER PREDICTABILITY

Sequence numbers track the bytes in a conversation, letting the receiver put them back in order. But they picked up a second job: proving both sides are genuinely connected. Only someone who received the SYN-ACK could know the server's sequence number—or so the reasoning went.

That reasoning has a flaw. It holds only if the sequence number is impossible to guess. If someone can guess it, they don't need to receive the SYN-ACK at all. They can predict it and complete the handshake blind.

Early TCP implementations chose sequence numbers poorly. Some systems incremented a global counter for each new connection. If you knew the counter's current value—perhaps from a legitimate connection you had just opened—you could predict the next value with high accuracy.

RFC 793 did address how to pick sequence numbers, but it framed the choice as a matter of reliability.[38] The specification noted: "To avoid confusion we must prevent segments from one incarnation of a connection from being used while the same sequence numbers may still be present in the network from an earlier incarnation." The hazard it had in mind was an old connection's leftover packets surfacing inside a new one. That someone might calculate the numbers deliberately was a later discovery.

The specification suggested using a clock-based scheme that would change sequence numbers over time. Four years later, in 1985, Robert Morris Sr.—the worm author's father, then at Bell Labs—published the first analysis showing that predictable sequence numbers were a security risk.[41] "Hard to predict" was not the same as "cryptographically random." Implementations varied. Some were weak.

4.2.6. POSTEL'S LAW

TCP embedded another principle in its design, one that would prove double-edged.

The principle later became known as the Robustness Principle: send perfectly formatted packets, but gracefully accept packets that are slightly malformed. If the intent is clear, accept it.

The principle helped the early internet survive—implementations had bugs, networks were noisy, and forgiveness kept connections alive.

But think about what "liberal in what you accept" means for an attacker. Every variation a protocol tolerates is a variation someone can probe. Every edge case is a potential way in. Postel's Law made the early internet work. It also made it vulnerable.

4.2.7. THE END-TO-END PRINCIPLE

One more design choice shaped TCP/IP's security profile: the end-to-end principle.[42]

Where should the intelligence live—in the network, or at the edges? Cerf and Kahn chose the edges. Routers should be simple. They should forward packets and nothing more. All sophisticated work—reliability, security, application logic—should happen at the endpoints.

When you send an email, your computer and the recipient's server handle encryption. The routers in between see only scrambled bytes.

They don't decrypt. They don't authenticate. They don't ask whether this packet should exist at all. That's not their job.

This made the network fast and flexible. New applications could be invented without changing infrastructure. HTTP didn't require router upgrades. Neither did email, file transfer, or video streaming.

But it also meant security was your problem. If you wanted encryption, you added it. If you wanted authentication, you added it. The network itself was just pipes.

The end-to-end principle made TCP/IP scalable. It also made TCP/IP trust-dependent. Every packet that reached your machine had passed through routers that neither knew nor cared whether that packet was legitimate. If your endpoint wasn't thinking about security, no one was.

4.2.8. THE UNSIGNED ENVELOPE

IP source addresses are claims, not proofs. TCP's handshake depends on sequence numbers, not identity. The entire design assumed that the machines completing a handshake were who they said they were, because in 1974 that assumption was nearly always correct.

The ARPANET connected a few dozen institutions. Everyone involved had met at conferences. The social layer—reputation, accountability, professional consequences—did the work that cryptographic verification would have done. That social layer didn't scale.

4.3. CHRISTMAS IN SAN DIEGO

Christmas Day, 1994. Tsutomu Shimomura was not at home.[43] He was in the Sierra Nevada, skiing, celebrating the holiday away from his computers. At 2:09 PM Pacific time, his computers were under attack.

Shimomura worked at the San Diego Supercomputer Center and ranked among the sharpest security researchers in the field. His machines contained tools for analyzing cellular phone networks, among other sensitive capabilities, and someone wanted those tools. The attacker knew what he was doing.

The attack required combining three techniques. Each exploited a different weakness in TCP/IP.

First: the SYN flood. Shimomura's network included a diskless workstation—in his own account of the attack, he calls it simply "x-terminal"—that trusted another of his machines, the server. The trust was expressed through a Unix file called .rhosts—a relic of simpler times that said, in effect, "if someone logs in from this machine, believe them."

The attacker started by crippling the server. He sent about thirty SYN packets, each the opening move of a TCP handshake he never intended to finish. The half-open connections piled up in the server's queue until it was full, and a full queue meant the machine could not answer anyone new. It stayed powered on and went quiet.

Why silence the machine? Because the next step required pretending to be that machine. If the server was awake, it would receive unexpected packets and send back error messages exposing the deception.

Second: IP spoofing. With the server incapacitated, the attacker sent a SYN packet to the x-terminal, but the source address was not his own. It claimed to be from the server—the machine the x-terminal trusted.

IP had no way to verify source addresses. The protocol accepts whatever address the packet claims. The x-terminal believed the connection request came from its trusted neighbor.

The x-terminal received the SYN and responded with a SYN-ACK. That SYN-ACK traveled to the server, the address listed on the incoming packet. But the server was drowning in connection requests. It could not respond.

Third: sequence number prediction. Now the attacker faced the hard part. He needed to complete the handshake by sending an ACK with the correct sequence number, but he had never received the SYN-ACK—it had gone to the server. He was blind, so he guessed.

The attacker had already probed the network, opening legitimate connections to learn how the target machine chose its sequence numbers. He had identified the pattern, calculated what the sequence number should be, and sent an ACK with that value. He was right.

The connection was established. As far as the x-terminal could tell, the server had just logged in. The trust relationship activated. The attacker sent a command:

```
echo '+ +' >> /.rhosts
```

Two characters and a space, appended to the root user's trust file. Those characters meant "trust everyone, from everywhere." The machine was open.

The attacker explored at leisure. He copied files, including the cellular monitoring software Shimomura had developed. Then he vanished. Days later, taunting voicemails appeared on Shimomura's system—"my technique is the best"—though who actually recorded them was never settled.

The attacker was Kevin Mitnick. Mitnick was already notorious—he had been arrested twice for computer crimes, had served time, had been released with strict conditions against using computers. None of it stopped him. He was compulsive, brilliant, and now in possession of tools that could intercept cellular phone calls.

Shimomura learned about the attack two days later, when a colleague noticed anomalies in the logs. What he found enraged him: someone had walked through his defenses using techniques he himself had contemplated, and the taunts on his voicemail turned professional curiosity into pursuit. He began hunting.

The chase lasted weeks. Shimomura worked with the FBI, with phone company technicians, tracing Mitnick's electronic footprints. The irony was exquisite: Shimomura used the same cellular monitoring capabilities Mitnick had stolen to track him down.

On February 15, 1995, around two in the morning, FBI agents arrested Kevin Mitnick at his apartment in Raleigh, North Carolina.[43] Shimomura had helped the radio surveillance team pin down the building, and he was there when the agents went in. At a court hearing the next day, Mitnick turned to him: "Hello, Tsutomu. I respect your skills." The hunt was over.

The attack revealed something troubling about TCP/IP. IP forwarded packets without verifying their source addresses, TCP completed handshakes based on sequence numbers, and the trust relationships in .rhosts files granted access based on IP addresses. Nothing broke. Nothing needed to break. The flaw lay in what the protocols assumed.

IP assumed source addresses were honest. TCP assumed sequence numbers were unpredictable. The trust model assumed IP addresses represented identity. Mitnick exploited all three assumptions simultaneously. IP spoofing gave him the false identity. Sequence number prediction let him complete the blind handshake. The trust relationship gave him root access. Three weaknesses, one attack, no bugs required.

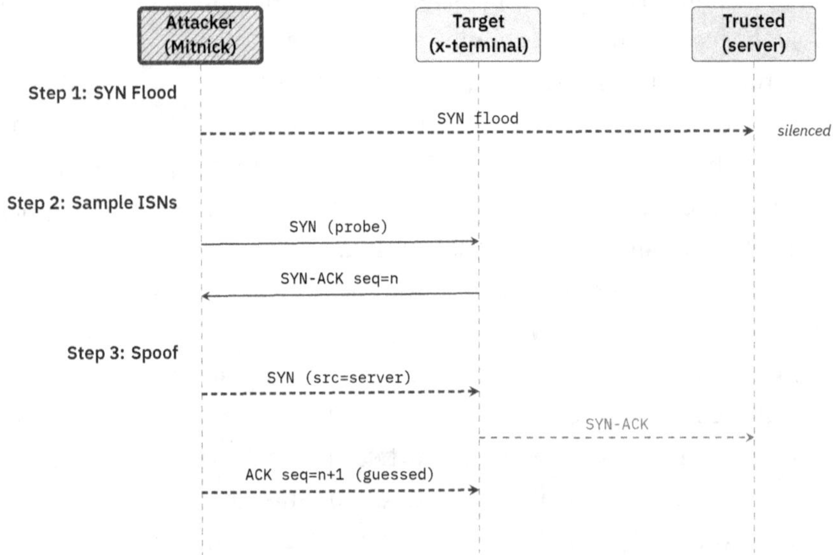

Figure 4.3: The Mitnick attack chain. Mitnick first silences the trusted machine with a SYN flood (Step 1), samples sequence numbers from the target (Step 2), then spoofs a connection from the trusted machine using predicted sequence numbers (Step 3). The SYN-ACK goes to the silenced machine, which cannot respond.

The response came quickly, at least by internet standards.

Researchers had documented TCP sequence number weaknesses years before the attack. Robert Morris described the vulnerability in 1985[41], and Steve Bellovin published a detailed analysis in 1989.[44] The Mitnick attack proved these theoretical concerns were practically exploitable. RFC 1948, published in May 1996, proposed cryptographically random initial sequence numbers.[45] Operating systems began implementing the fix.

SYN cookies—a clever technique for handling SYN floods without exhausting server resources—were invented and deployed. Network administrators learned to filter packets with spoofed source addresses at network borders. The .rhosts mechanism fell out of favor, replaced by `SSH` and other protocols that didn't trust `IP` addresses for authentication.

The protocols themselves did not change. RFC 791 and RFC 793 still describe `IP` and `TCP` as they did in 1981. But the implementations evolved. The design choices Cerf and Kahn made in 1973 were patched over, worked around, compensated for.

The patches are imperfect. `IP` spoofing remains possible on many networks. DDoS attacks—the descendant of Mitnick's SYN flood—still afflict the internet. Source address verification exists but is not universally deployed. The trust model that made the internet possible remains embedded in its foundations.

We cannot start over. Flag Day was the last chance to break everything at once, and that was 1983. Every computer on Earth now speaks `TCP/IP`. The protocols are frozen by their own success. So the fixes came as layers: `TLS` to encrypt, firewalls to filter, authentication protocols to verify what the handshake never could.

When the network grew into something larger, stranger, more adversarial, the protocols did not change. Only the world around them did.

The design from those hotel notepads still describes the handshake.

SYN, SYN-ACK, ACK. Three packets, connection established. Cerf and Kahn worked it out in 1973—on a conference-break envelope, on legal pads in a Palo Alto hotel lobby—and what they drew then is what runs now, on every smartphone, every server, every router between them. The internet handles billions of TCP handshakes per second. The envelope is long gone. The architecture on it is not.

What they could not sketch was the scale. The ARPANET had about 40 hosts when they started writing. The internet now connects five billion people. The assumptions built into those three packets—that source addresses are honest, that sequence numbers are unpredictable, that the machines completing a handshake are who they claim to be—were reasonable for 40 hosts. They endure on five billion. The gap between what the sketch imagined and what it became is not a design flaw. It is the measure of what two engineers in a hotel lobby accidentally built.

TCP/IP carried packets across the globe. But a packet arriving at its destination network still faced one more problem: how to find the specific machine? IP addresses were logical, abstract—Ethernet cables connected physical hardware. Another protocol, written by an MIT programmer who described the network as a "jungle," would solve that problem. Its trust model would prove just as brittle.

CHAPTER 5

THE FORGOTTEN PROTOCOLS

The world is a jungle in general,
and the networking game contributes many animals.

– David C. Plummer, RFC 826, November 1982

5.1. THE EMBARRASSING PROBLEM

David Plummer had an embarrassingly simple problem.

November 1982. Plummer was working at MIT with Ethernet cables snaking across the computer lab floor. Ethernet—the physical network standard that would connect most of the world's computers—had just arrived. The DEC, Intel, and Xerox consortium had published their specification two years earlier. Now 10-megabit coaxial networks were spreading through universities and research labs.[46] Plummer could see the future of local networking laid out before him. What he couldn't see was how to deliver a packet to the right machine.

The difficulty: the Internet Protocol gave every machine a logical address, a 32-bit number like 10.0.0.1. Ethernet gave every machine a physical address, a 48-bit number assigned to the network card at the factory—though it can be changed in software, a fact that would matter later. `IP` knew where a packet should go, Ethernet knew how to get it there—but nothing connected the two.

Consider a packet arriving at a router that determined the destination, 10.0.0.5, was on the local network. The router knew the `IP` address, but the Ethernet hardware needed a MAC address—the 48-bit hardware identifier like `00:1A:2B:3C:4D:5E`. Since the router had no idea which MAC address corresponded to 10.0.0.5, the packet could not be delivered.

The obvious approach was a table. An administrator could maintain a file listing every `IP` address and its corresponding MAC address, updated by hand whenever machines were added or moved. But tables didn't scale. By 1982, networks were already too large and too dynamic for manual mapping.

Plummer's solution was to ask.

The Address Resolution Protocol, published as RFC 826[47], worked by asking. When a machine needed to find the hardware address for an `IP` address, it simply broadcast the question to the local network. Some machine would answer. No central registry, no configuration files, no administrator required.

Plummer acknowledged the collaborative development. "The protocol proposed here is the result of a great deal of discussion with several other people," he wrote in RFC 826, "most notably J. Noel Chiappa, Yogen Dalal, and James E. Kulp." This was how the early internet worked: small groups hashing out solutions over whiteboards and email, crediting each other in the RFCs.

One assumption Plummer didn't question: the machines telling you their addresses were telling the truth.

Why would anyone lie? The machines on a local network were physically present inside one building, often the same room. They belonged to the same organization, plugged in by the same administrators. If someone claimed an IP address, you believed them.

The locked door was the authentication mechanism.

This assumption made sense in 1982. The internet had a few hundred hosts—the official count that May was 235. A local network might have a few dozen machines, all owned by the same university department. The concept of an attacker on the local network didn't fit the mental model.

The local network was, by definition, local. Trusted.

More than a year earlier, Postel had published a different protocol with a similar assumption: the Internet Control Message Protocol, ICMP, published as RFC 792.[48]

The problem ICMP solved was different from ARP's. IP was "best effort" delivery. Packets were sent into the network and might or might not arrive. If they didn't arrive, no one knew why.

ICMP gave the network a vocabulary for its own failures. A router with nowhere to forward your packet sent back "Destination Unreachable." One drowning in traffic said "Source Quench," meaning slow down, and a packet that circled too long came back labeled "Time Exceeded," which at least explained its fate. Engineers could finally see inside the black box of packet routing.

The most useful message type was the simplest. Type 8 was Echo Request: "Are you there?" Type 0 was Echo Reply: "Yes, I'm here." Together, they became the basis for the `ping` command, a tool network administrators still use daily, forty years later.

"ICMP messages are sent in several situations," Postel wrote: "when a datagram cannot reach its destination, when the gateway does not have the buffering capacity to forward a datagram, and when the gateway can direct the host to send traffic on a shorter route."

That last situation was the Redirect message. A router that saw a packet and knew a better path could say so: "Next time, send traffic for that destination to this other gateway." The sender updated its routing table and used the better path.

Postel included a disclaimer. "The Internet Protocol is not designed to be absolutely reliable. The purpose of these control messages is to provide feedback about problems in the communication environment, not to make IP reliable."

Control messages for routers, feedback for diagnostic tools, helpful infrastructure for administrators debugging problems. The expectation was that ICMP would serve the network itself. Error messages were helpful, not weaponized.

Together, ARP and ICMP occupied a strange position in the protocol stack, living below the applications users saw, below even TCP and UDP. They were infrastructure, invisible to anyone not running a network. Most programmers gave them no thought. Most users had never heard of them.

But both protocols shared the same premise that ran through every RFC of the era: the network connected a small group of cooperating institutions. ARP expected your neighbors wouldn't lie about their identity. ICMP expected error messages would be helpful, not hostile. Both expectations were encoded into protocols that would become as permanent as the internet itself.

The few hundred hosts connected by phone lines would become a world of strangers—over 300,000 hosts by 1990, roughly 70 million by 2000. The protocols that assumed everyone was trustworthy would remain unchanged, running on every device, vulnerable to anyone who chose to lie.

5.2. TRUST ON THE WIRE

5.2.1. THE ADDRESS GAP

Every networked computer has at least two addresses. The IP address tells the network where the machine lives in the global hierarchy—which network, which subnet. The MAC address, assigned to the network interface at the factory (though software can override it), is how devices on the same wire recognize each other.

These two addresses have nothing to do with each other. The IP address is assigned by software; the MAC address is stamped into hardware. When you want to send a packet to your neighbor at 192.168.1.5, you know the IP address, but the Ethernet hardware needs the MAC address—the 48-bit identifier that makes one network card distinguishable from another.

How do you find out? You ask—and you believe whatever answer you get.

The ARP exchange is a two-step dance.

First, the requesting machine broadcasts an ARP request. The broadcast goes to every device on the local network. The request says, in effect: "I'm looking for 192.168.1.5. If that's you, please tell me your hardware address. I'm at 192.168.1.1 with hardware address `AA:BB:CC:DD:EE:FF`."

Every machine on the local segment receives this broadcast. Most ignore it—the IP address in the request isn't theirs. But the machine at 192.168.1.5 recognizes itself and sends a response, directly to the requester: "That's me. My hardware address is `11:22:33:44:55:66`."

Now the requester has what it needs, and it writes the pair down. The IP address and the hardware address go into a local table, the ARP cache, so the next packet bound for 192.168.1.5 can go out without a broadcast at all.

Notice what's missing: nothing verified that the response came from the real 192.168.1.5, and nothing proved ownership of the IP address. The machine asked a question and believed the first answer it received.

Cache entries expire after a timeout—typically five to twenty minutes. When an entry expires, the next packet triggers a new ARP request. But for those five to twenty minutes, whatever is in the cache is treated as truth. Poison the cache once, and you control the traffic until the entry expires.

Sometimes a machine announces its own address without being asked. This is called gratuitous ARP: an unsolicited ARP reply that says "I'm 192.168.1.5 at hardware address 11:22:33:44:55:66."

Gratuitous ARP has legitimate uses. When a machine boots up, it can announce itself to the network, populating the ARP caches of any machines that were waiting for it. When a server fails over to a backup, the backup can send a gratuitous ARP to inform the network of the new hardware address for the same IP.

But no mechanism prevents a malicious machine from sending gratuitous ARP replies with false information. No verification confirms that the sender really owns the IP address it claims. The receiving machines write the new mapping into their caches, taking the announcement at face value. One forged packet, and every host on the segment believes the gateway is at the wrong address.

5.2.2. ICMP: THE ERROR VOCABULARY

ICMP rides inside IP. Every ICMP message is delivered as an IP packet, with the protocol field set to 1. (By comparison, TCP is protocol 6 and UDP—a simpler, faster cousin of TCP that doesn't guarantee delivery—is protocol 17.) The ICMP header starts with a Type field (what kind of message), a Code field (more specific details), and a checksum. The rest varies by message type.

`ICMP` speaks in message types, and each type tells your machine something about the network. The question is whether to believe it.

Type 8 is Echo Request—"Are you there?"—and Type 0 is Echo Reply—"Yes, I'm here." These two became the `ping` command: simple, helpful, and completely unauthenticated, since anyone can forge either side of that conversation.

Type 3 is Destination Unreachable, the network's way of saying your packet had nowhere to go—a dead host, or a closed port. It is also a convenient lie for an attacker who wants your connection to give up. Your machine accepts the message without asking who sent it.

Type `11` is Time Exceeded, sent when a packet bounces around too long, its time-to-live counter hits zero, and a router discards it. `Traceroute` depends on these messages—and so does an attacker mapping your network infrastructure.

Type 5 is Redirect. A router is telling you: "Send traffic for that destination through this other gateway instead." Your machine updates its routing table and obeys. What if the "router" is an attacker? What if the "better path" runs through their machine?

Every message type expects honest senders, and none of them verify identity.

From these building blocks, network engineers built two essential diagnostic tools.

`Ping` sends Echo Requests and listens for Echo Replies. If replies come back, the destination is alive, and the round-trip time gives you the latency. Silence suggests a problem, though not which one. The reply arrives with no evidence that it came from the machine you addressed.

`Traceroute` exploits the Time Exceeded message by sending a packet with TTL set to `1`; the first router decrements TTL to zero and sends back Time Exceeded, revealing itself. Then `traceroute` sends another packet with TTL set to 2, and the second router responds. The process continues, one hop at a time, mapping the path from source to destination.

These tools have been part of every network administrator's toolkit since the 1980s. They rely entirely on `ICMP` messages that can be sent by anyone, to anyone, about any packet—real or fabricated.

`ARP` and `ICMP` trust differently than `Telnet` or `FTP`—not the network path, not client declarations, but the identity of neighbors, the machines sitting next to you on the same wire.

When a machine broadcasts "I am 192.168.1.5," every other machine on the segment believes it. `ARP` includes no verification, no signature, no proof. The protocol cannot tell the difference between a legitimate announcement and a lie. `ICMP` trusts similarly: when a router says "Destination Unreachable" or "Use this better route," the recipient believes it.

The security model was physical. A machine that could broadcast on your local network had to be plugged into your building's wiring, which meant someone in your organization had run that cable and knew which office it served.

5.2.3. THE HONEST NEIGHBOR

`ARP` has no CVE—it cannot, because the protocol's trust model, that neighbors on a network segment are honest, is the vulnerability itself. There is nothing to patch, since the CVE system tracks bugs in implementations, not flaws in design. The specification did what it said. The world did something else.

5.3. THE AMPLIFICATION ATTACK

5.3.1. WHEN TRUST BECAME LIABILITY

Traffic on the University of Minnesota's network climbed one day in March 1998, and the central servers got slower along with it.[49,50] It looked at first like a crowd of users showing up at once. Then a system administrator looked at what the packets actually were: `ICMP` Echo Replies, thousands of them a second, arriving from hundreds of different sources.

They called it Smurf, named after the program that automated it[51]—a mechanism simple enough to fit on a single floppy disk.

The impact was immediate. For nearly two and a half hours, users across the university's four campuses experienced slow access to central servers or the internet. The university's security incident coordinator, Susan Levy Haskell, described the attack as a network traffic jam: "It was as if someone tried to push a river down a soda straw."[49]

The attack ran on directed broadcasts, a feature of the era: send one packet to a remote subnet's broadcast address and every machine on that subnet received it. The attacker aimed `ICMP` Echo Requests at those addresses and forged the source `IP`, filling in the victim's address instead of their own.

Every machine on the broadcast network received the Echo Request, every machine sent an Echo Reply, and every reply went to the victim—the spoofed source address.

If the broadcast network had 256 machines, one forged packet produced 256 replies. If the attacker found ten such networks and sent a hundred packets per second to each, the victim received 256,000 packets per second—all legitimate `ICMP` traffic from hosts that believed they were responding to a genuine `ping`.

The arithmetic favored the attacker. Someone on a slow dial-up connection could bury a target sitting on a fast T1 line, and the bandwidth doing the burying came from networks that had no idea they were involved.

Lists of vulnerable networks circulated in hacker forums, where attackers called them "Smurf amplifiers" and prized the big ones, since more machines meant more replies. Minnesota was on the receiving end of those lists: someone had forged the university's address into their pings, and hundreds of obliging networks aimed the replies at it.

ICMP was doing what the specification said it should do: Echo Requests received Echo Replies, error messages were helpful, and the protocol performed correctly. It just never anticipated someone lying about who was asking.

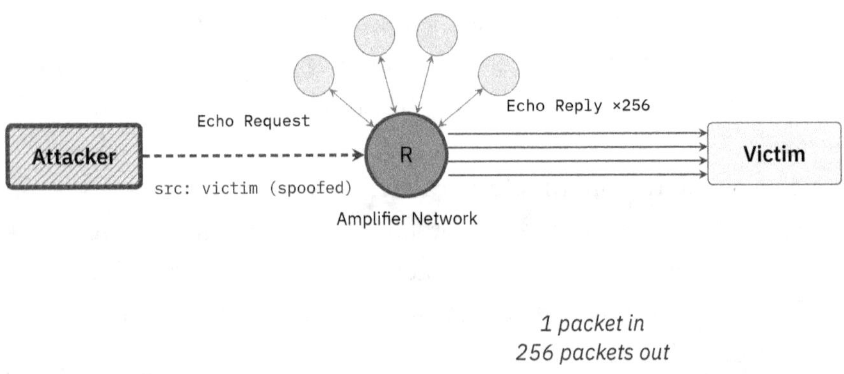

Figure 5.1: Smurf amplification attack. The attacker sends a single ICMP Echo Request to a broadcast network with the victim's IP as the spoofed source address. Every host on the amplifier network responds, flooding the victim with Echo Replies. One packet becomes 256.

The Smurf attack wasn't the first time ICMP became a weapon. Two years earlier, in late 1996, system administrators started noticing machines crashing for no apparent reason.[52] Windows workstations.

Unix servers. Macintosh computers. All dying the same way, freezing and requiring hard reboots.

The cause was called the Ping of Death. The exploit was almost embarrassingly simple.

The IP protocol specified that packets could be up to 65,535 bytes—the maximum value in a 16-bit length field. But ICMP Echo Requests were supposed to be small, a few dozen bytes at most. What happened if you sent an oversized Echo Request?

On a properly implemented system, nothing—the packet would be discarded. But many implementations had a bug: they allocated a fixed-size buffer for incoming ICMP data, trusting that the data would fit. When an oversized packet arrived, the data overflowed the buffer, memory was corrupted, and the system crashed.

The attack could be launched from a single command line. On Windows, `ping -l 65510 victim` oversized the packet past the legal limit. One command, typed from anywhere, could crash a remote machine.

Nearly every operating system needed a patch, and Microsoft, Apple, and the Unix vendors all shipped one. The demonstration lingered after the fixes landed. A protocol built for diagnostics could reach across the internet and crash a machine without so much as a login.

ARP's reckoning came more quietly, spreading through coffee shops and hotel lobbies rather than making headlines.

ARP cache poisoning, sometimes called ARP spoofing, took no more effort than sending a packet. Anyone on the victim's local network could forge an ARP reply claiming the gateway's IP address lived at the attacker's own MAC address. The victim's cache rewrote itself on the spot, and from then on the victim's outbound traffic went to the attacker instead of the gateway.

From there the attacker could read the traffic or change it, though the quietest option was to copy each packet and pass the original along to the real gateway. The victim's connection kept working, maybe a little slower, with every packet routed through a stranger's machine first.

This was an interception attack—sometimes called man-in-the-middle or MITM—at the network layer, before encryption could help. If the victim was browsing HTTP websites, everything was visible: usernames, passwords, session cookies, private messages. If the victim logged into their email, the credentials were captured. If the victim checked their bank balance, the numbers were exposed.

The attack required being on the same local network as the victim. In 1982, when Plummer wrote RFC 826, this seemed like a significant limitation. Local networks were corporate offices, university labs, research facilities—places you had to physically enter to join.

By the 2000s, local networks were everywhere. Coffee shop WiFi. Hotel business centers. Airport lounges. Conference venues. Coworking spaces. Anywhere that offered public wireless access, anyone could join the local network. The locked door had vanished, but ARP hadn't changed.

Tools made the attack easy to automate. The dsniff package included `arpspoof`, a command-line tool for forging ARP replies and poisoning a target's cache.[53]

Security researchers demonstrated the attacks at conferences, published papers, and warned about the risks of public WiFi, but most users had never heard of ARP and didn't understand what was at stake. The defenses, when they came, were partial and imperfect.

Administrators could pin the mappings down by hand, writing static ARP entries for the devices that mattered most. That works until the hardware changes, and on a network with a few thousand devices, the hardware is always changing.

Enterprise switches offered something better. Dynamic ARP Inspection watched DHCP hand out addresses, recorded which MAC address received which IP, and checked later ARP traffic against that record. The catch was the price of admission: managed switches and someone on staff who knew how to configure them. Coffee shops and home networks had neither.

The most widespread mitigation for ARP spoofing was HTTPS. If the traffic itself was encrypted, intercepting it revealed nothing useful. Encrypted packets would flow past, but their contents remained unreadable. The push to encrypt everything—HTTPS Everywhere, certificate transparency, browser warnings for unencrypted connections—was partly a response to the impossibility of securing the lower layers.

For ICMP, the Smurf attack prompted RFC 2644[54], which recommended that networks disable directed broadcasts. Ingress filtering, described in BCP 38[55], recommended that networks reject packets with obviously spoofed source addresses. If a packet claiming to come from 192.168.1.1 arrived on an interface where 192.168.1.0/24 wasn't reachable, the packet was clearly forged and should be dropped.

Both recommendations were sound, and neither was adopted everywhere. Networks that took the guidance stopped serving as Smurf amplifiers, and the rest remained available for abuse. The attack faded anyway, for a reason that had nothing to do with fixing it: attackers moved on to botnets, which could generate flood traffic directly and needed no amplifier at all.

The Ping of Death was patched in the operating systems themselves, where bounds checking, properly implemented, threw away oversized packets before they could overflow anything. It was the rare flaw in this story with a real fix.

ICMP Redirect attacks persisted longer, since a forged Redirect message could tell a victim to route traffic through a hostile machine, achieving the same interception position as ARP spoofing. Some operating systems started ignoring ICMP Redirects entirely, or accepting them only from the current gateway, but legacy systems remained vulnerable and the attack remained in penetration testers' toolkits.

Forty years after Plummer and Postel published their RFCs, the protocols run unchanged on every network.

We can watch them with a packet sniffer: connect to any WiFi network and capture traffic. `ARP` requests broadcast constantly—"Who has 192.168.1.1? Who has 192.168.1.254?"—while `ICMP` Echo Requests fly as someone pings a server and Time Exceeded messages appear as someone runs `traceroute`. The infrastructure of the 1980s, still operating, still trusting, still vulnerable.

The protocols cannot be fixed without breaking compatibility with billions of devices. `ARP` has no authentication because adding it would require changing every network card, every router, every switch. `ICMP` has no verification because the installed base of `IP` implementations assumes the current packet format.

So we compensate: encryption at the higher layers, networks chopped into segments, monitoring that flags `ARP` traffic that looks wrong, firewalls that drop `ICMP` arriving from outside. All of it costs money and takes people who know what they are doing, and none of it changes the design underneath, which still assumes honesty.

David Plummer, writing in 1982, noted that "hosts don't transmit information about anyone other than themselves." He meant it as a feature—no machine could lie about another machine's address—but a machine could lie about its own. On a network anyone can join, that lie is enough.

Jon Postel, in RFC 792, described `ICMP` as "feedback about problems in the communication environment." The feedback was genuine and the problems were real, but the feedback mechanism itself became the problem—error messages designed to help administrators became weapons for attackers.

A network that verifies every packet, authenticates every address, validates every error message—such a network would be slower, more complex, harder to build. The engineers of 1982 made reasonable choices for the networks they had. Those choices became permanent. The networks changed. The protocols didn't.

Right now, on your local network, ARP is asking who has the gateway address.

The question goes out as a broadcast, invisible, automatic, running whether your device is idle or busy. Some machine answers. Your device believes it without asking for proof. The mapping goes into the cache. Packets flow. You never see any of it.

This exchange has been happening on every Ethernet network since 1982. The protocol has not changed. The question is the same. The belief is the same. Billions of devices ask and answer these questions every second—on home networks, in corporate offices, at every coffee shop and hotel with WiFi. The locked door that Plummer assumed would protect these conversations is long gone. The conversations continue anyway.

The protocols of the 1980s, decades old, still believing every answer they receive. And ARP is not alone. While Plummer and Postel were designing how machines would find each other on local networks, another system had already taken shape—one that would become the internet's most-used application. It began with a researcher at BBN, a nearly forgotten key on a Model 33 Teletype, and a decision made in seconds that would outlast everything else he built.

==================================

CHAPTER 6

THE ELECTRONIC POST OFFICE

==================================

The objective of Simple Mail Transfer Protocol (SMTP) is to transfer mail reliably and efficiently.

— RFC 821, Jon Postel, August 1982

6.1. THE LEAST-USED KEY

Late 1971. Ray Tomlinson sits at his desk at Bolt Beranek and Newman in Cambridge, Massachusetts.[56] Printouts and manuals cover the desk; somewhere under them a cup of coffee has gone cold. BBN works out of a converted candy factory in an industrial neighborhood, which suits it—the place has no interest in looking important. The company employs some of the best computer scientists in the country. Since 1969 they have been building the ARPANET's guts: the Interface Message Processors, or IMPs.

Tomlinson is staring at his Model 33 Teletype keyboard. He has a problem nobody asked him to solve.

The ARPANET can connect computers. Researchers at UCLA can log into machines at MIT. But you cannot leave a message for someone who isn't there. Local mail programs exist—you can write to someone else who uses your same computer—but the network changes nothing. If you want to reach a colleague at Stanford, you still call them on the telephone.

Tomlinson has been working on a file transfer protocol. Along the way, he's modified a local mail program called SNDMSG to send messages between machines. The technical part works. Now he needs a way to address these messages—some notation indicating which user on which computer should receive them.

He looks at the keyboard. Forty-odd characters stare back. He needs a symbol that won't appear in anyone's name, something separating "user" from "host" in a way that's obvious. The percent sign? Already used. The dollar sign? Too closely associated with money. The ampersand? Too common in company names.

His eyes land on @.

It's the least-used character on the keyboard. It shows up in accounting contexts—"10 widgets @ $5 each"—but almost nowhere else. And it has a meaning that fits perfectly: "at." User at host. smith@bbn-tenexa.

Tomlinson sends test messages from one PDP-10 to another sitting a few feet away. He would later say there was no way to know which message first arrived intact: he typed whatever came to mind while debugging the program.[56]

The most important message in the history of communication, and nobody wrote it down.

The @ sign became the most recognized symbol of the digital age. Tomlinson had chosen it in a few seconds, without a committee meeting or formal proposal. A hack, in the original sense: a quick solution to a practical problem, implemented fast because it needed to exist.

What Tomlinson didn't design—what nobody designed—was any way to verify who was sending a message. When he typed QWER-

TYUIOP into his terminal, the message said it came from him because he said it came from him. The receiving computer believed it because computers, in 1971, believed what they were told.

Email spread through the ARPANET like a weed. The network had been built to share computing resources—expensive mainframes researchers could log into remotely. The funding agencies at DARPA expected packet switching to prove itself through remote computing. Email wasn't on anyone's roadmap.

But by 1973, a study found that 75% of ARPANET traffic was email.[57]

The finding shocked administrators. They had built a highway for compute jobs. Instead people were sending notes to each other. Researchers had discovered that sending messages was more useful than sharing computers. A physicist at Stanford could pose a question at 3 AM and wake up to answers from MIT, UCLA, and BBN. Email collapsed the tyranny of time zones and the telephone, which demanded both parties be present simultaneously.

Email became the application that justified the network.

The message format was not designed so much as accumulated. Different sites invented different conventions, and the ones that worked spread. Headers appeared—From, To, Subject, Date—and then Cc for carbon copies, an anachronism borrowed from typewriters and onionskin paper. Bcc followed, so a sender could hide some recipients from the others. None of this was a standard. It was whatever got the mail delivered.

Email mattered too much by the late 1970s to keep being a mess. Every site had its own habits about character encodings and line lengths, and habits don't travel. A message composed perfectly on one machine could arrive on another with its headers scrambled and its formatting gone. Somebody was going to have to write the rules down.

In August 1982, two RFCs appeared that would define email for the next four decades.[57] Postel wrote RFC 821, specifying `SMTP`—Simple

Mail Transfer Protocol—the rules by which mail servers relay messages.[58] David Crocker published RFC 822 the same month, defining the message rather than the transfer: the headers and address syntax at the top, then the blank line where the body begins.[59]

Together, these two documents built the electronic post office. RFC 821 defined how post offices pass mail. RFC 822 defined what letters look like.

Both were simple, direct, and built on a premise that would prove disastrous: senders tell the truth about who they are.

Postel, writing `SMTP`, wasn't designing for adversaries. The ARPANET connected universities and research labs—the same community that had built every protocol in this book so far. If a message purported to come from a researcher at MIT, it probably had. Forging email would have been professional suicide in a community small enough that everyone would have known. The word "security" appears exactly zero times in the original RFC 821 specification, and not because Postel was careless. Defending mail against people who wanted to break it was not the problem in front of him.

The protocol reflected that culture. A sending server announces itself with HELO, says where the mail is from with MAIL FROM, names its recipient with RCPT TO, and hands over the body. The receiving server checks none of it. It takes the sender's word, and in 1982 that was both the fast thing to do and the sensible one. The researchers wanted mail that worked, and they got it. They also got, without knowing, the architecture of spam and billion-dollar fraud.

RFC 821 defined just fourteen commands.[58] A programmer could read the specification in an afternoon and have a working mail server by evening. When something went wrong, you could telnet to port 25 and type the commands by hand, watching the server answer each one. That readability was deliberate—debugging is easy when the machines talk in a language you can read over their shoulder. Lying in a language that simple is just as easy.

6.2. THE ENVELOPE AND THE LETTER

6.2.1. HOW EMAIL WORKS

When we send an email, we're not really sending it. We're asking a series of servers to carry it for us, like passing a letter through a chain of post offices until it reaches the right one. The metaphor isn't perfect, but it's close. Email works through "store and forward": the mail program gives the message to a server, that server stores it temporarily, then forwards it to the next server, which stores it again, and so on until the message reaches the recipient's mailbox. The message might pass through three or four servers on its way across the internet.

The chain tolerates gaps. A phone call needs both parties on the line at the same moment; email doesn't, because every hop holds a copy. If the next server is down, the server holding the message waits and tries again—for days, if that's what it takes. So the mail moved even when the network didn't.

And in the 1970s, connectivity was always unreliable.

The store-and-forward design also meant each server in the chain had to believe the previous one. The message that arrives at hop three claims to have come from hop two, which claims it came from hop one. No server verifies these claims. The message passes through the system on faith.

SMTP governs the relay. The conversation runs in plain text that any programmer can read: one server opens a connection to another, and they talk in a pattern rigid enough to memorize. Nothing in that pattern asks for credentials, and nothing checks that either machine is what it says it is. Watch what's missing:

```
Server:  220 mail.example.com SMTP Ready
Client:  HELO sender.example.com
Server:  250 Hello sender.example.com
Client:  MAIL FROM:<alice@sender.example.com>
Server:  250 OK
Client:  RCPT TO:<bob@example.com>
Server:  250 OK
Client:  DATA
Server:  354 Start mail input
Client:  From: alice@sender.example.com
Client:  To: bob@example.com
Client:  Subject: Hello
Client:  This is the message body.
Client:  .
Server:  250 OK
Client:  QUIT
Server:  221 Bye
```

The client says HELO and claims an identity; the receiving host acknowledges without checking. The client announces who the mail is from—OK, no verification. The client names the recipient—OK again—then DATA, the message body, and a period to end.

Every server response starts with a three-digit code: 250 means "OK, I accepted what you said"—not "I verified what you said," just "I accepted it."

Codes starting with 4 mean temporary failures, while codes starting with 5 mean permanent ones. Postel specified exactly what each code meant, but he did not specify how to verify the claims that triggered them.

The response code system borrowed from FTP and would influence HTTP decades later. The codes let automated systems make decisions without parsing human-readable text. A sending server knows immediately whether the transaction succeeded—or at least, whether the receiving server accepted the claims it was given.

Two computers, speaking in plain English commands, passing messages between them. A programmer in 1983 could watch the conversation scroll by on a terminal and understand exactly what was happening. But look closely at that conversation. The client claims to be `sender.example.com`. The client claims the mail is from `alice@sender.example.com`. The server says OK to both. It doesn't check whether those claims are true. It can't. SMTP provides no mechanism for verification.

To understand email's vulnerabilities, we need to understand that every message has two separate parts: the envelope and the contents. The envelope consists of the SMTP commands—MAIL FROM and RCPT TO—the routing instructions that servers process along the way. They tell each server where the message came from and where it's going. The contents are different: the headers and body that come after DATA. The From: line, the To: line, the Subject:—these are what the recipient sees when they open the message. They're part of the message, not part of the envelope. But the envelope and the contents can say different things. They often do.

```
SMTP Envelope:                    Message Headers:
MAIL FROM:<attacker@evil.com>     From: ceo@yourcompany.com
RCPT TO:<victim@yourcompany.com> To: victim@yourcompany.
    com
                                  Subject: Urgent Wire
    Transfer
```

The envelope says the real sender is `attacker@evil.com`. The headers say the message is from the CEO. Most email programs show you the headers, not the envelope. The recipient sees only what the attacker wants them to see. This is the unsigned envelope from Chapter 4 again—except here the metaphor is literal, because "envelope" is the spec's own word: you can drop a letter in a mailbox with any return address printed on it, and the mail carrier will never verify you live there. You could impersonate anyone. That's how SMTP works.

Your server still has to find the destination. Sending to `bob@example.com`, it asks DNS who handles mail for example.com. The answer arrives as MX records—DNS entries that list the servers willing to accept incoming mail for a domain.

```
$ dig MX example.com
example.com.    3600    IN    MX    10 mail.example.com.
example.com.    3600    IN    MX    20 backup.example.com.
```

The lookup returns `mail.example.com` at priority 10 (lowest wins), so your server connects there to deliver the message. If that server is down, it tries the backup. One address can resolve to different servers at different times, which is how an organization moves its mail infrastructure without breaking anyone's address book. It also means an address points wherever DNS says it points, and DNS can be made to say things. Poisoning it is a story for Chapter 7; email's routing, meanwhile, rests on answers nobody checks.

6.2.2. THE SENDER'S WORD

SMTP's built-in expectation is perhaps the most consequential in this book: senders are whoever they say they are.

The MAIL FROM address accepts any value, and so does the From: header. The protocol provides no verification mechanism, no callback to the claimed domain, no cryptographic proof. A server receiving mail cannot distinguish a legitimate message from the CEO from a forgery sent by an adversary in another country.

> RFC 821 --- August 1982 --- Jon Postel
>
> The first step in the procedure is the MAIL command. The <reverse-path> contains the source mailbox. This command tells the SMTP-receiver that a new mail transaction is starting... It gives the reverse-path which can be used to report errors. If accepted, the receiver-SMTP returns a 250 OK reply.

Postel specified what the sender provides. He said nothing about verifying the sender's claims, and the silence was deliberate. In 1982, verification would have required infrastructure that didn't exist—public key cryptography was barely understood, and key distribution was an unsolved problem. The cultural reason mattered more. Among a few hundred researchers, honesty was less a hope than a fair description of the people at the other end of the wire.

What happens when senders lie? Spam is the most visible problem: anyone can impersonate anyone, so servers cannot reject mail from forged addresses. Spam filters must examine message content because they can't trust the envelope, and the industry has poured billions of dollars into building better filters. The attackers have responded by making their spam look more like legitimate mail. The arms race never ends.

Phishing goes further. An attacker can send mail that appears to originate from your bank, your employer, or your government. The From: header will show the spoofed address. Most users cannot detect the forgery. Security training tells employees to hover over links, verify unexpected requests, be suspicious of urgency. But people are busy. The requests seem reasonable. The email looks right. Training helps, but it's not enough.

Business email compromise takes it all the way. An attacker writes as the CEO, or as a vendor's accounts department, and asks for a wire transfer or a set of credentials. The recipient sees a familiar name at the top of the message and does what it says.

All three attacks exploit the same gap: SMTP accepts claims of identity without verification. The server followed its instructions perfectly. It just never expected adversaries.

6.3. THE FIRST SPAM

The first spam wasn't called spam—the word didn't exist yet.[60] On May 3, 1978, it was just an advertisement—and an outrage.

Gary Thuerk was a marketer at Digital Equipment Corporation, then twenty-one years old and headquartered in Maynard, Massachusetts. DEC had grown from three employees to tens of thousands, riding the wave of minicomputers that brought computing power out of glass-walled data centers and into engineering departments. Now Thuerk had new computers to sell: the DECsystem-20 and DECSYSTEM-2020, machines with built-in ARPANET support. He wanted to tell people about them. He had access to a list of ARPANET users on the West Coast—researchers, engineers, the people most likely to need such machines. Why not send them an invitation to a product demonstration?

The instinct was ordinary marketing. The ARPANET was small, its users mostly knew each other by name, and advertising on it had simply never occurred to anyone. The network was not a commercial place: the Department of Defense paid for it, and selling things over it felt like hanging a billboard in a university library. The Acceptable Use Policy did prohibit commercial activity. Enforcement was another matter. Thuerk saw a list of names and a product to sell them.

The message came out ugly for technical reasons. Addresses in 1978 were long—a username, then a machine name, with no DNS yet to shorten anything. Thuerk tried to fit all 393 into the To: field and the software choked. Addresses spilled down into the message body, so an already aggressive solicitation arrived looking like a malfunction too.

He composed his message:

```
MAIL-FROM: THUERK at DEC-MARLBORO
SUBJECT: INVITE YOU TO COME SEE THE NEWEST
         MEMBER OF THE DECSYSTEM-20 FAMILY

DIGITAL WILL BE GIVING A PRODUCT PRESENTATION OF
THE NEWEST MEMBERS OF THE DECSYSTEM-20 FAMILY...

WE INVITE YOU TO COME SEE THE 2020 AND HEAR ABOUT
THE DECSYSTEM-20 FAMILY AT THE TWO DIFFERENT TIMES
AND DIFFERENT LOCATIONS...
```

Thuerk sent the message to 393 ARPANET addresses.[60] It was, by any reasonable definition, an advertisement sent in bulk to people who hadn't asked for it. It was spam, before the word existed.

The reaction was swift, though not unanimous. Mark Crispin at Stanford called it "a clear and flagrant abuse of the directory." Jake Feinler at SRI objected that advertising gave networked companies an unfair edge over those without access. Richard Stallman, then at MIT, was contrarian even here: he first mused that a product demo "MIGHT have been interesting," then, after actually seeing the message, objected mainly to its bloated header. "Nobody should be allowed to send a message with a header that long," he wrote, "no matter what it is about." The decisive complaint came from Major Raymond Czahor of the Defense Communications Agency, who called the message "a flagrant violation of the use of Arpanet," a federal network reserved for government business, and warned that action would follow to prevent a repeat.

The outrage was genuine. These researchers had built something for science, for collaboration, for the free exchange of ideas. Thuerk had used it to sell computers. He had treated their shared resource as a marketing channel.

Thuerk defended himself. He was just trying to reach potential customers. The ARPANET was there, the addresses were there, and sending was free. Why wouldn't he use it? DEC sold $12 million worth of computers from those product demonstrations.[60] The message of the first spam was not lost on marketers: bulk email works. The ARPANET community could object all it wanted. Sending unsolicited messages cost nothing and produced revenue. The economics were irresistible.

Spam stayed a nuisance for twenty years, the kind of thing you complained about and deleted. Then the volume caught up with the network's growth. By the late 1990s the mail arrived in floods—"Make Money Fast" chain letters, Nigerian princes offering to share a fortune, advertisements for dubious pharmaceuticals—and clearing it out became part of the workday. That was the smaller problem. Fraud was moving in.

The word "phishing" appeared in the mid-1990s, for attacks that fished for credentials.[61] The name is "fishing" with the "ph" borrowed from "phreaking," the phone-hacking culture that got there first. The technique needed no cleverness. An email posing as America Online asked users to "verify" their password. The link led to a page that looked like America Online, and whatever was typed there went to the attacker. It worked because nothing in email proves who sent it. By the 2000s the copies were good: bank notices you could not tell from the real ones, IRS tax notices, a FedEx alert about a package that did not exist. Each was a link to a page built to harvest whatever the victim typed into it.

Then the attacks got personal. Rather than blast out a million generic messages, an attacker researches one target and writes for that target alone. The CFO gets a note about an upcoming board meeting; the executive assistant gets one that references a real travel itinerary. Everything around the lie is true, which is what makes the lie work.

The 2010s produced the expensive version, which the FBI calls Business Email Compromise—BEC. A crew starts with the org chart: who runs the company, who signs off on wire transfers. LinkedIn supplies much of it, and a company's own press releases and regulatory filings supply the rest. Then comes one email, apparently from the CEO, addressed to somebody in finance, with a subject line like "Urgent Wire Transfer" or "Confidential Request."

The body asks for a payment today, to an account the message supplies—a new vendor, an acquisition still under wraps. The CEO is traveling and needs it handled quietly. Everything the employee can check is real: the name, the details about the company, the address in the From: header. `SMTP` never verified that last one, and the header says whatever the attacker typed. So the transfer goes out, moves through a chain of banks, and is gone.

The FBI's Internet Crime Complaint Center counted $2.4 billion in BEC losses in 2021[62] and $2.7 billion in 2022.[63] Both figures are floors. Plenty of companies never report, out of embarrassment or fear of the regulators who would arrive next. The losses land on small businesses that lose their operating capital and on municipalities out millions in tax revenue. Nonprofits lose donations meant for people who needed them. Each number is also an employee who did exactly what the email said, and found out later what the email was.

Some cases are spectacular. In 2016, a Lithuanian man named Evaldas Rimasauskas identified a gap in how Google and Facebook processed invoices from their Asian hardware suppliers. He registered a company in Latvia with the same name as Quanta Computer, a real Taiwanese manufacturer that did business with both tech giants. Then he sent invoices—dozens of them, over two years—from forged email addresses that appeared to belong to Quanta. The invoices looked authentic, the payment requests seemed routine, and Google and Facebook, collectively, wired him more than $120 million—roughly $98 million from Facebook and $23 million from Google.[64] Rimasauskas was eventually caught and extradited, sentenced in December 2019 to five years in prison. But most BEC attackers operate from jurisdictions that don't cooperate with American law enforcement, and their victims never recover the money.

The attacks don't require technical sophistication—an attacker doesn't need to break encryption or exploit buffer overflows, just send an email from a forged address and convince someone to act on it. `SMTP` makes the first part trivially easy.

The email community has been bolting authentication onto a protocol that never asked for it, and the bolts have names: `SPF`, `DKIM`, `DMARC`.[65–67] `SPF`, the Sender Policy Framework, lets a domain publish a `DNS` record naming the servers allowed to send its mail. A receiver can look that list up. Mail claiming to come from `example.com` that arrives from a machine example.com never listed is, at minimum, suspicious.

`DKIM`—DomainKeys Identified Mail—signs the message itself, the way a wax seal once told you whether a letter had been opened on the road. The sending domain signs with a private key and publishes the matching public key in `DNS`, where any receiver can find it. Because the signature covers the headers and the body, changing a comma breaks it.

`DMARC` (Domain-based Message Authentication, Reporting, and Conformance) ties `SPF` and `DKIM` together and tells receiving servers what to do when checks fail: accept, quarantine, or reject. It also provides a reporting mechanism so domain owners can see who is sending mail purportedly from their domain. Together, these technologies can prevent some spoofing. If a company publishes strict `DMARC` policies and all its partners do too, attackers can't easily forge that company's email address.

Full `DMARC` enforcement remains rare. Plenty of domains publish no `DMARC` policy at all, and plenty more publish one that only asks to be told about failures rather than acting on them. Old systems can't run the checks. Perfectly legitimate mail fails `SPF` or `DKIM` all the time, because a mailing list forwarded it or a `DNS` record was entered wrong. The whole overlay is optional, and it shows.

`DMARC` working as designed does not help as much as it should. An attacker registers `examp1e.com`, with a digit where the letter belongs, and signs everything correctly, because the domain really is theirs. Or they steal a real employee's account and send from an address that passes every check there is. Authentication proves a message came from a particular domain. Users read it as proof the message is safe. Nothing in the specification closes that distance.

More than forty years after Thuerk's spam, more than twenty years after phishing became mainstream, email still lacks universal sender authentication. The patches help, but they're patches. The protocol underneath still accepts senders at their word. Modern email systems run machine learning models on every incoming message, analyzing writing style, link destinations, attachment types, sender reputation, and dozens of other signals. These systems catch most attacks. But "most" isn't "all," and every success teaches attackers what to avoid next time.

Email is the clearest case of a pattern that runs through this whole book. `SMTP` grew up among people who were honest with each other because dishonesty would have cost them something. Its designers saw no reason to build verification that the community already supplied. Then the community stopped being a community. A few hundred researchers became a few billion users, and whoever is impersonating a CEO for a wire transfer this morning does not worry about their standing among MIT professors. The protocol stayed put. `SMTP` in 2025 is structurally what `SMTP` was in 1982—same commands, same design, and MAIL FROM still accepts whatever the sender types into it.

The @ symbol that Ray Tomlinson chose in 1971 changed how the world communicates.

He picked it in a few seconds. No committee approved it. The character was sitting on the keyboard, almost never used, meaning exactly the right thing: "at." And the system he built around it connected people across distances and time zones in ways that telephone and letter could not. A physicist at Stanford could ask a question at midnight and wake to answers from three continents. Email made the global research community feel like a hallway.

The same openness that made any message possible made any forgery possible. Email connects and deceives through the same mechanism, the same fourteen commands, the same unverified MAIL FROM field. The spam folders that intercept billions of fraudulent messages every day are compensating for a design choice made before anyone imagined that strangers would ever use this system. The choice wasn't wrong for 1971. It just never changed. The mail still arrives—most of it real, some of it dangerous, none of it verified at the source.

Thuerk proved that the social costs of dishonesty vanish when the money is good enough. Forty years later, more than 350 billion emails cross the internet every day, and no one can be certain which ones to believe. The ARPANET was a professional network. The internet is not. The protocol doesn't know the difference.

Every one of those messages still has to find its destination—a machine somewhere that will accept mail for the name to the right of the `@`. In the early years a single file listed every host on the network, typed and retyped by hand. It worked until the network outgrew it—and the woman who kept that file went looking for something that could keep pace.

PART II

THE INTERNET

CHAPTER 7

THE PHONEBOOK

Host name to address mappings were maintained
by the Network Information Center (NIC)
in a single file (HOSTS.TXT) which was FTPed by all hosts.
The total network bandwidth consumed
in distributing a new version by this scheme
is proportional to the square
of the number of hosts in the network.

– RFC 1034, Paul Mockapetris, 1987

7.1. THE FILE THAT KEPT GROWING

In 1982, Elizabeth "Jake" Feinler had a problem that would not stop growing.

From her office at the Stanford Research Institute, Feinler ran the Network Information Center.[68] Her team maintained documentation, answered questions, and kept track of every computer on the ARPANET. Adding a new machine meant calling Jake's office. Someone wrote it down.

The file was called HOSTS.TXT. It listed every computer on the ARPANET: name, address, operating system, who to contact if something went wrong. When Feinler took over the NIC in 1972, the file held a few hundred entries. By 1982 it held thousands. By year's end, it would grow by another thousand.

In RFC 608, M.D. Kudlick described the process: "Jake Feinler at the NIC designed and maintains a source file... We shall write a program to generate the ASCII file."[69] Before anyone could download it, Feinler maintained it by hand.

The file spread by FTP: every site downloaded the whole thing from the NIC, so the bandwidth it consumed grew with the square of the number of hosts. Every new computer made the distribution problem worse, twice over.

The phone rang. Another sysadmin, another request. Could we add LOGIC? Sorry, there was already a LOGIC at MIT. How about LOGIC2? The administrator sighed.

Name collisions multiplied. The early ARPANET had a flat namespace. When the network had dozens of hosts, uniqueness was easy. With hundreds, every good name was taken.

Feinler pushed for a hierarchical system that would delegate naming authority.[68] Let MIT manage its own names. Let Stanford manage its own. The NIC would manage the top level.

The idea made sense, but the implementation didn't exist.

Hundreds of miles south, Paul Mockapetris was working on exactly this problem.[70]

Postel had asked him to look at the naming crisis. Several proposals were circulating, none of them close to consensus, and the working group had been meeting long enough that the discussions were starting to repeat themselves. Mockapetris decided to try something different.

He saw it as a question of authority. A file kept in one place meant a single point of control: the NIC approved every change, and a site wanting one address still had to take all of them.

Mockapetris proposed splitting both namespace and database. Names would be hierarchical, divided by dots. MIT's machines would live under `mit.edu`, Stanford's under `stanford.edu`. Each organization would maintain its own piece of the hierarchy, answering queries for names it owned and referring queries for names it didn't.

The root would be small—a handful of servers knowing the top-level domains. The top-level domains would know which organizations existed. Only the leaf servers would know actual addresses.

Delegation. Each level relied on the level below it. No one needed the complete list. When you asked "What is the address of `prep.ai.mit.edu`?" the query would cascade: root to .edu to mit.edu to ai.mit.edu to the answer. The room reached rough consensus. No one asked what happens if a nameserver lies.

Mockapetris wrote RFC 882 and RFC 883 in November 1983, defining the concepts and implementation of what he called the Domain Name System.[71,72] The two ran to more than a hundred pages between them, though the core of it fits in a sentence. A single file gave way to a constellation of servers, hierarchical and spread across the network, each one holding authority over a single branch of the namespace.

Postel endorsed the proposal immediately. DNS was buildable, and it solved the scaling problem without a central authority.

The first DNS servers came online in 1984. The .com, .edu, .gov, .mil, and .org top-level domains were established in January 1985. By

1987, Mockapetris had refined the specification into RFC 1034 and RFC 1035—the documents that define DNS to this day.[73,74]

Feinler watched the transition. Her NIC continued to operate, but its role changed. Instead of maintaining every host, it maintained the root. The phone still rang, but the questions were different: not "add this host" but "assign this domain."

By the end of the 1980s, HOSTS.TXT had been overtaken. The internet was growing too fast for any single file, and DNS had proven it could keep up.

The system rested on a simple premise: the phonebook entries were accurate. No verification, no cryptographic signature, no proof the answer came from the right source.

For twenty years, that faith held.

7.2. THE CHAIN OF PHONE BOOKS

7.2.1. HOW DNS WORKS

Every domain name is a question—and DNS answers it.

When you type `www.google.com` into a browser, your computer doesn't know what that means. Computers use IP addresses—numbers like 198.51.100.47—not names. DNS performs this translation billions of times per day, each one on faith.

Think of DNS as a chain of phone books. You want to find John Smith in Los Angeles. You can't look up "John Smith" directly; there are too many of them. Instead, you find the California phone book. That tells you which page covers Los Angeles. The Los Angeles section tells you which John Smith lives at which address. Each lookup refers you to the next level of detail.

DNS works similarly—your computer starts at the root and asks, "Who handles .com?"

The root doesn't know Google's address—that's not its job—but it knows who might: "Try the .com servers."

Your resolver asks the .com servers the same question: "Who handles google.com?" Same pattern, same answer: "Not me. Try Google's nameservers."

Finally, Google's nameserver has the answer: 198.51.100.47. Three hops, fifty milliseconds, and you're connected.

Each server passes the question down the chain. Each server *believes* the referral it receives. No one verifies anything. If any server in that chain lies, your computer believes it.

This is delegation—no one server knows everything, and no one checks whether the answers are true.

7.2.2. THE RESOLUTION PROCESS

Your computer doesn't do this work itself. It asks a resolver—a DNS server provided by your ISP or configured manually. The resolver follows the chain of referrals on your behalf, from root to authoritative server.

You make one query and wait. The resolver might make half a dozen queries to find the answer, each one accepting the referral before it. The complexity is hidden—and so are the places where trust can be violated.

7.2.3. CACHING

If every query went to the root, the root servers would collapse. There are only thirteen root server addresses, mapping to hundreds of physical machines through anycast.[75] Trillions of queries per day, thirteen addresses—impossible without caching. So DNS caches everything.

When your resolver learns that ".com" is handled by certain servers, it remembers. The next query for `google.com` skips the root entirely.

Each answer comes with a Time to Live (TTL)—how long it can be cached. A typical TTL might be 3600 seconds. For that hour, your resolver returns the cached answer without asking anyone.

Caching makes DNS fast and vulnerable. If someone can inject a false answer into the cache, that lie gets returned to every user for the duration of the TTL.

7.2.4. THE MESSAGE FORMAT

Every DNS message has a header, a question section, an answer section, and referral sections.

One field deserves attention: the transaction ID. Every query carries a 16-bit random number. The response must carry the same number. Think of it like a claim ticket at a coat check. You hand over your coat, you get a number. When someone returns with a coat, they need your number.

The coat check doesn't verify ID. Anyone with the right number gets the coat.

The transaction ID was designed for multiplexing, not security. It became the only thing standing between your DNS query and an attacker's forged response.

Sixteen bits. 65,536 possible values.

That's the lock on the front door.

7.2.5. THE UNVERIFIED ANSWER

DNS believes its answers. When a resolver receives a response, it accepts the content at face value—the response could come from anywhere, and the resolver has no way to tell the difference.

> RFC 1034 --- November 1987 --- Paul Mockapetris
>
> "The domain system is intentionally extensible. Researchers are continuously proposing, implementing and experimenting with new data types, query types, classes, functions, etc."

Mockapetris designed DNS to be extensible—security would come later. The base protocol assumed good faith from its participants.

For two decades, the lack of authentication was theoretical.

7.3. THE RACE CONDITION

Dan Kaminsky was twenty-nine when he found the hole in DNS.[76] It was early 2008, and he was Director of Penetration Testing at IOActive in Seattle.[77] He had a reputation for looking at old problems with fresh eyes.

Cache poisoning wasn't new. The technique was simple: race the legitimate response. Send a forged answer with the correct transaction ID before the real answer arrives. If you win, the resolver caches your lie.

Probability stood in the way. Sixteen-bit IDs gave one chance in 65,536. The resolver would only accept an answer while waiting—

perhaps a few hundred milliseconds. If you lost, you couldn't try again until the cached answer expired. With TTLs in hours, you might get a few attempts per day.

Kaminsky discovered how to try thousands of times per second.

Don't attack the name you care about—attack a name that doesn't exist.

Query for `aaaa.google.com`. There's no cached answer, so the resolver must look it up, and while it waits, you flood it with forged responses including additional records: "The nameserver for google.com is evil.com."

The forged responses carry random transaction IDs, and most are wrong—but you can send thousands while the resolver waits. If you lose, query for `aaab.google.com`. Another nonexistent name, another chance.

Each attempt takes milliseconds. Each failure costs nothing. Given seconds, anyone could poison any domain in any resolver's cache.

The attack didn't exploit a bug. It exploited the mathematics of a sixteen-bit identifier. DNS worked exactly as designed—but the design itself was flawed.

Kaminsky realized what he had. The flaw lived in the naming system itself, below any one vendor's code, which left every resolver on the internet exposed and with it every domain those resolvers answered for. Anyone who worked out the technique could send a bank's customers to a phishing page, or a software updater to malware.

He picked up the phone.

The first call went to Paul Vixie, president of the Internet Systems Consortium and maintainer of BIND—the most widely used DNS

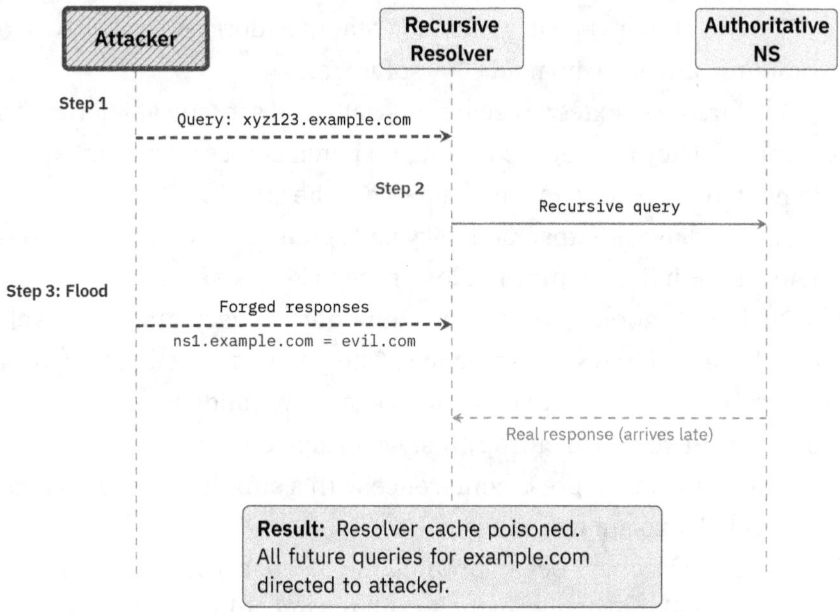

Figure 7.1: The Kaminsky DNS cache poisoning attack. The attacker queries for random nonexistent subdomains (Step 1), triggering recursive lookups (Step 2), then floods the resolver with forged responses faster than the legitimate response can arrive (Step 3). If a forged response has the correct transaction ID, the cache is poisoned.

implementation.[78] Vixie had been working on DNS since the 1980s, and he understood at once how bad it was.

"Usually, if somebody wants to report a problem, you expect that it's going to take a fair amount of time for them to explain it," Vixie later recalled. "In this case, it took 20 seconds for him to explain the problem, and another 20 seconds for him to answer my objections. After that, I said, 'Dan, I am speaking to you over an unsecure cell phone. Please do not ever say to anyone what you just said to me over an unsecure cell phone again.' "

The two of them began contacting other vendors—Microsoft, Cisco, Nominum, anyone who made DNS software.

On March 31, sixteen researchers gathered secretly at Microsoft's campus.[78] They needed a coordinated patch across all major DNS implementations before anyone figured out the attack.

They had five months. Kaminsky had agreed to wait until Black Hat in August. But five months is a long time to keep a secret.

On July 8, 2008, the patches came out.[79] Every major DNS vendor released updates the same day. The patches added source port randomization—attackers now had to guess two random numbers, not one. Thirty-two bits of entropy instead of sixteen.

Kaminsky held a press conference with a simple message: patch now, and I'll explain why at Black Hat.

Some researchers began probing the patches. On July 21, Halvar Flake guessed the attack correctly and posted online.[80] Matasano Security accidentally confirmed it on their blog—the post was removed within five minutes, but it had been mirrored. The secret was out.

By the time Kaminsky took the stage on August 6, organizers had moved him to the largest venue. It was standing room only.

He walked through the attack: query random names, flood with forged responses, redirect the domain. "I stumbled across something that lets you rewrite DNS for any domain. The entire internet."[81]

The patches held. Source port randomization made the attack harder by a factor of 65,000. Attackers would need minutes or hours instead of seconds.

But the underlying vulnerability remained. Randomizing ports was mitigation, not a fix. The only real solution was cryptographic authentication.

DNSSEC had been standardized in 1999.[82,83] It added digital signatures to DNS responses, but deployment stalled—the signatures added complexity and broke some things, so a decade after standardization, almost no one used it.

Kaminsky spent years advocating for DNSSEC. He became a leading voice in internet security, pushing for fixes to protocols designed without adversaries in mind.

On July 15, 2010, the root zone was signed with DNSSEC.[84] But the chain of trust was incomplete. Most top-level domains weren't signed. Most resolvers didn't validate.

DNSSEC adoption has grown slowly, and most queries still travel without validation.[85] The rest accept whoever answers first.

Dan Kaminsky died on April 23, 2021, at forty-two.[76] At twenty-nine, he had helped save the internet's phonebook. The security community mourned him as a researcher, an advocate, and a friend.

The Kaminsky attack remains the most significant DNS vulnerability ever discovered, the moment when the internet confronted the fragility of its naming infrastructure.

DNS was designed to translate names to numbers, and it does. It scales to billions of queries, survives failures, and distributes authority across the internet.

It also accepts every answer it receives. Mockapetris built a protocol for researchers who knew each other. The phonebook worked because everyone in it was honest.

The patches accumulate, but the vulnerability persists.

In October 2025, a new cache-poisoning flaw surfaced in BIND 9, the same software Paul Vixie had once maintained. CVE-2025-40780 was a weak random number generator: it let an attacker predict the very source ports and query IDs that Kaminsky's 2008 fix had made random.[86] The defense that closed the door in 2008 had quietly swung open again. Seventeen years later, the phonebook could still be poisoned.

DNS resolves trillions of queries every day. The phonebook Mockapetris built for a community of a few thousand researchers still translates names to numbers for five billion users, across every language, every device, every network on the planet. Mockapetris published RFC 882 and RFC 883 in November 1983. The core design hasn't changed.

Kaminsky had spent the years after his disclosure advocating for DNSSEC, for cryptographic validation, for the kind of authentication that Mockapetris never had reason to include. He believed the phonebook could be secured. A third of queries are validated now. Two-thirds are not. The root zone is signed, and every year the validated fraction grows by a few percentage points. Kaminsky would have kept pushing.

The phonebook keeps working. It still believes the first answer it hears, and the faith that held for the twenty years before Kaminsky found the flaw is still, mostly, honored. Most nameservers answer honestly because the people running them gain nothing by lying, and the operators are many but not quite anonymous to one another. There is no version of the internet that works without a phonebook that does. The system goes on as it always has, on borrowed trust.

DNS tells the internet where things are. But knowing where isn't enough. Distributed systems also need to know when—when a message was sent, when a certificate expires, when a transaction happened. In 1979, a researcher noticed that networked computers couldn't agree on what time it was.

CHAPTER 8

THE CLOCKWORK

The intent of the service for which this protocol is designed is to connect a few primary reference clocks, synchronized by wire or radio to national standards, to centrally accessible resources such as gateways.

— RFC 958, David L. Mills, September 1985

8.1. THE CLOCKS THAT DISAGREED

Nobody else seemed to notice the problem David Mills was chasing.

It was 1979, and Mills was building systems that synchronized satellite transmissions with ground stations.[87] The work required precision timing. He knew how hard it was to get two clocks to agree.

Then he paid attention to the ARPANET. A network of computers spread across a continent, each with its own clock drifting at its own rate. A log at MIT might say an event happened at 10:42:17. A log at Stanford: 10:43:02. Which came first? Nobody could tell.

For most purposes, this didn't matter. But Mills could see where the internet was heading. Distributed systems need to know order.

Databases need to resolve conflicts. Authentication systems need to timestamp tickets that expire in minutes. Without synchronized clocks, these systems couldn't work.

A time protocol already existed—RFC 868 returned a 32-bit timestamp—but it wasn't enough.[88]

Network delay defeated simple approaches. A timestamp that left the server at noon might arrive fifty milliseconds later—or five hundred. If you set your clock to whatever timestamp the server reported, you'd be off by half the round-trip time. On the ARPANET, that could mean seconds of error.

Mills wanted milliseconds.

His insight: exchange four timestamps instead of one—enough to separate clock offset from network delay.

RFC 958, published in September 1985, defined the Network Time Protocol.[89]

The design was a chain of custody for time. **Stratum 0** sat at the head of it—atomic clocks at national laboratories, GPS satellites, radio stations carrying NIST's signal—and everything below inherited from above. A server wired straight to an atomic clock passed the time down to servers that were not, and they passed it down again, until it reached machines that would never see an atomic clock.

An atomic clock counts cesium atom vibrations—9,192,631,770 oscillations per second, so stable that this rate defines the second itself. The best atomic clocks lose less than one second over millions of years.

Mills moved to the University of Delaware in 1986, and NTP moved with him.[90] He refined the protocol through three RFCs, culminating in RFC 1305 in 1992—over a hundred pages of phase-locked loops, oscillator drift, filtering algorithms.[91]

But the work wasn't abstract. The first NSFNET backbone, built in 1986, ran on "Fuzzballs"—DEC PDP-11s running software Mills had written by hand. For a stretch, a national network's routing depended on one professor's code. The global timekeeping infrastructure began the same way: a personal project, tended by one man.

He wrote code too. The reference implementation, `ntpd`, turned NTP from paper into software, and Mills maintained it himself for three decades. The internet's timekeeping ran on software that one man in Delaware kept alive.

Colleagues called him "Father Time." He had given the internet a shared clock, and the clock carried his assumptions. Time sources tell the truth. NTP servers provide accurate time. Clients accept what servers give them.

In 1985, this made sense. The network connected researchers who had no reason to lie about the time. There was no profit in it, and time wasn't yet a weapon.

So Mills designed for that world. The protocol lacked authentication. Clients couldn't verify that a server was legitimate, and responses could be spoofed. The security model, like every protocol in this book, was the community itself. It would take twenty years to discover what happened when the community grew beyond recognition.

8.2. FOUR TIMESTAMPS

8.2.1. HOW NTP WORKS

Every computer has a clock. Every clock is wrong.

A computer's clock is driven by a quartz oscillator—and these drift. Temperature changes and manufacturing variations mean no two crystals vibrate at exactly the same rate, and the drift accumulates.

NTP disciplines these clocks: continuously comparing them against reliable references and nudging them back into alignment. Milliseconds over the internet, microseconds on local networks.

Choosing which time source to believe is NTP's central problem.

NTP organizes sources into layers, called strata. At the top, stratum 0: GPS satellites, atomic clocks at national laboratories, radio stations broadcasting from NIST. These are the reference sources, the ultimate authorities.

Stratum 1 servers connect directly to stratum 0—a GPS antenna on the roof, a cable to a server. These machines touch the source—thousands of them worldwide. Your computer believes them.

Stratum 2 servers synchronize to stratum 1, stratum 3 to stratum 2. Each layer adds a hop—a place where the chain could be broken or bent. A stratum 2 server trusts that its stratum 1 source is honest—nothing proves otherwise.

Stratum 16 means "unsynchronized"—a clock that has lost contact with any reference.[92] But there's no stratum for "liar." A server advertising stratum 1 could be an attacker in a closet, and NTP can't tell the difference.

Stratum	Source
0	Reference clock (GPS, atomic, radio)
1	Directly connected to stratum 0
2	Synchronized to stratum 1
3	Synchronized to stratum 2
...	
15	Maximum usable stratum
16	Unsynchronized

Table 8.1: The NTP stratum hierarchy

The result: a single stratum 1 server serves dozens of stratum 2 servers, each serving thousands of clients. The load spreads naturally, and the system scales without central coordination.

8.2.2. THE TIME EXCHANGE

The next problem: I ask you what time it is. You say "12:00." How long did your answer take to reach me? If I set my clock to noon when your message arrives, I'm wrong by the transit time.

NTP's solution: exchange four timestamps instead of one. The client notes when it sends the request (T_1). The server notes when the request arrives (T_2) and when the response departs (T_3). The client notes when the response arrives (T_4).

Four timestamps—two are yours, two are mine. Together they reveal the round-trip delay and the clock offset.

Notice who controls what. The client measures T_1 and T_4—its own clock. The server reports T_2 and T_3. The client accepts those numbers on faith. A lying server can report any T_2 and T_3 it wants.

The **round-trip delay** measures transit time:

$$\text{delay} = (T_4 - T_1) - (T_3 - T_2)$$

Total elapsed time on the client's clock, minus the time the server claims it spent processing. The **clock offset**—how far the client's clock differs from the server's—comes from averaging the forward and return legs:

$$\text{offset} = \frac{(T_2 - T_1) + (T_3 - T_4)}{2}$$

The math requires symmetric routing and honest servers—but internet routing is asymmetric. Servers don't need to be honest.

NTP clients typically synchronize to multiple servers. Redundancy protects against failure—if one server goes offline, others remain. They sometimes disagree.

Mills called unreliable sources **falsetickers**: machines that report bad time, whether through malfunction, misconfiguration, or attack. A broken clock doesn't know it's broken. It reports its time with the same confidence as a working one. NTP needs to identify which sources to rely on.

NTP settles the question by **intersection**. Each server's estimate arrives wrapped in an uncertainty bound, a range where the true time probably lies, and somewhere in the pile of ranges there is usually a region where most of them agree. The protocol finds that region and throws away whatever falls outside it. The discarded sources are the falsetickers; the survivors, the **truechimers**, are what the final estimate gets built from.

The algorithm is self-organizing: bad servers get ignored while good servers rise to the top.

The requirement: the majority must be honest. If an attacker controls more than half the servers a client uses, the attacker's time becomes the consensus. The falseticker becomes the truechimer.

Once NTP knows the offset, it adjusts the local clock. But you can't just jump.

If your clock is 500 milliseconds slow, the obvious fix is to leap forward 500 milliseconds. This is called **stepping**—but stepping breaks things. Programs measuring elapsed time see negative intervals. Log files have timestamps that repeat or skip. Cryptographic protocols reject valid messages because the time changed mid-handshake.

NTP prefers to **slew**: speed up or slow down the clock gradually. If you're 500 milliseconds slow, run slightly fast until you catch up. Time keeps moving forward, just at a different rate, and no one notices.

For small offsets—under 128 milliseconds—NTP always slews. For larger gaps, the protocol steps the clock forward or backward in a single jump. If your clock is off by an hour, you can't wait days to drift back.

The danger: slewing is gradual, but the direction comes from the server. An attacker who controls your time source controls which way your clock drifts. Over hours or days, they can walk your clock anywhere they want—forward to make certificates expire, backward to make revoked certificates valid again.

Mills spent decades refining the algorithms that manage this discipline. RFC 1305 devotes fifty pages to feedback loops and oscillator modeling. The goal wasn't just setting the correct time once—it was training the local clock to keep better time on its own.

8.2.3. THE HONEST CLOCK

NTP servers included a feature for administrators: the `monlist` command. Send it to any NTP server, and it returns a list of the last 600 clients—addresses, packet counts, timestamps. Everything an administrator might need.

Everything an attacker might exploit.

The request was small—40 bytes—but the response could be enormous: 100 packets, tens of thousands of bytes. An amplification factor of 556 to 1.

For every byte you send, the server sends 556 back—and it sends them wherever you claim to be from. The server doesn't verify your address; it simply believes the source field in your packet.

NTP servers accept requests at face value.

> RFC 958 --- September 1985 --- David L. Mills
>
> "There is no provision for peer discovery, acquisition, or authentication in NTP. Data integrity is provided by the IP and UDP checksums."

UDP checksums detect transmission errors—cosmic rays flipping bits, electrical noise corrupting packets. They don't detect intentional forgery. Anyone who can inject packets can pose as a stratum 1 server synchronized to an atomic clock.

Mills built for a research network where lying about the time would have been pointless vandalism. Adding authentication in 1985 would have required cryptographic infrastructure that didn't exist. The trade-off was reasonable then—but the network changed while the protocol stayed the same.

8.3. 400 GIGABITS PER SECOND

On March 18, 2013, Spamhaus went to war.

Spamhaus was a nonprofit organization that maintained blacklists of spam sources. Internet service providers used these lists to filter email. If Spamhaus said an IP address was a spam source, millions of mail servers would refuse to accept mail from it. The organization had made powerful enemies.

One of them was CyberBunker, a Dutch hosting provider with a libertarian philosophy: they would host anything except child pornography and terrorism. Spamhaus added CyberBunker's IP ranges to their blacklist. CyberBunker responded with what would become the largest distributed denial-of-service attack in history.

The attack reached 300 gigabits per second, enough traffic to disrupt major internet exchanges in London and elsewhere.[93] The method was DNS amplification: small queries to DNS servers that generated large responses, all directed at Spamhaus through IP address spoofing. The technique was already known. The scale was unprecedented.

When the attack finally subsided, security researchers took stock of what they had witnessed. `DNS` wasn't the only amplifiable protocol. Other `UDP`-based services had similar properties. The researchers started looking at `NTP`.

Brian Krebs learned about the new attack method the hard way.

On February 12, 2014, the security journalist's website disappeared. For roughly ten minutes, 200 gigabits per second of traffic flooded his servers.[94] The attacker wasn't trying to keep him offline permanently. This was a demonstration—proof of capability for admission to Darkode, an invitation-only crime forum. The attacker, who went by "Rasbora" online, later boasted in private channels: "If all else fails and you just want it offline, PM me." He was reportedly a teenager.[94]

Around the same time, Cloudflare reported an even larger attack against one of their European customers.[95] The traffic peaked at 400 gigabits per second—enough to cause network congestion across parts of Europe. The attack used 4,529 `NTP` servers spread across 1,298 networks on six continents. Each server dutifully responded to what it thought were legitimate monitoring queries. The queries had been spoofed.

The French hosting giant OVH was hit at roughly the same time. Founder Octave Klaba reported an `NTP`-amplification attack exceeding 350 Gbps.[96] The irony was bitter: OVH's own `NTP` servers were among those being exploited to attack others.

The weapon was a command called `monlist`. It asked an `NTP` server to list its recent clients—a useful diagnostic tool. A 40-byte request could generate up to 22,000 bytes in response, a 556-to-1 amplification factor. The 400-gigabit attack used 4,529 `NTP` servers, each contributing roughly 87 megabits—all triggered by spoofed requests that may have originated from a single machine. No need to compromise thousands of computers into a botnet. Just a list of `NTP` servers and the ability to spoof source addresses.

The list was easy to find—scanning the internet for open NTP servers was trivial. Most ran default configurations, and most default configurations included `monlist`.

The vulnerability wasn't new. Security researchers had warned about `monlist` for years, and it was assigned CVE-2013-5211 after being exploited in the wild by December 2013.[97] US-CERT issued an alert in January 2014.[98] The warnings came too late. Millions of NTP servers ran publicly accessible `monlist` endpoints, configured by administrators who had set them up years earlier and forgotten about them.

Disabling `monlist`, or restricting it to trusted addresses, was enough; version 4.2.7 of the reference NTP implementation dropped the feature from its defaults. The hard part came after that. Administrators had to update their own servers and restart them, and no central authority could make them do it. The internet's timekeeping infrastructure was a collection of independent operators running their own machines, many of whom had switched on a helpful monitoring feature years earlier and never thought about it again.

Months passed, and surveys found that the number of NTP servers with `monlist` enabled dropped from hundreds of thousands to tens of thousands. The attacks became less powerful, but they didn't stop. As long as any amplifying servers remained, attackers would use them.

The deeper problem was architectural. NTP ran over UDP, a protocol that didn't verify sender addresses. Any packet with a spoofed source address matching the victim's IP would be accepted. The same amplification pattern would appear in SNMP (Chapter 12) and other UDP protocols—any service that answered queries from strangers could be turned into a weapon.

IP spoofing had been a known issue since the 1980s. BCP 38, published in 2000, recommended that networks filter outbound traffic to prevent spoofed addresses from leaving.[55] More than a decade later, the recommendation remained optional. Networks that allowed spoofing became amplification platforms.

Mills, watching from Delaware, had seen this coming. He had worked on NTP security extensions for years, and the extensions existed—but they weren't deployed. The same administrators who forgot about `monlist` weren't about to configure cryptographic authentication.

Time manipulation offered another attack vector. Anyone who could control a victim's NTP traffic—through a rogue server, through interception, through BGP hijacking (Chapter 13)—could control their clock.

The consequences rippled through time-dependent security. TLS certificates have expiration dates; shift the victim's clock, and valid certificates become invalid or expired certificates become valid. `Kerberos` tickets have five-minute windows; push the clock outside the window, and authentication fails. Log files become unreliable when timestamps can't be verified. Forensic analysis falls apart when the timeline is corrupted.

In 2015, researchers from Boston University demonstrated that NTP's lack of authentication made it possible to shift clients' clocks by years.[99] The attack exploited a "kiss-o'-death" packet that NTP used to tell clients to back off, repurposed to convince clients that their upstream servers had failed. The client would then accept time from an attacker-controlled source. A certificate revoked in 2012 would suddenly appear valid to a victim who thought it was still 2012.

Network Time Security, RFC 8915, was published in September 2020.[100] The protocol adds cryptographic authentication to NTP, letting clients verify that responses come from legitimate servers and haven't been tampered with. It uses the same TLS certificates that protect web traffic. It addresses both the amplification problem (authenticated servers can reject spoofed requests) and the time manipulation problem (clients can verify server identity).

Adoption has been slow—NTS requires servers to obtain certificates and clients to support the new protocol. Most operating systems still default to unauthenticated NTP. Most public time servers don't offer NTS. The infrastructure that should have been secured decades ago remains largely open.

The helpful features of 1985—open access, detailed monitoring, willing responses to anyone who asked—became the vulnerabilities of 2014. Trust, once granted, is hard to revoke.

David Mills died in January 2024, at eighty-five.[90] The obituaries called him the internet's "father time." Forty-five years of his working life went into keeping billions of devices in step, and the result made distributed computing possible. Every timestamp online sits on top of it.

His clocks still run. Whatever checks the time against a network source—a phone, a server stamping its logs, a certificate measured against its expiration date—passes through the stratum hierarchy Mills designed. At NIST and USNO the reference clocks still tick, and the GPS satellites still broadcast. The Fuzzball in his den is long gone, but the protocol it ran has replicated itself across millions of servers on six continents. The borrowed seconds keep extending.

On December 17, 2025, hurricane-force winds drove a utility to cut power across Boulder, Colorado, and NIST's timekeeping laboratories sat dark for the better part of three days.[101,102] UTC(NIST) drifted by 4.8 microseconds—the cause was weather, not an attack or a software failure. Even stratum 0 runs on electricity. The recovery went the way Mills had designed it to go: NIST keeps clocks in more than one location, the stratum hierarchy routes around what stops answering, and the drift corrected. His system survived its own foundation going dark.

Somewhere, a stratum 2 server is asking a stratum 1 server what time it is. The answer comes back unsigned, unverified, accepted on faith. The clock adjusts. The seconds tick forward. Mills is gone, but the handshake he wrote still runs, billions of times a day, keeping the whole machine in time.

NTP taught distant machines to agree on the time, each trusting the stratum above it to answer honestly. But time was the simplest thing the network learned to share. Years earlier, two graduate students in North Carolina had wired their campuses together to pass something messier from machine to machine—human conversation—on the same terms of trust: every server relaying whatever it received, and vouching for none of it.

CHAPTER 9

THE NEWSGROUP

Given the strains of running a nationwide distributed network on machines with limited capacity and via long distance telephone, we utterly relied on the ease of writing shell scripts to experiment with protocol variants.

— Steve Bellovin, on the origins of Usenet[103]

9.1. THE POOR MAN'S ARPANET

Tom Truscott wanted what he couldn't have.

In 1979 he was a graduate student at Duke, watching the ARPANET from the outside. It ran to the elite institutions—MIT, Stanford, Berkeley—and Duke had no way onto it.

But Duke had Unix machines, and Unix machines could exchange data.

Truscott and a fellow grad student, Jim Ellis, had an idea. What if they built their own network? Computers that dialed each other overnight, when long-distance rates were cheap, and exchanged messages in batch. A poor man's ARPANET.

The technology already existed. UUCP—Unix-to-Unix Copy—could transfer files over phone lines, and universities were already using it to exchange email and share software. It was slow and unreliable, but it was cheap.

Truscott and Ellis imagined a system for distributing messages to multiple recipients. A user at Duke posts an article. When Duke's machines dial UNC overnight, the article copies over. UNC copies to its neighbors, neighbors to theirs, until the article has propagated through the network.

They called it Usenet.

Steve Bellovin volunteered to write the software.[104] He wrote the first version in a few evenings—three pages of shell scripts that were crude but functional.

The first Usenet connection went live in late 1979, carrying about ten articles per day: Unix bugs, system administration tips, department gossip.

Truscott and Ellis presented at a USENIX conference in January 1980.[105] Their pitch: a network anyone could join. You just needed a Unix machine, a modem, and a phone line.

Sites joined, and the network grew from three nodes to thirty to three hundred. By 1983, Usenet connected over five hundred sites, with traffic growing from ten articles per day to thousands.

Usenet was radically decentralized—no master server, no central authority. Every site stored its own copy and decided which neighbors to exchange with.

Articles propagated through flood-fill: when a site received a new article, it forwarded copies to all neighbors, who forwarded to theirs, until a single post had generated thousands of copies.

The Path header tracked where an article had been, with each site prepending its name as the article passed through. If you received an article with your site already in the path, you'd already seen it.

Articles were organized into newsgroups. `net.unix`. `net.jokes`. `net.lang.c`. By 1987, administrators reorganized it into the "Big Seven": comp, misc, news, rec, sci, soc, talk.[106]

Usenet worked because everyone followed the rules.

The rules were called netiquette: don't post advertisements, don't spam, don't forge headers, stay on topic. The enforcement mechanism was community pressure—violators would be flamed, their administrators contacted. Five hundred sites, a few thousand users, shared norms.

RFC 977, published in February 1986, standardized the Network News Transfer Protocol—NNTP—for exchanging articles over TCP/IP rather than UUCP.[107]

NNTP was simple: commands like GROUP to select a newsgroup, ARTICLE to retrieve a message, POST to submit a new one. The standard accepted that information in article headers was accurate. The From line showed who sent the article. The Date line showed when. The Path showed the route it had traveled.

9.2. FLOOD-FILL

9.2.1. HOW USENET WORKS

How do you run a bulletin board with no central server?

You make copies—lots of copies. When you post a Usenet article, your server forwards it to its neighbors, who forward it to theirs, until the article exists on thousands of servers worldwide. One post becomes many copies.

This differs sharply from email, where one copy travels from sender to recipient. With Usenet, thousands of copies flood outward until every server has everything.

The implications cut both ways. No one can censor Usenet—there's no central authority to pressure, no single server to shut down. But no one can moderate it either. Once something propagates, it's everywhere. And since every server accepts every other server's articles, a single lie propagates as efficiently as the truth.

9.2.2. THE ARTICLE FORMAT

A Usenet article looks almost identical to an email message. Headers at the top, blank line, body below:

```
Usenet Article Header

From: alice@example.com (Alice Smith) Newsgroups:
comp.lang.c Subject: Question about memory
allocation Date: 15 Apr 1994 09:30:00 GMT Message-
ID: <1994Apr15.093000.12345@example.com> Path:
news.server.com!upstream!example.com!alice
```

Look at that `From` header. It says Alice Smith sent this article.

No one verifies it.

The receiving server accepts whatever the `From` line claims. If you want to post as the professor who runs the newsgroup, you change one line of text. The protocol has no mechanism to check.

The `Path` header traces the article's journey, with each server prepending its name as the article passes through:

```
Path: final.server!middle.server!origin.server!user
```

Servers use this to avoid loops—if your site is already in the path, you've seen it before. But the path is just text that anyone can type. The chain of provenance holds together only because everyone agrees to be honest about it.

9.2.3. FLOOD-FILL PROPAGATION

How does one post reach thousands of servers? The same way rumors spread through a village: everyone tells everyone.

When your server receives a new article, it checks the Message-ID. If the article is new, the server stores it, adds its name to the Path, and forwards copies to every neighbor, each of whom does the same. The article floods outward until it reaches the whole network.

This is beautiful for sharing information. It's terrifying for controlling it.

A single post generates traffic proportional to servers times connections—in the early days, with hundreds of servers and kilobyte messages, the load was manageable. But later, with millions of users posting binary attachments and pirated movies, the math became brutal.

Worse: removing content is nearly impossible. Once an article propagates, it exists on thousands of independent servers. No central authority can delete it.

The internet remembers—even when you wish it wouldn't.

9.2.4. CONTROL MESSAGES

With no central authority to call, Usenet administered itself through articles that doubled as commands. A control message arrived looking like any other post—headers, body, Message-ID. But a server that accepted one would act on it—creating a newsgroup, deleting one, or removing an article from its spool. The sender could be sitting at any site on the network.

`newgroup` created a newsgroup—someone wanted to discuss Python programming? Send a `newgroup` message, and every server obediently creates `comp.lang.python`. No one approves it, and no one verifies that the sender has the right.

`rmgroup` deleted groups from every server—useful for cleaning up spam-ridden discussions, but also useful for silencing conversations you didn't like if no one could prove you weren't authorized.

Most dangerous was `cancel`. It removed a specific article from every server worldwide. The stated purpose: let users delete embarrassing posts, let administrators remove spam. The actual effect: anyone who knew an article's Message-ID could forge a cancel and erase it everywhere.

How did servers know which control messages to obey? They checked the `From` header—the same header that no one verified, the same header you could fill with any text you wanted.

If your server accepted articles purportedly from a certain administrator, it obeyed. If someone forged that administrator's name, your server obeyed anyway. The mechanism designed to let administrators remove spam could also let attackers censor dissent.

9.2.5. THE GOOD-FAITH FORUM

Usenet added a new dimension to the familiar pattern: faith in the community's ability to police itself.

Every header was accepted at face value, and control messages—commands to delete articles network-wide—carried no cryptographic authentication. The enforcement mechanism was entirely social: netiquette, peer pressure, and the expectation that administrators would discipline their own users.

The protocol they shipped had no authentication mechanism at all.[107] A standardized `AUTHINFO` extension arrived in 2006, but it authenticated a reader to a server; the specification explicitly did not authenticate the identity of an article's author.[108] The control-message trust problem remained.

9.3. THE DEATH OF THE COMMUNITY

On April 12, 1994, Laurence Canter and Martha Siegel broke Usenet.[109]

Canter and Siegel were immigration lawyers in Phoenix who wanted to advertise their services for the green card lottery. Television was expensive, but Usenet was free.

They posted "Green Card Lottery- Final One?" to every newsgroup they could find. Over five thousand copies flooded across the network in ninety minutes.

The reaction was immediate and furious.

Usenet had seen spam before, but previous incidents had been mistakes or pranks. Canter and Siegel were commercial, deliberate, and unrepentant.

Their ISP, Internet Direct, crashed under the flood of complaint emails—angry users sent thousands of messages demanding action, and some sent email bombs. Internet Direct terminated the lawyers' account, but Canter and Siegel simply signed up with another provider.

They received death threats and harassing phone calls as the internet's fury descended.

But the lawyers didn't care. They later claimed the advertisement had generated between one hundred thousand and two hundred thousand dollars in business.[109] The outrage was free publicity. They wrote a book teaching others to do the same.[110]

Years later, Canter remained unapologetic. "Somebody would have done it if we hadn't." He was probably right.

The Green Card spam proved that spam worked—commercial incentive outweighed social pressure. Netiquette depended on caring about reputation, but Canter and Siegel cared about money.

The flood-fill design that made Usenet work also made it vulnerable: a single post propagated to thousands of servers, and the network amplified abuse as efficiently as it amplified discussion.

The community fought back. Arnt Gulbrandsen wrote a "cancelbot"—software that detected spam and automatically removed it.[111] Others built similar tools.

No part of a cancel message proved who had sent it. The same forgery that wiped out an advertisement could erase anything else, and before long people were cancelling each other's posts. The "cancel wars" had begun, waged with the one tool Usenet had for keeping itself clean.

Then came Eternal September.

Every September, new students discovered Usenet without knowing the norms. The regulars would sigh, correct them, and by October the newbies had learned.

Starting in September 1993, commercial providers began pointing their subscribers at Usenet, and unlike university students, they kept coming. America Online opened its own Usenet gateway the following spring, pouring millions more through the door. There was no October. The influx never stopped.

Dave Fischer named it on January 25, 1994: "September 1993 will go down in net.history as the September that never ended."[112]

The flood swamped the community's ability to socialize new users—the regulars were outnumbered, and the cultural norms dissolved.

By the late 1990s, Usenet's character had changed. The binary newsgroups—alt.binaries.*, where users shared software, images, and later, pirated movies and music—came to dominate traffic. Discussion continued in the traditional groups, but the volume of binaries dwarfed it. A 2010 study of European ISP traffic found that more than ninety-nine percent of Usenet bytes were yEnc-encoded binary files.[113]

The major internet service providers began dropping Usenet. AOL stopped carrying it in 2005.[114] Verizon, Time Warner, and Sprint followed in 2008, responding to pressure from New York Attorney General Andrew Cuomo about illegal content in the binary groups.[115]

The network that had pioneered internet discussion was becoming a liability.

In May 2010, Duke University—where Tom Truscott and Jim Ellis had conceived Usenet thirty-one years earlier—shut down its Usenet servers.[116] The birthplace of the network no longer saw a reason to participate.

Usenet has not gone away. Commercial providers sell access, Google Groups holds decades of the archive, and articles move from server to server exactly as RFC 977 said they should. Only the community that made those articles worth reading is missing.

The network that believed in its users learned the hard way: that belief could not survive at scale. The social pressure that enforced good behavior required a community small enough to know each other. When millions joined, the community dissolved into a crowd. The crowd had no norms, no reputation system, nothing to punish defectors.

Tom Truscott and Jim Ellis had built a poor man's ARPANET. They got what they asked for: a network anyone could join. They hadn't anticipated what would happen when everyone did. Spam proved that economic incentives could overwhelm social norms. Eternal September proved that community doesn't scale. The binary groups proved that people would use any free distribution network for whatever they wanted to distribute. The question was never whether Usenet's model would fail—only when.

Usenet could not solve abundance: strangers arrived faster than the community could absorb them, and the norms went under. The researchers at MIT had a different problem. Their campus network was small and controlled, its users students and faculty, and none of that helped. Every password on it crossed the wire in plain text, readable by anyone with a packet sniffer and an Ethernet tap.

CHAPTER 10

THE TICKET

This is accomplished ... under the assumption that packets traveling along the network can be read, modified, and inserted at will.

— RFC 4120, The Kerberos Network Authentication Service, July 2005

10.1. THE DIGITAL BADGE

The password went across the wire in plain text, visible to anyone watching.

It was 1983. MIT was building Project Athena[117]—workstations across campus connected to shared services. Students would log into any terminal, access their files, check their email. The network would make computing democratic. Making it secure was a harder problem.

When a student typed a password, it traveled across the campus network to a server. Ethernet was fast and completely unencrypted. A student with a packet sniffer could sit in a dorm room and collect passwords all day.

Steve Miller and Clifford Neuman confronted the problem.[118,119] Authentication for Project Athena was their assignment, and the obvious answer—encrypt the password before it goes on the wire—lasted only until someone asked which key to use. Ten services meant ten keys and ten separate arrangements. The campus kept adding services.

Miller and Neuman's insight was that a user should authenticate once and then carry a credential—a digital proof of identity—to present to each service.

Working alongside Project Athena's technical director Jerome Saltzer and MIT network manager Jeffrey Schiller, Miller and Neuman designed a digital badge system. A user authenticates once to a trusted server, which issues a ticket—an encrypted token that can be presented to any service. No password crosses the wire after initial authentication.

They named it after the three-headed dog guarding the gates of Hades. `Kerberos`.

Project Athena launched in 1983, funded by IBM and DEC.[117] Students could sit at any terminal, log in, and see their files, while the security challenges remained invisible—exactly as Miller and Neuman intended.

`Kerberos` version 4, described in a 1988 USENIX paper, became the first version distributed outside MIT when it was released publicly on January 24, 1989.[118,119] The protocol spread beyond MIT, and a 1994 overview documented implementations across Unix, Macintosh, and PC systems.[120] Microsoft made `Kerberos` the default authentication protocol for Windows domain services beginning with Windows 2000, while retaining `NTLM` as a negotiated fallback.[121]

The RFC came later—Kerberos version 5 was published as RFC 1510 in 1993[122] and updated as RFC 4120 in 2005.[123] The campus project was now an internet standard.

> RFC 4120 --- July 2005 --- Kerberos Network Authentication
>
> A client sends a request to the authentication server (AS) for "credentials" for a given server. The AS responds with these credentials, encrypted in the client's key. The credentials consist of a "ticket" for the server and a temporary encryption key (often called a "session key").

The design did not hide where the weight sat. Each Kerberos network needed a Key Distribution Center, a KDC, and into that one machine went the secret key of every user and every service. It was the registration desk that issued the badges, and it held the faith of everyone carrying one.

Control the KDC, control everything.

10.2. TICKETS AND TRUST

10.2.1. HOW KERBEROS WORKS

Think of an amusement park.

You arrive and show ID, and the attendant wraps a wristband around your arm. For the rest of the day, you show the wristband to access rides instead of showing ID again. The wristband says: this person already proved who they are.

`Kerberos` follows this model. Your password is the ID, the Key Distribution Center issues wristbands, and the services—file servers, email, printers—check your credential.

How do you prove your identity without sending your password over the wire? With a shared secret—a key that both parties know. Either side can encrypt messages only the other can read. In `Kerberos`, the KDC stores a secret key for every user and every service, derived from passwords but never transmitted.

The registration desk has a copy of every badge.

`Kerberos` uses these keys in three exchanges: prove your identity, obtain permission, then access the resource.

The Authentication Service Exchange (AS Exchange). Call it the "prove who you are" step. You sit at your workstation and type your username and password. Your computer sends a message to the Key Distribution Center: "I am alice@EXAMPLE.COM and I want to prove it."

The KDC finds Alice in its database, and with her the secret key derived from her password. Then it writes her a master pass. The Ticket Granting Ticket, or TGT, says that "Alice has proven her identity," and the KDC locks it with its own secret key. A session key rides beside the ticket; both are wrapped in Alice's key, and the package travels to her workstation.

When it arrives, Alice's workstation derives the same secret key from her password. It uses this key to decrypt the package. If her password was correct, decryption succeeds. She now has a TGT that she cannot read (it is encrypted with the KDC's key) and a session key she can use to talk to the KDC.

The password never crossed the network. Alice proved she knew it by successfully decrypting a message. If she typed the wrong password, the decryption would have failed. The KDC never sees her password either—it only stores the derived key.

That TGT lives in memory. Alice's workstation keeps it cached, ready to present whenever she needs access to a service. For the next eight to ten hours—the default ticket lifetime—anyone who can read that memory has Alice's master pass.

The Ticket Granting Service Exchange (TGS Exchange). Alice wants to access a file server. Her workstation contacts the KDC again, presenting the TGT: "Here is my proof. I want a ticket for fileserver.example.com."

The KDC decrypts the TGT with its own key. Inside, it finds Alice's identity and verifies that the TGT has not expired. Then it creates a service ticket for the file server, encrypted with the file server's secret key, and sends it back.

Notice what the KDC does not verify: whether Alice is still at her workstation.

The Application Protocol Exchange (AP Exchange). Alice's workstation contacts the file server and hands over the service ticket. The ticket is not enough on its own. Her workstation must also send an *authenticator*—a timestamp encrypted with the session key, which only Alice received. The file server opens the ticket with its own secret key, takes out the session key, and tries it on the authenticator. A recent timestamp and a clean decryption prove that Alice holds the session key.

This sounds secure. But both the ticket and the session key sit in Alice's workstation memory. Anyone who can read that memory has everything they need to impersonate her. The ticket alone cannot authenticate—but together with the session key, it might as well be a bearer token.

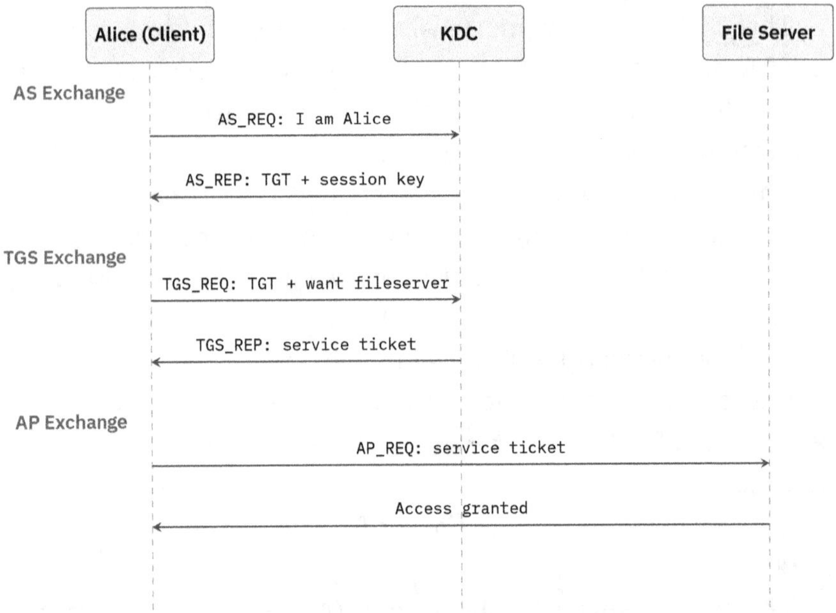

Figure 10.1: The Kerberos ticket flow. Alice authenticates once to the KDC, receives a Ticket-Granting Ticket, then uses it to obtain service tickets for individual resources — never sending her password over the network.

10.2.2. WHY TIME MATTERS

Every `Kerberos` ticket contains timestamps—the TGT records when it was issued and when it expires, and service tickets have their own validity windows. The default tolerance for clock skew between machines is five minutes.

This makes `Kerberos` depend on `NTP`, the Network Time Protocol we discussed in Chapter 8. If clocks drift too far apart, authentication fails. A ticket that looks valid to the server might appear expired to the client, or vice versa.

The timestamps serve a purpose: they prevent replay attacks, since an attacker who captures a ticket cannot use it forever. After the ticket expires, it's worthless, and the five-minute window keeps the replay threat small.

The time dependency creates its own vulnerabilities. Anyone who can manipulate a machine's clock can make valid tickets appear expired, or make expired tickets appear valid. The timestamps assume clocks are honest. In a hostile environment, that assumption fails.

10.2.3. THE CENTRAL AUTHORITY

`Kerberos` inverts the usual pattern. Instead of extending good faith to every node equally, it concentrates all reliance on a single point: the Key Distribution Center.

> RFC 4120 --- Environmental Assumptions
>
> Principals MUST keep their secret keys secret. If an intruder somehow steals a principal's key, it will be able to masquerade as that principal or to impersonate any server to the legitimate principal.

The KDC knows every secret—it holds the keys for every user, every service, every machine in the network. The three-headed dog guards everything, and whoever controls the dog controls every gate.

The designers knew this. They expected the KDC to be the best-defended machine on the network, isolated and hardened, reachable only by administrators someone had vetted. On Project Athena, where the administrators knew each other by name, that expectation was sound. The networks that came after were much bigger than a campus.

10.3. THE GOLDEN TICKET

Benjamin Delpy was a security researcher in France who wanted to understand how Windows stored credentials. In 2011, he released a tool called mimikatz[124] to demonstrate that Windows stored passwords in a way that could be extracted. The tool worked too well.

Mimikatz could extract `Kerberos` tickets from Windows memory. When you log into a Windows workstation, the operating system caches your TGT in RAM, and mimikatz could read that RAM and copy the ticket out. Once copied, the ticket could be used from any machine—a technique called pass-the-ticket. Anyone who compromised one workstation could steal the TGT of any user who had logged in.

Pass-the-ticket was devastating—it bypassed password security entirely. Change your password every hour—it wouldn't matter. Your ticket was already stolen.

But pass-the-ticket was just the beginning.

In a Windows domain, the Key Distribution Center ran on domain controllers, and the KDC's secret key was stored in an account called krbtgt. An attacker who gained administrative access to a domain controller could extract the krbtgt password hash. With that hash, they could forge TGTs for any user, with any permissions, for any duration. The golden ticket attack.[125]

In 2014, Delpy built the technique into mimikatz, naming it for Willy Wonka: the golden ticket, a pass that opened everything, forever.

A golden ticket was not stolen but created. The adversary generated a TGT asserting domain administrator privileges, set an expiration twenty years in the future, and began accessing resources. The KDC never issued this ticket, but because it was encrypted with the correct key, every service treated it as legitimate.

Discovery does not end a golden ticket. Defenders can reset every user password in the domain, delete the accounts they know are compromised, and patch the hole the attacker came in through. The attacker still has the krbtgt hash, and new administrator tickets cost nothing to mint.

Remediation requires resetting the krbtgt password twice, with at least ten hours between resets, and both disruptions ripple across authentication for the entire domain. Surgery while the patient is awake.

10.3.1. THE NATION-STATE PLAYBOOK

Criminals were not the only ones forging golden tickets. Nation-state attackers adopted the technique as a standard tool for persistent access.

Take APT29, the group U.S. intelligence agencies attributed to Russian state actors and the one better known as Cozy Bear. They used `Kerberos` attacks heavily.[125] Phishing or a software flaw got them onto a network; lateral movement—machine to machine—carried them to the domain controllers. Once they had the krbtgt hash, they could sit through the cleanup.

The SolarWinds attack of 2020 demonstrated the technique at scale.[126,127] Attackers compromised the software supply chain of SolarWinds, a company that made network management tools used by thousands of organizations, including government agencies. The malicious update gave attackers initial access. From there, they moved to domain controllers, extracted `Kerberos` keys, and forged tickets that let them access email and documents for months.

The attackers did not stop at Kerberos. What worked on tickets worked on SAML tokens, the credentials that carry an identity from an on-premises domain out to cloud services.[128,129] Microsoft's Azure Active Directory trusted the tokens that arrived correctly signed. An attacker holding the SAML signing certificate could forge tokens for Azure that bypassed multi-factor authentication.[130]

Organizations believed a line ran between their data center and the cloud, and another between their own network and Microsoft's. The lines were bookkeeping. A golden ticket on-premises came out the far side as a golden SAML token.

10.3.2. THE DESIGN CHOICE

Kerberos was made for a campus where every machine had an owner someone could name. Miller and Neuman expected that the network contained authorized users and legitimate services, and they built for a KDC that would be protected, administrative access that would be restricted, keys held only by people who deserved them.

The premise held for Project Athena, for university networks in the 1980s, and more or less for enterprise networks in the 1990s. It did not hold for networks connected to the internet, penetrated by nation-states, running software with unknown flaws. The three-headed dog guarded the gates, but someone found the side entrance.

The ticket-based model that made single sign-on possible also made persistent compromise possible, and the architecture that simplified authentication also concentrated the target. Own one machine—the domain controller—and you own the entire network.

Microsoft's answer was to add layers. Protected Users groups cut down on ticket caching and Credential Guard holds tickets in a hardware enclave, while advanced auditing watches for ticket use that looks wrong. None of that touches the design underneath, drawn as it was for a different threat model.

The KDC is still the center of the design, and the krbtgt key still opens everything in it. The architecture endures.

Steve Miller left MIT years ago. Clifford Neuman became a professor at USC, where he continued working on distributed systems and security.[131] The protocol they designed to solve a campus authentication problem became the authentication layer for most corporate networks in the world.

They solved the problem they set out to solve: passwords no longer cross the wire in plain text, users authenticate once and move from service to service without logging in again, and the digital wristband works.

They could not anticipate attackers who would steal the wristbands, counterfeit them, target the registration desk itself. `Kerberos` was built for a community. The community became a battleground.

Golden tickets became standard tools in nation-state attacks, and mimikatz made credential theft trivial. The krbtgt key that protected every Windows domain became the prize that attackers sought above all others. Ransomware operators needed to own an entire domain before encrypting it, and the golden ticket gave them exactly that.

The wristband never stopped working. Billions of Windows logins each day pass through `Kerberos`, and the ticket system that Miller and Neuman designed in an MIT lab still authenticates the world's corporate networks. Somewhere, an employee is sitting down at a workstation, typing a password once, and opening every door on the network. The three-headed dog still guards the gate.

`Kerberos` concentrated trust in a single server. Other protocols tried the opposite: no center at all, no authority, just an open channel and the hope that everyone on it would behave.

CHAPTER 11

THE CHAT ROOM

IRC has been designed over a number of years
for use with text based conferencing.
This document describes the current IRC protocol.

— RFC 1459, Jarkko Oikarinen and Darren Reed, May 1993

11.1. ARCTIC TWILIGHT

In August 1988, Jarkko Oikarinen was a summer trainee at the University of Oulu, in northern Finland.[132] The sun barely set at that latitude in summer. He had been coding through the long twilight. His assignment: improve the chat feature on the bulletin board system. Instead, he built something entirely new.

The BBS chat was limited—it ran on a single machine, and Oikarinen wanted more. He imagined users anywhere joining the same conversation, multiple conversations at once, each in its own channel.

He called it Internet Relay Chat.

The first IRC server ran on tolsun.oulu.fi, where Oikarinen tested it from other machines in the department. A few students joined, but what mattered was that the room could now be anywhere.

His nickname was WiZ—on IRC, your handle mattered more than your legal name.

The idea wasn't entirely new. Other real-time chat systems existed. Bitnet Relay Chat let users on Bitnet—a separate academic network—talk in groups. The Unix `talk` program allowed two people to type at each other, their words appearing letter by letter on split screens. A Finnish programmer named Jyrki Kuoppala had written `rmsg`, a multi-user messaging system.

Oikarinen's contribution was synthesis. He took the multi-user model from Bitnet Relay, the internet's TCP/IP infrastructure, and the Unix tradition of small, composable programs, and created something that could scale. Servers connected to servers. Users connected to any server and could talk to anyone else who had logged in. Messages relayed through the mesh. The whole thing worked like a distributed party line.

By 1989, IRC had escaped Finland. Servers appeared across Scandinavia, then at MIT in the United States.[133] The network grew through word of mouth and academic connections. A researcher would discover IRC, set up a server at their institution, link it to the existing network, and suddenly everyone at that university could join the global conversation.

The growth was explosive. When Oikarinen finally standardized the protocol in RFC 1459, he noted the strain: "[The network] is striving to cope with growth. Over the past 2 years, the average number of users connected to the main IRC network has grown by a factor of 10."[134]

The early culture was anarchic in the best sense. Channels formed around topics: programming, science fiction, philosophy, music. Anyone could create a channel just by joining one that didn't exist. Anyone could claim a nickname just by using it. The only rules were the ones each community enforced for itself.

This worked because the early users shared norms. They were researchers, students, hobbyists who had found their way onto the academic internet. They wanted to talk, not to fight. When conflicts arose, they worked them out or ignored each other. Social pressure kept people in line.

Shared norms worked until the community grew too large to know itself.

By August 1990, the network had grown large enough to need governance. A server called "eris" had a wildcard line allowing anyone to connect servers, causing chaos. Operator Greg Lindahl led a split, and the remaining operators called themselves the Eris-Free Network—EFnet.[135] It became the first major IRC network, the mother from which all others would descend.

January 1991 brought a moment that hinted at IRC's potential.[136] American forces began bombing Baghdad in the first Gulf War. Users in Israel typed reports as SCUD missiles fell on Tel Aviv. Updates appeared in IRC channels before they reached television newsrooms. For a few nights, the network became the fastest news source on the planet.

The same openness that let Israelis report missile strikes let anyone pretend to be anyone. The architecture that carried news would carry commands to criminal botnets. The protocol that enabled global conversation enabled global attacks.

Oikarinen and his collaborators published the protocol specification as RFC 1459 in May 1993.[134] The document described what IRC had already become: a text conferencing system with channels, nicknames, and a mesh of servers. It codified the trust assumptions that had governed the network since August 1988.

Two premises held the network together. Users would identify themselves honestly, and server operators would link only reputable servers. Crime was not something the design had to account for.

11.2. CHANNELS AND COMMANDS

11.2.1. HOW IRC WORKS

Think of `IRC` as a party spread across many rooms. Each door has a name on it—`#linux`, `#python`, `#randomchat`—and none of them lock. Walk in and start talking; that is the whole entrance procedure. A few rooms have bouncers, but the bouncer is another guest who ended up with the power to throw people out.

The party happens across a network of servers. When you connect to `IRC`, you connect to one server in the mesh. That server is linked to others, which are linked to still others. A message you send travels from your server to every other server that needs to see it, then down to the clients in the relevant channel. The servers relay your messages. That's where the name comes from.

11.2.2. CONNECTING AND IDENTIFYING

When you connect to an `IRC` server, you introduce yourself—but no one checks whether you're telling the truth.

```
NICK alice
USER alice alice localhost :Alice Smith
```

The NICK command claims a name. The USER command provides a username, hostname, and "real name" (though no one verifies this). Once these complete, the server welcomes you with a burst of information: the server name, the network rules, the message of the day.

Your full identity on `IRC` is a triple: nickname, username, and hostname. You might appear as:

```
alice!alice@isp.example.com
```

This triple identifies you in channel bans, private messages, and server logs.

What's missing: proof.

You chose your nickname. You provided your username. The hostname comes from your connection, but that can be masked or spoofed. No password, no certificate, no proof that alice is who she claims to be. The server takes your word for it.

11.2.3. CHANNELS AND MESSAGES

Channels are where conversation happens, and they start with #—`#linux`, `#python`, `#secretcommands`. That last one could exist, because anyone can create a channel just by joining it.

```
JOIN #chat
PRIVMSG #chat :Hello everyone!
PART #chat :Goodbye
```

JOIN enters a channel. If the channel doesn't exist, you create it—no approval needed. PRIVMSG sends a message to a channel or a person. PART leaves.

When you send a message to `#chat`, your server forwards it to every other server with users in that channel. Those servers deliver it to their local users. Milliseconds. Global reach.

The protocol doesn't care what the message contains. "Hello everyone!" and "!ddos yahoo.com 80 60" travel the same way. The infrastructure that carries conversation will carry commands.

11.2.4. OPERATORS AND POWER

Channels have operators, marked with an @ before their nickname. Operators can kick users, ban them, set channel modes, and appoint other operators.

```
MODE #chat +o bob
KICK #chat alice :Spam
MODE #chat +b *!*@bad.net
```

Give bob operator status; remove alice from the channel for spam; ban everyone connecting from bad.net. Three commands, and you have total control.

Who decides who becomes an operator? The first person to join an empty channel. Or anyone an existing operator trusts enough to promote. No vetting. No appeals process. Just power, granted by whoever holds power.

Operator status is temporary—it lasts only while you're in the channel. If every operator leaves, the channel is ungoverned, and the next person to join could claim control. So people built defenses: bots that sat in the channel around the clock holding the @, scripts that rejoined the instant a user dropped. The popular channels were fought over.

11.2.5. THE NETSPLIT PROBLEM

IRC networks are trees of servers. When a link between servers fails, the tree splits in two. Each side continues operating independently, unaware of the other. Users on one side can't see users on the other.

When the link comes back, chaos follows.

Both sides may have users sharing a nickname. Both may have granted operator powers to different people in one channel. The servers must reconcile these conflicts. The typical solution: kill the colliding nicknames and force both users to reconnect.

Attackers turned this into a weapon. They would cut a server link deliberately, wait for key users to drop off one side, then take the nicknames and channels those users had left unattended. "Riding the split" became an art form.

11.2.6. THE OPEN DOOR

What did IRC verify? Nothing. What did it expect? Good faith from everyone.

> RFC 1459 --- May 1993 --- Internet Relay Chat
>
> IRC itself is a teleconferencing system, which (through the use of the client-server model) is well-suited to running on many machines in a distributed fashion.

The RFC describes a teleconferencing system. No built-in registration verified identities. Server operators could see all traffic and impersonate any user. The specification expected a community of enthusiasts who shared norms about acceptable behavior.

In 1993, using a chat system to control malware would have seemed absurd. But the features that made IRC good for conversation—real-time messaging, channels for coordination, global reach—would make it perfect for crime.

11.3. THIRTY MILLION MACHINES

The screen showed IP addresses scrolling upward—each one a compromised computer, all waiting for instructions.

The early 2000s. A botnet operator sat at a keyboard, logged into an IRC channel whose name was a string of random characters. The server was either a hacked machine or a cheap VPS paid for with a stolen credit card. No legitimate user would ever have found the place.

In the channel, thousands of bots waited, each a program running on someone else's computer. Some were home PCs taken over by a malicious email; others were corporate workstations a worm had walked into, or servers whose software was years past its last patch. They had names like `[XP-HOME]39842`.

The operator typed:

```
!ddos yahoo.com 80 60
```

The bots began flooding Yahoo's servers. Sixty seconds of coordinated attack from thousands of machines.

This was what IRC became: infrastructure for crime.

11.3.1. THE BOTNET EVOLUTION

IRC bots started as helpers—they managed channels, kept logs, kicked troublemakers, enforced rules. Useful, even beloved.

Then someone realized that a bot could run on a compromised machine, connect to a secret channel, wait for commands, and bring thousands of friends.

GTBot appeared in 2000.[137] Written in mIRC script, crude but effective. An infected machine would connect to a specified IRC server, join a hidden channel, and wait. The operator issued commands through normal IRC messages.

SDBot followed in 2002, written in C++ and more sophisticated.[138] The source code leaked, and soon thousands of variants existed—the barrier to entry had dropped to zero.

Agobot raised the bar in 2003. It offered over five hundred configuration options, could evade antivirus software, hide as a rootkit, and use encrypted channels. Its creator, Axel Gembe, was arrested in Germany in May 2004[139], but by then the model had spread beyond any single author's control.

11.3.2. THE MAFIABOY ATTACKS

In February 2000, a fifteen-year-old Canadian who called himself Mafiaboy demonstrated what distributed denial-of-service attacks could do.[140]

On February 7, Yahoo went offline. The site had been the web's most visited destination, and it simply stopped responding—about an hour of downtime, millions of users locked out.

The next day Amazon buckled, and eBay and CNN after it, all drowning under floods of traffic. The attacks were distributed denial of service—DDoS. The coordination happened in IRC channels: compromised machines sat waiting for commands, and when the operator named a target, thousands of them flooded it at once, far more traffic than any one attacker could generate alone.

Michael Calce—Mafiaboy—had bragged about his exploits in `IRC` channels, and the FBI was in those channels too, building a case. Investigators had traced the communications by mid-February, and Canadian police eventually arrested him at his Montreal home.

One widely repeated estimate put the damage above a billion dollars, though that figure—from a single market analyst—was disputed, and prosecutors calculated far less. Whatever the number, Calce was a teenager with no financial motive. He did it because he could.

11.3.3. BREDOLAB: THE CRIMINAL EMPIRE

If Mafiaboy was an amateur, the operators of BredoLab were professionals—and by their era, the professionals had outgrown `IRC`. The early botnets had marshaled their machines in `IRC` channels, easy to find and easy to cut off once defenders learned where to look. BredoLab's operators moved the command channel to the web, hiding their orders inside ordinary-looking web requests, relayed through a shifting maze of proxy servers. The same evolution that pushed conversation off `IRC` pushed crime off it too.

By 2009, BredoLab controlled an estimated thirty million infected computers. The malware spread through spam emails, through compromised websites, through malicious advertisements. Each infected machine phoned home over the web, awaiting commands.

The operators didn't use the botnet themselves—they rented it out. Want to send spam? Pay per million messages. Want to launch a DDoS attack? Pay per hour. Want to steal banking credentials? The botnet could be configured for that too. Kaspersky estimated the operator earned up to $139,000 per month renting access.[141]

BredoLab was a service business.

In late October 2010, the Dutch National High Tech Crime Unit coordinated an international takedown.[142] They seized 143 command-and-control servers. The botnet operator, Georgy Avanesov, was arrested at Yerevan's Zvartnots Airport in Armenia, and in May 2012 was sentenced to four years in prison.[143] No one had ever taken down a larger botnet.

But by then, the model had proven itself. `IRC`-based botnets continued for years afterward.

In May 2021, the Freenode `IRC` network—home to thousands of open-source projects—collapsed after a hostile takeover by its new owner.[144] Staff resigned en masse. Users migrated to a new network called Libera.Chat. Within weeks, Freenode was dead.

The incident demonstrated `IRC`'s final vulnerability: lacking any central authority, governance structure, or legal framework, a network could be seized or destroyed at the whims of whoever controlled the domain name. A system that welcomed everyone couldn't protect itself from anyone.

Millions of machines once answered to `IRC` commands, as botnets turned conversation into attack infrastructure. The network that connected Finnish students became the nervous system of criminal enterprises. The major chat platforms moved on, built their own protocols, added encryption and moderation and corporate governance. The world `IRC` was built for is gone.

And yet—it is two in the morning UTC, and in `#linux` on Libera.Chat someone wants to know how to compile a kernel module. A bot logs the question. Three strangers answer it. No one is paid to be there and no company runs the server, and the channel has been open under one name or another for thirty years. The protocol underneath still trusts whoever shows up.

IRC connected people to each other. The machines carrying all that conversation—the routers and switches and servers—were multiplying past the point where anyone could manage them by hand. Someone needed to build a way to ask them how they were doing.

CHAPTER 12

THE COMMUNITY STRING

Security issues are not discussed in this memo.

— RFC 1157, May 1990

12.1. THE SIMPLE QUESTION

Jeffrey Case wanted one thing: to know what was happening inside his network.

It was 1987, and Case was a researcher at the University of Tennessee with a growing collection of routers and gateways to look after. Each device had its own console and its own commands, so checking the network meant walking from machine to machine and logging in at every stop. Ten devices made for a tedious afternoon. A hundred would have been impossible.

Other administrators had the same problem. The internet had thousands of routers and switches and servers by then, and every one of them generated logs and could fail without warning. You could not walk a network that size.

That November, Case and three colleagues published RFC 1028 and called it the Simple Gateway Monitoring Protocol. The name was honest. A management station could query a gateway for information, and the gateway would respond. SGMP ran over UDP and asked almost nothing of the machine it ran on, which mattered on devices with limited memory and processing power. A router that could barely spare the cycles to forward packets had none to spare for anything clever.[145]

The protocol spread quickly, and within months vendors were adding SGMP support to their routers. Gateways were only part of the problem, though. The Internet Engineering Task Force wanted something that could manage any device on the network, and in 1988 it formed a working group to extend SGMP into a full management framework.

The result was SNMP, the Simple Network Management Protocol. RFC 1157 arrived in May 1990, and it became the standard way to monitor and control network devices. Case was the first name on it, alongside Mark Fedor, Martin Schoffstall, and James Davin, the same team behind SGMP. They kept the "S."[146]

The design philosophy was explicit. "The SNMP explicitly minimizes the number and complexity of management functions realized by the management agent itself," the RFC stated, a goal it called "attractive in at least four respects." The authors listed those four: lower development cost, broader remote management, fewer restrictions on management tools, easier understanding for developers. Security appeared nowhere.

A router's job was to forward packets. Every cycle spent on management was a cycle not spent on routing. SNMP would be lightweight, easy to implement, and universally deployable. Administrators needed to monitor their networks now; they could worry about security later.

Authentication, in SNMP's design, came down to a single string of characters. The protocol called it a "community string," a name chosen because SNMP organized devices into communities that shared management policies. In practice the string was a password, and the whole test was whether the string in the request matched the one the device held. Match, and it answered.

The RFC used "public" as an example community string for read-only access and "private" for read-write access. The examples were meant to be illustrative, placeholders that administrators would replace with their own values. Instead, they became defaults.

Device manufacturers shipped their routers and switches with "public" configured for read access and "private" for write access. Administrators, busy with a thousand other problems, left the defaults in place. They meant to change them later. Meant to secure their networks properly once things calmed down. Things never calmed down.

The community string traveled with every SNMP request, in cleartext. Anyone who could capture network traffic could read it, and anyone who knew it could query the device. SNMP drew no distinction between a legitimate administrator and someone who had guessed the password. Know the magic word and you were authorized. The word was usually "public."

RFC 1157 contained a section titled "Security Considerations." It consisted of a single sentence—the one that would become the chapter's epitaph.

It worked. By the mid-1990s SNMP was everywhere—routers, switches, servers, even network-attached printers. A management system could query thousands of devices at once, aggregate their statistics, page an administrator when a link failed, and reconfigure the equipment from a desk. The walk was over. Administrators watched a dashboard instead, one screen showing the state of an entire infrastructure.

Fedor had organized all that device knowledge hierarchically—every piece of information on every device had a precise address that could be queried remotely. Routing tables, interface statistics, connection logs, ARP caches, configuration data, and in a few vendors' implementations, passwords.

With the community string, you could read all of it. With the read-write community string, you could change it.

12.2. MANAGERS AND AGENTS

12.2.1. HOW SNMP WORKS

Every network device keeps a running record of what it does. Interface counters tally the packets passing through, error logs note what went wrong, and routing tables describe the paths data takes. ARP caches remember which hardware address belongs to which IP address. Together they add up to a picture of your network that no documentation captures.

SNMP exists to ask questions and hear answers. The protocol divides the world into managers and agents. A manager is the software that wants information: the monitoring dashboard, the alerting system, the configuration tool. An agent runs on the device being managed: the router, the switch, the server. The manager asks; the agent answers.

How does the agent tell a legitimate administrator from an intruder scanning the network?

It doesn't. Anyone who knows the password—a short string of characters—is treated as authorized. The agent cannot tell the difference between your monitoring system and an attacker in another country. Both look the same: a UDP packet arriving on port 161, carrying a request and a password.

If the password matches, the agent answers. If the agent has something urgent to report—a link going down, a threshold being exceeded—it can send a trap to the manager on UDP port 162. Traps are unsolicited messages that let the network cry for help, but they also announce that something valuable is listening.

The operations are elementary and dangerous.

A **GET** request retrieves a single value. "What is the system uptime?" The agent responds: 86400 seconds. One day since the last reboot. Anyone who asks with the right password learns how long the device has run untouched—and a router that hasn't rebooted in a year probably hasn't been patched in a year either.

A **GETNEXT** request retrieves whatever comes next in the database. Call it again and again, starting from the root, and you walk through every piece of information the agent knows: routing tables, interface statistics, ARP caches, configuration data. Attackers map networks this way, one query at a time, as the device reveals everything.

A **SET** request changes a value. "Disable interface 3." If you have the write password, the agent obeys. No login screen, no audit trail, no confirmation that you should be allowed to do this. Just a UDP packet and a password.

A **TRAP** flows in the opposite direction—the agent notifies the manager that something happened. A link failure. A reboot. An authentication failure, when someone guessed the wrong password. Ironically, the trap reveals that the device exists and is worth attacking.

12.2.2. THE MANAGEMENT INFORMATION BASE

What exactly can an attacker read? Everything the device knows about itself—and everything it knows about your network.

SNMP organizes what a device knows into a tree called the Management Information Base. It starts at a single root and divides into branches, and the leaves at the far end hold the actual data. Every leaf has an address: a sequence of numbers separated by dots, called an Object Identifier. Any one fact about the device can be requested by number, the way a clerk pulls a file by its shelf code.

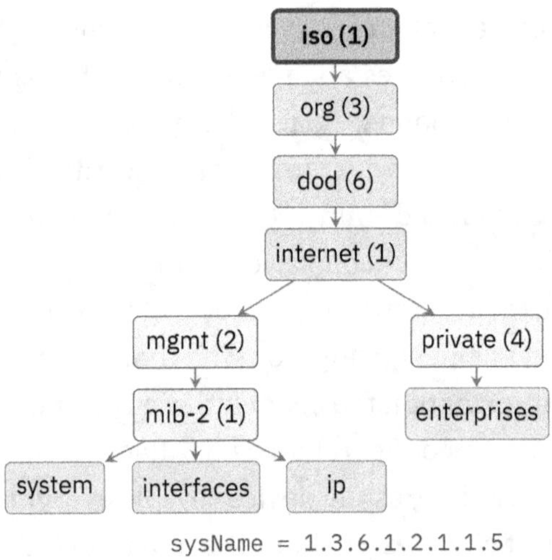

Figure 12.1: SNMP MIB tree structure. Object Identifiers form paths from root to leaf.

The address `1.3.6.1.2.1.1.5.0` points to the device's hostname. The address `1.3.6.1.2.1.2.2.1.10.3` points to how many bytes have arrived on interface 3. Hundreds of addresses, hundreds of pieces of information.

Each branch reveals more about your network.

System identity tells an attacker what they have found, and interface statistics show them the traffic patterns. The IP routing table lays out the topology. TCP connection data names the services that are running and who is talking to them, and the ARP cache maps IP addresses onto physical hardware—the skeleton of the local network.

Vendors extend the tree with their own branches, and some of those branches contain configuration data—a few even contain passwords.

An SNMP walk—GETNEXT requests, one after another, starting from the root—enumerates everything. One guess at the password, and the device tells you its secrets. For a legitimate administrator, this is visibility. For an attacker, reconnaissance on request.

12.2.3. THE COMMUNITY STRING

Authentication in SNMP version 1 has one component: the community string. Every request includes it, and every response requires it to match what the agent expects.

> RFC 1157 --- May 1990 --- SNMP Authentication
>
> "Each SNMP community is named by a string of octets, that is called the community name for said community. An SNMP message originated by an SNMP application entity that in fact belongs to the SNMP community named by the community component of said message is called an authentic SNMP message."

The language is formal, almost bureaucratic. But the mechanism is bare: if the string matches, the request is "authentic." No usernames. No cryptographic signatures. No challenge-response. Just a password, sent in the clear with every packet.

Most agents recognize two community strings. The read-only one permits GET and GETNEXT, which is enough to look around but not to change anything. The read-write one permits SET requests as well, and a SET reconfigures the device. An administrator might pick "monitoring" for reading and "configure" for writing.

Or they might leave the defaults: "public" and "private."

Millions did.

SNMP sends these strings as plaintext in UDP packets—no encryption, no hashing—so the password travels in the clear, readable by any device on the path. Capture one SNMP exchange, and you have the key. Use that key, and the device cannot tell you from its legitimate administrator.

12.2.4. THE DEFAULT PASSWORD

SNMP's security model stands out for its self-awareness—and its surrender.

RFC 1157 acknowledged that security mattered. It defined authentication services and noted their importance. Then it provided an escape hatch: "Some SNMP implementations may wish to support only a trivial authentication service that identifies all SNMP messages as authentic SNMP messages."

You could implement real security, or you could skip it—and most implementations skipped it. The trivial authentication service—community strings sent in cleartext—became the standard, and the escape hatch became the main entrance.

The working group knew this was a problem, and they debated cryptographic approaches for years. In 1996, SNMPv2 added bulk retrieval operations.[147] Its community-based administrative framework, SNMPv2c, kept community strings.[148] SNMPv3 finally arrived in 2002 with real authentication and encryption.[149,150]

By then, the damage was done. Millions of devices were deployed with "public" and "private" as their passwords, and SNMPv3 was complex enough that administrators who had grown up with the defaults found it bewildering. Many didn't bother upgrading.

What sets this apart from the earlier chapters is that the engineers knew authentication mattered. They argued about how to build it and eventually did, but the 1990 standard shipped without any. Surveys taken more than twenty years later still turned up millions of devices answering to "public," an example value from RFC 1157 that had quietly become production configuration.

12.3. THE DEVICES ANSWER BACK

Security cameras across the East Coast went dark one October morning in 2016. DVRs rebooted. Home routers dropped connections. The devices weren't failing—they were attacking.

The target was Dyn, the company providing DNS services to some of the internet's largest websites: Twitter, Netflix, GitHub, Reddit, Amazon. All of their names resolved through Dyn's servers, and on this morning, those servers were drowning.

The traffic came from everywhere. Homes, small businesses, security cameras, printers, thermostats, baby monitors with factory-default configurations. The devices had been conscripted into a botnet called Mirai.[151]

Mirai was not sophisticated—its source code was almost insultingly simple. The botnet spread by scanning for devices running `Telnet` with default passwords, trying 62 combinations like admin/admin, root/root, and guest/guest. When one worked, it logged in, downloaded itself, and started scanning for more victims.

But `Telnet` was just the beginning. The internet was full of devices answering queries without any login. `SNMP` was one of them.

Anyone scanning with "public" could query any device that hadn't changed defaults. The response revealed identity, contact information, sometimes location—and more usefully, network configuration. Anyone who could walk the MIB could map the entire network.

The reconnaissance was free. Shodan, a search engine for internet-connected devices, indexed `SNMP` responses, and a query for devices answering to "public" returned millions of results.[152] Some were old routers forgotten in closets, but plenty were live infrastructure still carrying traffic. The example community string had become a skeleton key.

The amplification attacks came next. Three things made them possible: `UDP`, forged source addresses, and responses far larger than the requests that triggered them.

`SNMP` runs over `UDP`, the User Datagram Protocol. `TCP` sets up a connection before it sends anything. `UDP` fires the packet off and hopes it lands, which makes it quick and cheap—exactly what `SNMP`'s small questions needed.

But `UDP` has a weakness: it does not verify where packets came from. The source address in a `UDP` packet is whatever the sender claims it is, and an attacker can write any address they want in that field. This is called `IP` spoofing.

The attack works like this: an attacker sends an `SNMP` query to a device but lies about where the request came from. Instead of their own address, they write in the victim's. The device receives the query, prepares a response, and sends it to the victim. The victim never asked for this data. They drown in answers to questions they never asked.

This technique becomes devastating when the response is larger than the request. Attackers call this **amplification**. If you can send a 60-byte request and generate a 6,000-byte response, you have multiplied your attack power by 100. Your bandwidth becomes a hundred times more destructive.

SNMP was well suited to amplification. A GETBULK request—added in SNMPv2 to retrieve multiple values efficiently—could ask for many OIDs at once. US-CERT listed a measured bandwidth amplification factor of 6.3 for an SNMPv2 GETBULK request, while Cloudflare cited a theoretical factor as high as 650.[96,153] The actual multiplier depended on the query and the responding device, but the asymmetry favored the attacker.

The pattern was familiar from NTP (Chapter 8) and DNS (Chapter 7)—any UDP protocol that answered queries from strangers. But SNMP had a particular advantage: the devices running it were everywhere, often forgotten, rarely updated, almost never firewalled. Scans in 2014 found millions of devices responding to SNMP queries on port 161.[152] Many still do.

The attacks were not merely theoretical. In February 2014, Cloudflare reported an NTP amplification attack that peaked just below 400 gigabits per second. The company also reported evidence that attackers had begun experimenting with SNMP as a DDoS vector, and US-CERT listed SNMPv2 among the UDP protocols known to enable reflected amplification.[96,153] The devices Case had designed to answer administrators' questions could now be made to answer attackers' questions and flood their victims with the responses.

The fix was well known. Turn SNMP off on the devices that had no use for it, change the community string on the ones that did, and keep port 161 behind a firewall. The obstacle was that a device still running defaults had usually dropped off every inventory years earlier. The cameras had gone in with the wiring contract, and the routers had been left alone since installation. The printer had always worked and so had never come up in a meeting.

The trouble was the architecture, not the configuration. SNMP took the community string as proof of membership, a reasonable reading when infrastructure was private and the password stayed inside the organization. Its designers assumed that reaching a router at all meant you were already inside. Then every device got a route to the internet, and "public" turned out to be no harder to guess than "password123."

RFC 1157's one sentence about security considerations had aged badly. The very things that let administrators put SNMP on every device in the building—cheap to implement, trivial to switch on—let strangers query those same devices from anywhere in the world.

In 2017, US-CERT published an advisory: SNMP remained a significant threat.[154] Disable it where possible. Use SNMPv3 with authentication and encryption where necessary. Block UDP port 161 at network boundaries. The recommendations were the same ones security researchers had been making for years. They continued to go unheeded.

Case went on to found SNMP Research, a company that built network management tools.[155] The standard he helped create became the foundation of an industry. The monitoring dashboards that network administrators rely on today descend from one elemental idea: devices should answer questions about themselves.

The community string persists. Newer devices may ship with randomized defaults, or refuse to enable SNMP until somebody configures it, but the installed base is vast and changes slowly. Millions of routers still respond to "public" on port 161 and hand over their routing tables.

RFC 1157 used "public" as an example. Just a placeholder, never meant for production. It shipped in every manual, on every default configuration, an invitation that no one revoked.

In October 2025, security researchers documented Operation Zero Disco, an attack campaign exploiting an SNMP flaw in Cisco devices.[156] Cisco estimated nearly two million devices ran the vulnerable software. The flaw lived in the SNMP subsystem, reachable with nothing more than a read-only community string. Often, that string was still the example value from 1990, thirty-five years later.

Somewhere right now, a router on the edge of a network that no one remembers installing is listening on port 161. It will answer any question, from anyone, as long as they know the word. The word is "public." It has always been "public."

SNMP let a network watch its own machines. But the internet was never one network—it was thousands of them, each run by strangers, somehow agreeing to carry one another's traffic. How they reached that agreement, and how much of it rested on nothing but trust, got worked out over lunch in Austin, on the backs of two napkins.

PART III

THE WEB

CHAPTER 13

THE ROUTING TABLE

The primary function of a BGP speaking system is to exchange network reachability information with other BGP systems.

— RFC 1105, Kirk Lougheed and Yakov Rekhter, June 1989

13.1. LUNCH IN AUSTIN

It was lunchtime in Austin, Texas, and two engineers were redesigning the internet on napkins.

By 1989, the infrastructure was in place. DNS translated names. NTP synchronized clocks. SNMP monitored the machines. The academic internet hummed along, eighty thousand hosts strong, managed by engineers who recognized each other at conferences. But commercial networks were knocking at the door: PSINet, UUNET, companies that wanted to sell connectivity, not share it. The research network was about to become a marketplace. It would need a new kind of routing.

Kirk Lougheed had flown in from Cisco's Menlo Park offices. Yakov Rekhter had come from IBM's T.J. Watson Research Center.[157] They were attending the twelfth IETF meeting, where the people building the internet argued about how it should work. The formal sessions had broken for lunch, but the real work was happening at a restaurant table.

Stating the problem was easy; the fix was not. The ARPANET had been one network under one organization. By 1989 the internet was a patchwork: the NSFNET backbone linking universities, PSINet and UUNET carrying commercial traffic, regional networks reaching the smaller institutions. Each ran its own equipment and hired its own administrators, and each had opinions about where traffic ought to go. The term for such a network was "autonomous system"—one that made its own routing decisions.

The existing protocol, `EGP` (Exterior Gateway Protocol), assumed a simpler topology: the ARPANET at the center, everything else connected like spokes on a wheel. The internet wasn't a wheel anymore. It was becoming a mesh, with networks connecting in complicated patterns. `EGP` couldn't express those patterns or handle policy: the rules about who could send traffic through whom, who paid whom, who trusted whom.

Lougheed and Rekhter sketched on napkins. They drew circles for autonomous systems, lines for connections between them. They wrote out the information each network would share with its neighbors: which destinations it could reach, and through which path.

The path was the key insight. `EGP` said "I can reach this network." The new protocol would say "I can reach this network through these autonomous systems." With that information, networks could prefer shorter paths, avoid competitors, and detect loops. If your own network appeared in the path, something had gone wrong.

They called it the Border Gateway Protocol, `BGP`. The name was straightforward: it ran on border routers, the machines at the edges of each autonomous system, the gateways between networks.

Lougheed worked at Cisco, which meant he had access to routers. Within months, he had a working implementation running on Cisco hardware. Rekhter implemented BGP for the NSFNET backbone. By late 1989, BGP was carrying real traffic.

RFC 1105, published in June 1989, laid out the design.[158] The document ran seventeen pages. It described four message types: OPEN, to establish a connection between BGP speakers; UPDATE, to exchange routing information; NOTIFICATION, to signal errors; and KEEPALIVE, to confirm the connection was still alive. The protocol ran over TCP—the reliable transport protocol from Chapter 4—which meant it inherited TCP's reliability. If a BGP message got lost, TCP would retransmit it. The engineers didn't have to build that machinery themselves.

The design was elegant: two routers would connect over TCP port 179,[158] exchange OPEN messages, agreeing on parameters, then exchange their complete routing tables. After that, they'd send UPDATE messages whenever routes changed. The rest of the time, they'd exchange KEEPALIVEs: heartbeats proving the connection was alive.

Underneath the simplicity sat an assumption. An autonomous system announced "I can reach 192.0.2.0/24," and the receiving router believed it, because the announcement arrived with no proof attached and no certificate to check. Operators would tell the truth about the routes they could carry, the protocol assumed, since lying would disrupt the network and everyone wanted the network to work.

BGP picked up a nickname: "the two-napkin protocol." Two paper napkins, a sketch between the plates, and the result ended up routing the entire internet; the story has been retold enough times to count as legend.[159] The lunch table had no nation-states at it. Lougheed and Rekhter never imagined that the trust they encoded would one day route traffic for adversaries.

The internet of 1989 had about 100,000 hosts. A decade later, it would have more than fifty million. The community of network operators who met at IETF meetings would become an industry of thousands of companies, including some that would rather route traffic through their surveillance infrastructure than deliver it honestly. The napkin protocol would scale beyond anyone's imagination. The underlying premise would not.

RFC 1105 was only the first draft of the idea. `BGP-2` followed in 1990[160], `BGP-3` in 1991[161], and `BGP-4` in 1995.[162] Each revision picked up what the previous one had missed: classless addressing, better route aggregation, finer control over policy. In January 2006, RFC 4271 revised and replaced the 1995 `BGP-4` specification.[163] By then `BGP` was carrying traffic for billions of users, and what two engineers had drawn on napkins touched every packet crossing the internet.

The core premise never changed. Your neighbors tell the truth about what they can reach. If you can't rely on your neighbors, you shouldn't be peering with them.

The question nobody asked at that Austin lunch was simple: What happens when the neighborhood changes?

13.2. LONGEST PREFIX WINS

13.2.1. HOW BGP ROUTES THE INTERNET

Picture a world map where every major city manages its own roads. Los Angeles doesn't know Tokyo's roads, and Tokyo doesn't know Los Angeles's. But they both need to move traffic between them.

That's the internet's routing problem. Each city is an autonomous system (AS): a network under unified administrative control, like a transportation district. Los Angeles County manages its roads, and Orange County manages its own—neighbors, but separate. AT&T, Comcast, and Google each manage their own networks the same way.

Every AS gets a number: a name it uses to identify itself. AT&T is AS 7018, Google is AS 15169, and the U.S. Department of Defense operates AS 721. When they announce routes, they attach these numbers identifying who claims to control each piece of the internet—claims, not proof.

Neighboring districts exchange traffic by sharing road maps: "To reach San Diego, take I-5 south." BGP works the same way. The maps get traded by routers sitting at the network borders—the on-ramps and off-ramps between districts.

These border routers are BGP speakers—the name is literal, they speak BGP to each other. When two AS networks agree to share traffic, they establish a peering session, like postal offices exchanging mail. Once the session is established, each side believes what the other announces.

Once connected, the BGP speakers trade routes. A route is a promise: "I can reach these addresses, and here's the path." The path is expressed as a list of AS numbers, like highway directions listing which counties you'll pass through. If Google announces a route to YouTube's addresses, the path might be `15169 36561`. Traffic enters AS 15169 (Google), then reaches AS 36561 (YouTube, a Google subsidiary). Two hops.

These paths grow longer as they spread. AT&T might receive that route and announce it to its neighbors as `7018 15169 36561`. Now the path shows three hops: "Come through AT&T, then Google, then YouTube." Each network adds itself to the front, like stamping a passport.

> RFC 1105, Section 2 --- June 1989
>
> This network reachability information includes information on the autonomous systems (AS's) that traffic must transit to reach these networks. This information is sufficient to construct a graph of AS connectivity from which routing loops may be pruned and policy decisions at an AS level may be enforced.

The AS path does two jobs. One is loop prevention: a BGP speaker that receives an announcement carrying its own AS number knows the route has come back around, and it throws the announcement away. The other is policy. An AS can favor shorter paths or steer around a competitor. It can also refuse to transit traffic through a particular network—because of politics, or money, or its own security.

But notice what the AS path doesn't do. It doesn't prove that any of those networks actually handled the packet. The path is a list of claims, not a chain of receipts.

13.2.2. THE ROUTE SELECTION ALGORITHM

When multiple routes exist to the same destination, BGP picks a winner—and the winner captures the traffic.

That's the key insight: if you can make your route look better than the legitimate route, packets flow to you, and BGP doesn't verify whether you deserve them.

How does BGP pick the winner? Through a hierarchy of preferences, the most important being LOCAL_PREF, local preference. Network administrators assign this number to express how much they favor a given route—higher numbers win.

Why prefer one route over another? Cost and politics—a path through a cheap peer might get LOCAL_PREF 100. A path through an expensive transit provider might get LOCAL_PREF 50. The highway is faster, but the back roads are free.

If LOCAL_PREF ties, the shorter AS path wins. Fewer hops usually mean faster delivery. A three-hop path beats a five-hop path, all else being equal.

But here's what matters: the competition is about appearances, not legitimacy. The route that *looks* best wins, whether or not the announcer actually controls the destination.

Let's trace a packet from a laptop in Chicago to a YouTube video server in California—watch for the trust.

The laptop sends the packet to the home router, addressed to 208.65.153.47, a YouTube server. The router doesn't know where that is, so it sends everything to the ISP—let's say Comcast.

Comcast's edge router receives the packet. It looks up 208.65.153.0/24 in its BGP routing table and finds an entry: "To reach this prefix, send to Google (AS 15169) via the Chicago exchange point." The router forwards the packet to Google's router at that exchange.

Google's router receives the packet. It looks up the same prefix and finds an internal route: "To reach 208.65.153.0/24, send to the Los Angeles data center." Google's internal network carries the packet across the country.

At the Los Angeles data center, another router receives the packet. This one has a more specific entry: "208.65.153.0/25 is handled by rack 47." The packet reaches the correct server. Total time: about 60 milliseconds.

Three autonomous systems handled that packet: the ISP, Google, and YouTube's internal network. Every router along the way looked the answer up in a BGP-derived table. The entries in those tables came from neighbors, who had gotten them from neighbors of their own.

At no step did anyone verify that those routes were legitimate. The ISP accepted Google's announcement. Google accepted YouTube's. The chain stretched from Chicago to California, every link relying on good faith.

13.2.3. LONGEST PREFIX MATCH

Here's where the trouble starts.

Routing tables do not list individual addresses. A router that receives a packet looks up the destination and finds a prefix—a whole block of addresses. Highway signs are the same: they read "Downtown—Next Exit" rather than "123 Main Street, Apartment 4B." A routing table entry is that kind of instruction: everything starting with 208.65 goes this way.

Prefixes use a notation like 208.65.152.0/22, where the /22 specifies how many bits identify the network. A /22 covers 1,024 addresses, a /24 covers 256, and a /25 covers 128.

Remember those numbers—they're about to matter.

Consider overlapping prefixes: suppose one route announces 208.65.152.0/22 (a block of 1,024 addresses) and another announces 208.65.153.0/24 (a subset of 256 addresses). Both announcements are valid, both point to the same address space—which one wins?

The routing rule is simple: the most specific prefix wins. This is called longest prefix match. If the highway sign says "California—This Way" and another sign says "Los Angeles—Next Exit," you take the more specific exit. Routers follow the same logic. A /24 beats a /22 because /24 is more specific.

Overlapping prefixes are allowed on purpose. A large provider can announce one big block while its customers announce smaller pieces inside it, and traffic engineers can split a prefix to balance load. The flexibility is a feature.

Until it becomes a weapon.

Anyone who announces a more specific prefix captures traffic, even if they don't own that address space. If YouTube operates 208.65.152.0/22 and I announce 208.65.153.0/24, traffic to those 256 addresses flows to me instead. The routers don't know I'm lying. They just see a more specific sign and follow it.

This is not a theoretical vulnerability—it's an instruction manual.

BGP has no authentication layer. When an AS announces a route, other ASes simply believe it. The protocol doesn't verify that you own the addresses you claim, that your AS path is real, or that you intend to deliver the traffic rather than swallow it. BGP verifies nothing.

The reasoning made sense in 1989. Autonomous systems connected through peering agreements—contracts specifying what traffic each side would accept and forward. If someone lied about their routes, they'd violate the agreement, their peers would notice, and they'd be disconnected. Reputation and business relationships would enforce honesty.

But peering is transitive. If AS A peers with AS B, and AS B peers with AS C, then A will receive routes that originated from C, filtered and re-announced by B. The path might be `B C destination`. AS A has no relationship with C. It cannot verify C's announcements. It relies on B, and B relies on C, and somewhere down that chain, someone might be lying.

The internet of 2008 had over 30,000 autonomous systems. The web of trust had become so tangled that no one could trace it.

Years later, Yakov Rekhter reflected on what he and Lougheed had sketched that day in Austin. "There was no concept that people would use this to do malicious things." The napkin protocol had been meant for a handful of ISPs that trusted each other. What they built was the routing layer for five billion strangers.

On a Sunday afternoon in February 2008, that premise would be tested.

13.3. TWO HOURS OF DARKNESS

It was Sunday, February 24, 2008, and YouTube was disappearing.

At the company's operations center in San Bruno, California, engineers watched their traffic graphs collapse. YouTube normally served over 100 million videos a day. The drop was not confined to one region; the site had gone unreachable everywhere at once.

The problem had started half a world away, in Pakistan.

The Pakistani government had a problem with YouTube. A video had been uploaded that authorities considered blasphemous. The Pakistan Telecommunication Authority ordered local internet providers to block access. Pakistan Telecom, the country's largest telecommunications company, was ordered to make YouTube disappear.

The engineers at Pakistan Telecom faced a technical question: how do you block a website? One option was DNS filtering: manipulate the domain name system so that queries for youtube.com return nothing.

But that's easy to circumvent. Users can change their DNS settings to use foreign servers.

Pakistan Telecom chose a more aggressive approach. They would hijack YouTube's IP addresses at the routing level. If traffic to YouTube's addresses never left Pakistan, users couldn't reach the site even if they knew the right IP.

YouTube operated its content from a block of addresses in the 208.65.152.0/22 range. To intercept that traffic, Pakistan Telecom announced a more specific prefix: 208.65.153.0/24. They configured the route to point to a "null route," a dead end where packets would be discarded. From the perspective of BGP, Pakistan Telecom was telling the world: "We can reach 208.65.153.0/24. Send us your traffic." What happened to that traffic after it arrived was Pakistan's problem.

The null route worked perfectly inside Pakistan. Pakistani users trying to reach YouTube had their packets swallowed, and the censorship was complete.

Then the route leaked.

Pakistan Telecom bought its international connectivity from PCCW, a Hong Kong telecommunications company, and the BGP session between them was configured to share routes. On a normal day Pakistan Telecom announced only what it was authorized to announce: its own address space and its customers'. This time a configuration let the internal null route to YouTube's prefix out the external session as well.

PCCW received the route and saw 208.65.153.0/24 being announced by Pakistan Telecom. The route was more specific than YouTube's legitimate announcement of 208.65.152.0/22. PCCW's routers did exactly what BGP requires: they preferred the more specific prefix, updated their routing tables, and announced the new route to their peers.

From PCCW, the false route spread to Asia's major carriers. Within minutes, it had reached European networks. A few minutes more, and it was in North America.[164] The AS path grew longer with each hop, but the route remained valid. No one questioned whether Pakistan Telecom actually controlled YouTube's addresses. The protocol had no mechanism for questioning.

By 18:47 UTC, YouTube was unreachable from most of the world's internet. Traffic destined for the video platform flowed toward Pakistan and vanished.

Operators traded notes on NANOG, the mailing list where the internet's plumbing gets coordinated, and worked out what they were seeing. "Routing to Pakistan?" one wrote, watching the traceroutes terminate in Islamabad. The world's cat videos were being handed to a null route in South Asia.

YouTube's engineers saw the problem immediately in their monitoring systems: inbound traffic had crashed. The site was up, their servers running fine, but no one could reach them because the traffic was being absorbed somewhere upstream, somewhere beyond their control.

The standard response to a BGP hijack is to announce an even more specific prefix. If the attacker has claimed /24, announce two /25s. BGP's longest-prefix-match rule will route traffic to the more specific announcements, away from the hijacker.

YouTube began announcing 208.65.153.0/25 and 208.65.153.128/25, two halves of the hijacked space, each more specific than Pakistan Telecom's /24. Traffic started coming back as the announcements spread. Propagation is not instant, though. Some networks converged quickly, and networks with longer paths to YouTube's real address space needed more time to learn the legitimate routes.

Meanwhile, PCCW had identified the source of the problem. They began filtering Pakistan Telecom's announcements, refusing to accept or propagate routes to YouTube's address space. Without PCCW as a path, the false route lost its reach. Networks that had been sending traffic through Pakistan's null route switched to other paths.

By 21:01 UTC, approximately two hours after the hijack began, YouTube had recovered. The video platform was reachable again. The null route in Pakistan, which had only been meant to block local users, had instead blacked out YouTube for most of the planet.

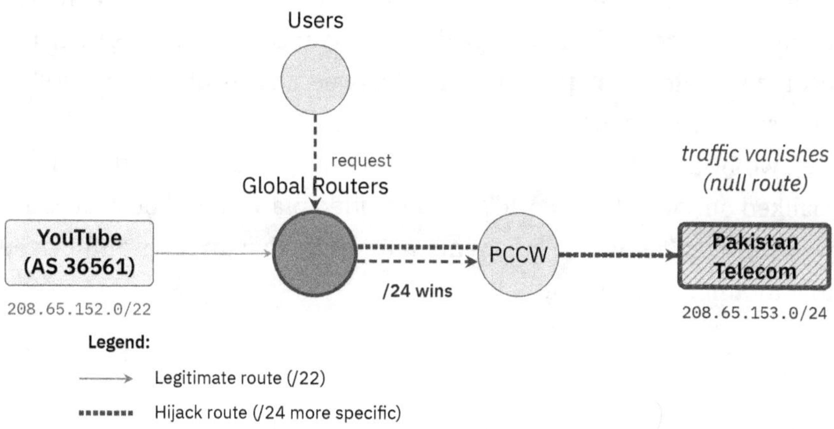

Figure 13.1: The Pakistan/YouTube BGP hijack. Pakistan Telecom announced a /24 prefix for YouTube's address space, more specific than YouTube's legitimate /22. BGP's longest-prefix-match rule caused global routers to prefer the false route, sending worldwide traffic into a null route.

Pakistan Telecom called it an accident. Their engineers had configured an internal null route for censorship purposes and failed to prevent it from leaking to external peers. A configuration error, not an attack.

The explanation was plausible. BGP misconfigurations are common, and networks announce routes they shouldn't all the time. The damage is usually small—a few thousand users lose connectivity to one destination for a few minutes, until someone notices and backs the change out. Pakistan's mistake differed in one respect: the target. YouTube was among the web's most popular destinations, and millions of people tried to reach it during those two hours and failed.

But the accident revealed something important: intent doesn't matter. Whether Pakistan Telecom was trying to censor YouTube or trying to attack it or trying to intercept its traffic, the mechanism was identical. Announce a more specific prefix, and let BGP do the rest. The protocol couldn't tell the difference between a mistake, a censorship order, and an attack.

Two hours. That's how long a misconfigured router in Pakistan blacked out one of the world's largest video platforms. The root cause was simple: BGP has no mechanism to verify that an AS is authorized to announce a given prefix.

13.3.1. THE AFTERMATH

The Pakistan incident accelerated discussions about BGP security that had been simmering for years. Engineers had long known that route hijacking was possible. What they lacked was motivation to fix it.

The countermeasure is RPKI, Resource Public Key Infrastructure. It runs a cryptographic chain of trust from the regional internet registries, which hand out address blocks, down to the networks that use them. A network publishes a Route Origin Authorization—a ROA, a signed statement saying "AS 36561 is authorized to announce 208.65.152.0/22." Other networks check announcements against the ROAs, and an announcement of YouTube's prefix by Pakistan Telecom, with nothing signed behind it, can be thrown out.

RPKI was standardized in 2012.[165] By 2024, roughly 50% of announced routes had a matching ROA.[166] That leaves half the routing table unverified, and publishing is only part of the work: plenty of networks never check the ROAs that do exist, accepting announcements whether or not anything cryptographic backs them.

The incentives run the wrong way. Deploying RPKI costs engineering time up front and maintenance forever after. The payoff lands mostly on everyone else's side of the ledger: dropping invalid announcements keeps other people's traffic from being pulled through you, by accident or by attack. Engineering time is scarce in a competitive industry, and shared infrastructure loses to whatever is more immediate.

The Pakistan-YouTube incident was dramatic because of its scale. But smaller hijacks happen regularly. In March 2022, a Russian ISP routing through Rostelecom briefly announced Twitter's address space.[167] In 2018, traffic to Amazon's Route 53 DNS service was hijacked to steal cryptocurrency.[168] In 2019, European mobile traffic was routed through China Telecom.[169] In January 2024, a hacker used infostealer malware to compromise Orange Spain's RIPE account, then altered its routing and RPKI settings, knocking out about half the company's traffic.[170] Some incidents are mistakes. Some are crimes. BGP cannot tell the difference.

13.3.2. THE PERSISTENT THREAT

In February 2013, a security firm called Mandiant published a 74-page report with a map of a single building: a 12-story office tower at 208 Datong Road in Shanghai.[171] The building, Mandiant alleged, housed Unit 61398 of the People's Liberation Army—a signals intelligence unit responsible for systematic intrusion into American companies and government agencies.

Kevin Mandia, who founded the company that bore his name, had been tracking Chinese intrusions for years. His investigators had traced hackers across dozens of breaches, watching their working hours (Beijing time), their language (simplified Chinese), their targets (defense contractors, energy companies, technology firms). The patterns pointed to a single organization, and the IP addresses pointed to a single neighborhood in Shanghai, where the building at 208 Datong Road was large enough to house hundreds of hackers.

The report named names: Wang Dong, using the handle "Ugly Gorilla," and Mei Qiang, also known as "SuperHard"—specific individuals whom Mandiant linked to specific intrusions, allegedly at the direction of the Chinese military. A year later, the U.S. Department of Justice indicted five alleged officers of Unit 61398, marking the first time the United States had criminally charged foreign government officials for network espionage.[172]

The indictments were largely symbolic—the officers would never face trial in an American court—but the Mandiant report changed the conversation. Nation-state hacking was no longer an open secret; it was documented, publicly attributed, and backed by detailed evidence.

While the hackers at 208 Datong Road were stealing secrets through compromised networks, China Telecom was achieving something potentially more troubling through BGP. Between 2016 and 2017, researchers documented multiple incidents in which traffic destined for networks outside China was routed through China Telecom.[173] In one case, traffic from Canada to Korean government sites transited China for about six months. In another, traffic bound for a financial institution in Milan was briefly rerouted through mainland Chinese infrastructure.

Were these accidents? Configuration errors happen constantly in BGP. But unlike the Pakistan incident, where the hijack was brief and immediately noticed, some of these routes persisted for months. The traffic passed through infrastructure where it could be copied, analyzed, or modified. Even when packets eventually reached their destination, they had passed through territory where China's intelligence services had complete visibility.

The BGP incidents highlighted an exposure that no patch could fix. Nation-states operate legitimate networks. China Telecom is a major carrier with peering relationships across the globe. When a Chinese network announces routes, other networks accept them because that's how BGP works. To the protocol, a routing optimization and a surveillance operation look identical.

Unit 61398 and the BGP incidents were two routes to the same destination. One breaks into networks one at a time and leaves traces on every machine it touches. The other redirects traffic at the routing layer, quietly, without much caring whose traffic it is. Both rely on the same blind spot: the expectation that remote systems are secure and that BGP announcements are legitimate.

The napkins are lost.

Lougheed and Rekhter never kept them. The restaurant in Austin is long gone. What survived is the protocol they sketched—and it now routes over a million prefixes through more than 75,000 autonomous systems.[174] A couple of handwritten sheets became the routing layer for the planet.

The system works because, usually, network operators tell the truth. The exceptions are brief enough and rare enough that the internet survives them. But survival isn't the same as security. The napkin protocol now connects adversaries: nation-states with intelligence services, companies with competitive interests, criminals with financial motives. All of them can announce routes, and all of them can redirect traffic. The sketches in Austin never imagined them.

The premise that made BGP work—that your neighbors would tell the truth—was reasonable for the internet of 1989, where operators knew each other at conferences and reputation enforced honesty. That internet is gone. The protocol is not.

Lougheed and Rekhter had solved the problem of getting packets where they needed to go. But arrival was only half the story. Once a packet reached the network's edge, someone still had to open the door.

In Pleasanton, California, an engineer named Carl Rigney was building a different kind of trust. His protocol would guard WiFi networks, VPN connections, and enterprise systems for three decades, all of it resting on a single shared secret.

CHAPTER 14

THE SHARED SECRET

Transactions between the client and RADIUS server are authenticated through the use of a shared secret, which is never sent over the network.

— RFC 2865, Remote Authentication Dial In User Service, June 2000

14.1. THE MODEMS WOULDN'T STOP

The modems wouldn't stop ringing.

It was 1991. Steve Willens had a problem. Livingston Enterprises, the company he led from Pleasanton, California, made terminal servers—the boxes between dial-up modems and the network.[175,176] When someone picked up their phone, dialed a local number, and waited for the carrier tone, a Livingston PortMaster answered. It asked for credentials, checked them against a list, connected the caller to the internet.

The list was the bottleneck. Livingston's largest dial-up customer was Merit Network, half a continent away in Ann Arbor, Michigan, and

Merit had thousands of users; every PortMaster it deployed had to know every valid username and password.

Merit was old for the internet. Three Michigan universities—the University of Michigan, Michigan State, and Wayne State—had founded it in 1966 as a shared computing project, back when a "network" meant a cable strung between two mainframes on two campuses.[177] By 1991 Merit ran two networks at once. One was NSFNET, the National Science Foundation's backbone—the federally funded spine that tied the country's regional networks into a single internet. The other was MichNet, a statewide dial-up service that let anyone in Michigan reach the network through a local phone number: a student in an Ann Arbor dorm, a professor at a kitchen table, an engineer at a company across the state. MichNet was the fastest-growing part, and every new bank of modems made the list problem worse.

None of it scaled. Adding one user meant touching every terminal server, and a single password change had to reach dozens of machines. One disk failure could take the whole user database with it. The credentials were everywhere, and no copy could be trusted to be current.

So Merit went looking. In 1991, an engineer named John Vollbrecht—who managed the group that kept MichNet running—drafted a request describing what Merit needed and sent it to seven or eight vendors: a way to check dial-in credentials against one central list instead of a copy on every box.[176] Steve Willens at Livingston answered, and Merit gave Livingston the contract. Carl Rigney, an engineer there, started sketching a solution.

The insight was simple: separate the database from the equipment. Store credentials in one place, and when a user dials in, have the terminal server ask a central authentication server: is this username valid? Is this password correct? The server says yes or no, and the terminal server follows orders.

Rigney called it RADIUS: Remote Authentication Dial-In User Service—an unwieldy name for a simple idea.

A PortMaster running RADIUS didn't need a user database or disk space for credentials—it simply asked questions and accepted answers. All intelligence lived in the RADIUS server, which could run on a Unix machine with proper backups and administration. Add a user once and every terminal server would recognize them; change a password once and it changed everywhere.

The protocol did more than authentication. Rigney built in authorization—what the user was allowed to do—and accounting—what the user actually did. The three functions formed what network engineers would call the **AAA model**: Authentication, Authorization, and Accounting. RADIUS handled all three.

Merit deployed RADIUS in 1992, and it worked. Users dialed in, the PortMasters queried the central server, and access was granted or denied in milliseconds. The user database lived in one place, password changes took effect instantly, and when Merit added new dial-up points of presence, they just pointed the new equipment at the existing RADIUS server.

Other organizations noticed. Internet service providers were sprouting across the country, each of them hitting the same wall Merit had hit: thousands of dial-up users and no central place to check them. RADIUS was an answer they didn't have to invent.

Livingston published the protocol specification and released a reference implementation. They weren't trying to keep RADIUS proprietary—their business was selling terminal servers, and RADIUS made those servers more valuable. An open protocol meant that customers could run whatever RADIUS server they wanted, that competitors could build compatible equipment, and that RADIUS would spread.

It spread.

By the mid-1990s `RADIUS` had become the de facto standard for dial-up authentication. Every major ISP ran it, and the equipment vendors built to it. Wherever a customer dialed in, the same question got asked first: are you who you say you are?

The IETF standardized the protocol in 1997 as RFC 2138[178], then updated it in June 2000 as RFC 2865.[179] The acknowledgments section was brief: "RADIUS was originally developed by Steve Willens of Livingston Enterprises for their PortMaster series of Network Access Servers." Merit stayed with the protocol as it grew up. Vollbrecht and his Merit colleague Allan Rubens helped shepherd it through the standards process, and Rubens's name went onto RFC 2865 beside the Livingston engineers—the byline reads "Merit" next to "Livingston," Ann Arbor next to Pleasanton.

Rigney was listed as the first author. He had designed the protocol to solve a practical problem for a paying customer. He had no illusions about perfect security. The goal was something that worked, that scaled, that could be implemented on the limited hardware of early 1990s terminal servers.

The security model was built to fit those constraints. A terminal server and a `RADIUS` server shared a secret, which is to say a password, though no one called it that. The secret both vouched for the terminal server and "encrypted" the user's password on the way across, by a method that was good enough for 1991.

The RFC described the method precisely. `MD5`, or Message Digest 5, is a one-way fingerprint function: any input goes in, a fixed 128-bit code comes out. Feed it the shared secret followed by the Request Authenticator—a random 16-byte value that changes with every request—and the result is 16 bytes of noise. That noise is XORed with the user's password, XOR being reversible scrambling, and the scrambled password travels in the packet. The `RADIUS` server knows the secret, so it can generate the same noise and take it back out.

```
RFC 2865 --- Section 5.2 --- Password Hiding

Call the shared secret S and the pseudo-random 128-bit
Request Authenticator RA. Break the password into 16-octet
chunks p1, p2, etc.
b1 = MD5(S + RA)    c(1) = p1 xor b1 b2 = MD5(S + c(1))
c(2) = p2 xor b2
```

That was obfuscation, not encryption. Anyone who held the secret could recover a password instantly, and enough captured traffic gave an attacker a start on guessing the secret itself. The RFC acknowledged the concern: "The User-Password hiding mechanism described in Section 5.2 has not been subjected to significant amounts of cryptanalysis in the published literature."

But the RFC went ahead anyway, because in 1991 the threat model was different. `RADIUS` traffic flowed over private networks, between equipment that organizations controlled. The secret stayed between machines racked a few feet apart, never transmitted across hostile territory. The premise was that if an attacker could read your `RADIUS` traffic, you had bigger problems.

That premise survived dial-up. It wouldn't last forever.

14.2. THE NIGHTCLUB BOUNCER

14.2.1. HOW RADIUS WORKS

Think of a nightclub with a guest list—except the bouncer doesn't have it.

What the bouncer has is a radio. When you show up and give your name, he calls the manager inside and asks whether you're on the list. The manager checks, then radios back: yes, let them in and give them a VIP bracelet, or no, turn them away.

The bouncer is the Network Access Server, the NAS, the manager is the `RADIUS` server, and the radio channel is the network connection between them. The radio code they use to confirm each other's identity—that's the shared secret. The bouncer and the manager share a code word, and anyone claiming to have the guest list must prove they know the code.

`RADIUS` follows this pattern. A user connects to the NAS and provides credentials, and the NAS packages those credentials into a request and sends it to the `RADIUS` server. The server consults its database, makes a decision, and sends back a response, which the NAS enforces without question.

What the NAS doesn't do: verify the response independently. The bouncer trusts the voice on the radio. If someone else gets on that frequency and says "let them in," the bouncer lets them in.

When you type your username and password, the NAS constructs an `Access-Request` packet. Your username travels in clear text—there's no point hiding it, since the server needs to look it up—but your password gets scrambled using `MD5` and the secret key.

The NAS sends the packet over `UDP` and waits. No `TCP` connection sits underneath, and nothing guarantees the packet arrives. If no response comes back, the NAS asks again; a primary `RADIUS` server that stops answering may be abandoned for a backup. `UDP` made that failover easy, and it also meant no one verified where a packet came from.

The request can go to any server that shares the secret. But how does the NAS know that the response came from a legitimate server?

Three responses are possible. An `Access-Accept` means you authenticated successfully. An `Access-Reject` means authentication failed—wrong password, disabled account, unknown user—and the game is over.

An `Access-Challenge` means the server wants more information—maybe a second factor, like a code from a hardware token. The exchange can continue through multiple rounds until the server reaches a final decision.

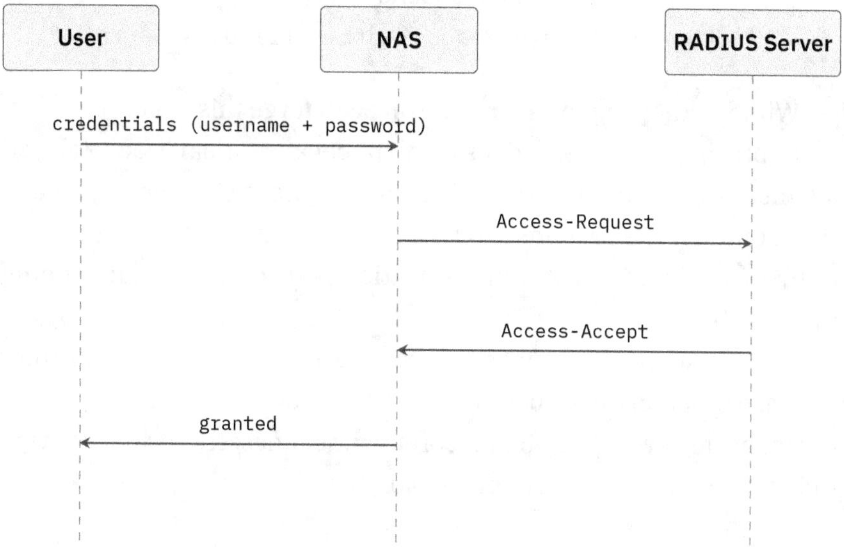

Figure 14.1: RADIUS authentication flow. The Network Access Server proxies user credentials to the central RADIUS server, which holds the user database. The shared secret between NAS and server is never sent over the network.

The problem: the NAS lacks any mechanism to confirm a response is legitimate. The server could be spoofed. An attacker could inject a fake `Access-Accept`, granting access to someone who should have been rejected.

RADIUS addresses this with the Response Authenticator. When the server constructs a response, it computes an MD5 hash—there's that word again—over the entire response packet, the Request Authenticator from the original request, and the secret. The result goes in the Authenticator field. When the NAS receives the response, it performs the same calculation. If the hashes match, the response is authentic.

The formula looks like this:

```
ResponseAuth =
MD5(Code+ID+Length+RequestAuth+Attributes+Secret)
```

Without knowing the secret, no one can forge this hash.

Capturing a response doesn't help, because it can't be replayed against a different request—the Request Authenticator changes each time, binding the response to both the request and the secret. The entire security of RADIUS authentication rests on this binding being unforgeable.

MD5 was supposed to make forgery impossible. The designers knew the hash function wasn't perfect, but they believed the secret key would compensate—even if MD5 had theoretical weaknesses, an attacker who didn't know the secret couldn't exploit them.

14.2.2. THE SHARED KEY

RADIUS rests on two premises: that the network between the NAS and the authentication server is safe, and that MD5 cannot be broken.

Why UDP instead of TCP? The answer was speed—you're staring at a login prompt, waiting for access, and TCP's reliability guarantees take time with their acknowledgments, retransmissions, and congestion control. With UDP, RADIUS controls its own timing: if a response doesn't arrive in two seconds, send another request, and if the server is dead, fail over immediately.

UDP made the implementation simpler, too—early RADIUS servers were single-threaded, following a straightforward pattern of receive, process, respond. In 1991, simpler meant it would actually get built.

But UDP has no concept of a connection and no way to verify a source address—anyone can put a forged source IP on a packet and send it. So the RADIUS server takes it on faith that a request came from a real NAS, and the NAS extends the same courtesy to whatever answers. Neither side is required to check, and by default neither does.

The secret is supposed to compensate, proving that both ends are legitimate while the MD5 hashing ensures that responses cannot be forged. But if someone positions themselves between the NAS and the authentication server, the first premise collapses. If someone finds a way to forge MD5 hashes, the second premise collapses too.

The RFC made the bargain explicit: both sides must know the secret, and both sides must keep it.

This secret authenticates the transaction, but it has to be distributed somehow. Administrators type it into configuration files on both ends. The RFC recommends at least 16 bytes of random data.

In practice? “radius123.” “companyname.” “secret.”

Recommendations are not requirements.

And the secret has to remain secret, since every device that shares it can impersonate every other device that shares it. When a new access point joins the network, it gets the secret; when an old access point is decommissioned, the secret should change. It almost never does.

14.3. BLAST-RADIUS

The paper appeared on July 9, 2024, under an unassuming title: "RADIUS/UDP Considered Harmful".[180] The content was less modest—they had found a way to forge RADIUS responses, turning rejected authentication attempts into accepted ones. The vulnerability had existed since 1991.

The research team spanned institutions: Sharon Goldberg from Cloudflare; Mike Milano from BastionZero; Miro Haller, Nadia Heninger, and Adam Suhl from UC San Diego; Dan Shumow from Microsoft Research; and Marc Stevens from CWI Amsterdam.[180] They had been working together since late 2023, following a trail that led back to MD5. Among them were some of the world's foremost experts on hash function cryptanalysis; Stevens had spent fifteen years on MD5 collisions alone. Their proof of concept computed a chosen-prefix collision in under five minutes on CPU and GPU clusters. The paper estimated that about $50 per hour in cloud resources could exceed the computing capacity they had used. Engineering and debugging a larger deployment, at hundreds of dollars per hour, could push the total into the tens of thousands.

They named it Blast-RADIUS. CVE-2024-3596.[181]

The vulnerability centered on the Response Authenticator, the fingerprint that proved a response was genuine. That fingerprint is computed from the shared secret, and an attacker who doesn't know the secret shouldn't be able to produce one. Everyone believed that held even as MD5 weakened. Whatever turned up in the literature, the secret was still in the mix.

The belief was wrong. Cryptographers had been chipping away at MD5 for decades: theoretical cracks in 1996, then in 2004 a team from Shandong University demonstrated practical collisions, two different inputs that produced the same fingerprint.[182] Marc Stevens went further in 2007, showing that two messages could be crafted in advance so their hashes came out identical.[183] Two different keys opening the same lock, when the lock was supposed to be unique to every door.

Blast-RADIUS turned that weakness into an attack. What the attacker needs is a position on the wire between the access point and the RADIUS server, and a user about to log in. The user's request gets captured and passed along, and the server does what it should: the credentials are invalid, so it sends back an Access-Reject.

That rejection never arrives. The attacker blocks it and builds a fake Access-Accept in its place, which needs a fingerprint that will match whatever the access point computes when it checks. The attacker still has no idea what the secret is. Everything else that goes into the hash was captured from the original exchange, though, and that is enough to work the MD5 weakness. The forged message can be shaped so its fingerprint comes out identical to the one a real response would have produced.

The computation is expensive—not laptop-in-a-coffee-shop expensive, but well-funded-research-lab expensive. Finding the right forgery takes three to six minutes on specialized hardware costing tens of thousands of dollars. That sounds like a barrier, but RADIUS is patient. The NAS will wait for a response, retransmitting periodically. The server has already sent its Access-Reject, but the attacker holds it back. Three to six minutes is plenty.

When the collision is found, the attacker sends the forged Access-Accept to the NAS, which computes the Response Authenticator, finds that it matches, and accepts the response as genuine. An unauthorized user has been authenticated. The protocol worked exactly as designed—the cryptography failed.

RADIUS authenticates far more than dial-up modems—that use case faded with the rise of broadband—but RADIUS adapted, and in 2024 it was everywhere.

Enterprise WiFi networks use RADIUS—when you connect your laptop to a corporate wireless network and enter your username and password, that authentication goes to a RADIUS server. The protocol is called 802.1X, and it runs on WPA2-Enterprise and WPA3-Enterprise networks at every Fortune 500 company, every university, every hospital.

VPN authentication uses RADIUS—when employees connect to the corporate network from home, the VPN gateway often validates their credentials through RADIUS, and the same applies to network device management for the routers, switches, and firewalls that require administrator login.

ISP subscriber authentication uses RADIUS—when you plug in your home router and it connects to your cable or DSL provider, RADIUS is often involved in verifying your service.

The researchers estimated that "billions of devices" relied on RADIUS. The vulnerability affected all of them.

Alan DeKok had spent two decades with RADIUS and had created FreeRADIUS, the open-source server that handled more RADIUS authentication than any other implementation.[184] When the researchers contacted him in February 2024, he understood the implications immediately.

The fix was theoretically simple. RADIUS had always supported an optional attribute called Message-Authenticator, which used HMAC-MD5 instead of plain MD5 when present in a request, binding the message to the secret key in a way that resisted collision attacks. If servers required Message-Authenticator on all packets, Blast-RADIUS wouldn't work.

"Optional" is a powerful word. For thirty-three years Message-Authenticator had been optional—equipment deployed in 2005 didn't include it, equipment deployed in 2015 often didn't either. Administrators configured their systems to work, not to enforce security requirements that nobody demanded.

Making Message-Authenticator mandatory meant breaking compatibility with decades of deployed equipment. But leaving it optional meant leaving the vulnerability open.

Coordinated disclosure started in February 2024. The researchers worked down a list of every major vendor: Microsoft, Cisco, Aruba, Palo Alto, Juniper, Fortinet, `FreeRADIUS`. Each of them had to write a patch, test it, and ship it, then revise documentation and warn customers.

The public disclosure came on July 9. Patches followed immediately: `FreeRADIUS` required Message-Authenticator by default; Microsoft updated its Network Policy Server; networking vendors pushed firmware updates.

Updating `RADIUS` infrastructure isn't like updating a web browser. The servers sit buried in data centers, managed by teams that might not know they exist. The access points are scattered through campus buildings, installed by contractors who moved on years ago, and a VPN concentrator carrying thousands of production connections is not something anyone volunteers to reboot.

The long-term fix is `RadSec`, which is `RADIUS` carried over `TLS`, specified in RFC 6614.[185] Put the whole exchange inside a `TLS` connection and the collision attacks stop mattering, because the encryption hides the traffic and the certificates prove who is on each end. `RadSec` has been available since 2012, and adoption is still limited: it means new infrastructure, certificates to manage, configurations to change. `UDP` requires none of that.

The Blast-`RADIUS` paper concluded with a section on responsible disclosure. The researchers had waited five months between contacting vendors and going public, working with implementers to develop patches and coordinating timing so that fixes would be available when the vulnerability was announced.

They also reflected on what the vulnerability meant. `MD5`'s weaknesses had been known for twenty years before anyone demonstrated a practical attack on `RADIUS`. In between, the protocol ran on faith: that the cryptography would hold, and that the attackers who could break it wouldn't bother.

That faith had held for thirty-three years. Now it was gone.

Carl Rigney designed `RADIUS` to solve a practical problem: authenticating dial-up users for Merit Network. He succeeded. The protocol scaled from thousands of users to billions of devices, outliving the modems it was built for and adapting to WiFi, VPNs, and enterprise networks.

The shared secret at the heart of `RADIUS` was a design choice, not a design flaw. In 1991, nobody doubted that the communication between a terminal server and an authentication server would stay private—the `RADIUS` traffic stayed inside the organization's network, the threat was external attackers, and internal links were trusted.

The trusted zone shrank. Networks joined the internet, employees started working from home, and access points went up in buildings reached over paths that nobody controlled. The same secret sat on every one of those devices, and every administrator who configured one had it. It went unchanged for years, because changing it would break something.

`MD5` aged, too. The hash function that looked adequate in 1991 was showing cracks by 1996, and by 2024 a research team could forge a fingerprint that `RADIUS` would accept. Every cryptographic algorithm runs on a clock like that—published, trusted for a while, then broken—

which is why a protocol built on one needs a way to swap it out. RADIUS had none.

The vulnerability wasn't about speed or timing. RADIUS relied on cryptography, with the secret key and MD5 hash supposed to make forgery impossible. When MD5 broke, the foundation broke with it.

The thirty-three-year-old vulnerability waited for someone to exploit it.

Someone did.

Every corporate WiFi login, every VPN connection, passes through the protocol Rigney designed for dial-up modems.

Most of the people who log in to a company network have never heard of RADIUS. They type a username and password, wait a moment, and the connection opens. Somewhere in a data center a server answered the question and went back to waiting, all of it finished before the browser loaded its first page.

The world moved—employees working from home, access points spreading across campuses and hotels and airports—and still the secret stayed the same. The protocol that Rigney sketched for a dial-up problem now stands at the door of nearly every corporate network, still trusting the shared secret, still serving without being seen.

RADIUS decided who could join the network. Before that question could even be asked, a machine needed something more basic: an address. In offices everywhere that still meant one person keeping one list, and a growing certainty that doing it by hand could not last much longer.

CHAPTER 15

THE FIRST RESPONSE

A host should not act as a DHCP server
unless explicitly configured to do so
by a system administrator.

— RFC 2131, Ralph Droms, March 1997

15.1. THE LIST

Somewhere in every building with a network, there was a list.

In 1992 that list might be a text file on a server, a worksheet in Lotus 1-2-3, or a sheet of paper taped to the side of a monitor. The format hardly mattered. What mattered was that one person kept it and everyone else depended on it. The list recorded which IP address belonged to which machine—one line per computer, an address paired with a name, a location, and whoever used it.

Every address on a network has to be unique—the IP address, and the hardware address underneath it. Give two machines the same one and things fail in ways that take hours to diagnose.[186] So someone had to hand out addresses one at a time and record every assignment.

When a computer arrived, the keeper of the list found a free address, wrote it down, and walked over to type the numbers into the machine by hand. When a computer moved, the list was edited and the machine reconfigured. When a computer left, its address was supposed to be crossed off and returned to the pool. Often it wasn't—so the list slowly filled with addresses marked taken but actually free, and machines running on addresses that appeared on no list at all.

The list was never quite right. Someone in marketing hired a contractor, and word never reached the person who kept the file. A machine moved to another office, and its line stayed where it was. Each mistake was small on its own; the trouble was that the network kept growing, and every new machine was one more chance for the file and the building to disagree.

Portable computers made it worse. Machines like the Compaq LTE had started appearing on the desks of people who traveled, and a laptop that connected at headquarters on Monday and a branch office on Thursday needed a different address in each place—each site its own network, its own list, its own keeper, its own drift. A machine that moved could not be pinned to one line in one file.

None of this was a private struggle. The original DHCP specification called manual host configuration "error-prone" and made preventing duplicate network-address assignments an explicit design goal.[187] Automation would not eliminate every configuration mistake, but it could replace a patchwork of human-maintained lists with a service that allocated addresses and tracked when they could be reused.

The problem had a partial solution, and it came from a surprising place: diskless workstations.

In the mid-1980s, some organizations deployed computers without hard drives. These thin clients booted over the network, downloading their operating system from a central server. The cost savings were significant, but the machines faced a bootstrapping problem. A computer without a disk couldn't store its network configuration. When it powered on, it didn't know its own address.

Bill Croft and John Gilmore solved this with the Bootstrap Protocol, BOOTP, published as RFC 951 in September 1985.[188] BOOTP was simple. A diskless machine would broadcast a request: "I need an address." A server with a table of hardware-to-IP mappings would respond: "You're this address. Boot from this server." The workstation would configure itself and proceed.

BOOTP solved the bootstrapping problem, but it didn't solve the list problem. BOOTP servers required static tables, one entry for every machine, maintained by hand. An administrator still had to assign each address. A visitor with a laptop still couldn't connect. The table just lived on a server instead of in a spreadsheet or a text file.

Ralph Droms saw the next step. A computer science professor at Bucknell University in central Pennsylvania, he had been working on network configuration since the late 1980s, trying to make networks easier to manage. By 1993, he had a proposal: extend BOOTP with dynamic allocation.

The concept was straightforward. Instead of maintaining a table of permanent assignments, the server would maintain a pool of addresses. When a machine requested an address, the server would pick one from the pool and loan it out. The loan would have a time limit, called a lease. When the lease expired, the address would return to the pool.

Dynamic allocation solved the laptop problem. A laptop connecting at headquarters would receive an address from the local pool; the same laptop connecting at a branch office would receive a different address from that site's pool. No administrator needed to update a list. No one needed to know in advance which machines would connect.

Droms called it the Dynamic Host Configuration Protocol, DHCP. He published the specification as RFC 1531 in October 1993[187], reissued it shortly after as RFC 1541 to correct errors introduced in editing[189], and revised it again as RFC 2131 in March 1997.[190] RFC 2131 remains DHCP's core IPv4 specification.

The protocol did more than assign addresses. Everything the keeper of the list used to type by hand—the subnet mask, the default gateway, which DNS servers to ask, what domain, which time servers—now arrived in the same exchange as the address itself. A machine could power on knowing nothing and come up fully configured.

The exchange followed a four-step pattern the community would call DORA—four packets, and you're connected.

Nothing in those four packets said who was allowed to answer. Physical presence on the wire implied authorization to offer configuration.

Droms wrote in RFC 2131: "DHCP is built on a client-server model, where designated DHCP server hosts allocate network addresses and deliver configuration parameters to dynamically configured hosts."[190]

Designated. The word did a lot of work. Any machine on the local segment could run a DHCP server and respond to discovery requests; the base protocol supplied no credentials by which a client could distinguish an authorized server from an impostor.

In 1993, this assumption made sense. Local networks were corporate. Access required physical presence in the building, past the front desk, through the locked door. If someone connected a rogue DHCP server, they were an employee, and they had probably made a mistake, not mounted an attack.

DHCP spread rapidly. Microsoft added client support to Windows 95. Unix vendors added it to their distributions. Home routers shipped with DHCP servers enabled by default. By the end of the decade, most computers on most networks received their addresses automatically.

The list problem was solved. The people who had maintained those lists by hand were, quietly, freed from the task. The network configured itself.

Two decades later, in public WiFi hotspots across the world, attackers would exploit exactly this automation. The fastest server would win—and the fastest server wouldn't always be the legitimate one.

15.2. THE FIRST RESPONSE WINS

15.2.1. HOW DHCP WORKS

RADIUS relies on cryptography, but DHCP relies on something simpler: speed.

You power on your laptop in a hotel lobby with no IP address, no gateway, no DNS server—you know nothing about this network. Within seconds, you're browsing the web. How?

Your computer shouts into the void: "Is anyone out there? I need an address." Any DHCP server within broadcast range can answer, and your computer accepts whatever arrives first.

Think of it like checking into a hotel. You arrive at the front desk without a room assignment. The hotel has a block of rooms available. The clerk assigns you one, gives you a key, and tells you where to find the elevator, the restaurant, and the pool. You keep the room for the length of your stay. When you leave, the room goes back into the pool.

But here's where the analogy breaks. At a hotel, the front desk is clearly marked, so you know you're talking to the actual hotel. With

DHCP, anyone in the lobby can pose as the front desk—and your computer cannot tell the difference.

Network engineers call the exchange DORA: Discover, Offer, Request, Acknowledge. Four packets. Let's trace what happens—and what's missing.

Your computer broadcasts a Discover message. It has no address yet, so the packet goes out from 0.0.0.0 and is addressed to 255.255.255.255—everyone on the local network. "I need an address," it announces, and every DHCP server that hears it can answer, whether it belongs to the hotel or not.

Servers respond with Offers. "I could give you 10.0.0.47," says one. "I could give you 10.0.0.112," says another. Each offer includes not just an address but a full configuration: gateway, DNS servers, lease duration. The client collects one or more offers and selects one.

The selected offer is not an authenticated offer. The protocol gives the client no cryptographic basis for trusting it.

Your computer broadcasts a Request: "I'll take the address from that first server." All servers hear this, so the ones who lost know their offered addresses are still available.

The winning server sends an Acknowledge: "Done. Here's your configuration." Your network interface comes up, and you're connected.

Four packets, a few hundred milliseconds, no verification at any step.

15.2.2. LEASES AND CONFIGURATION

Why not just assign addresses permanently? Because networks change—servers move, DNS entries update, and people come and go. Leases force your computer to check back periodically, picking up new configuration if anything has changed.

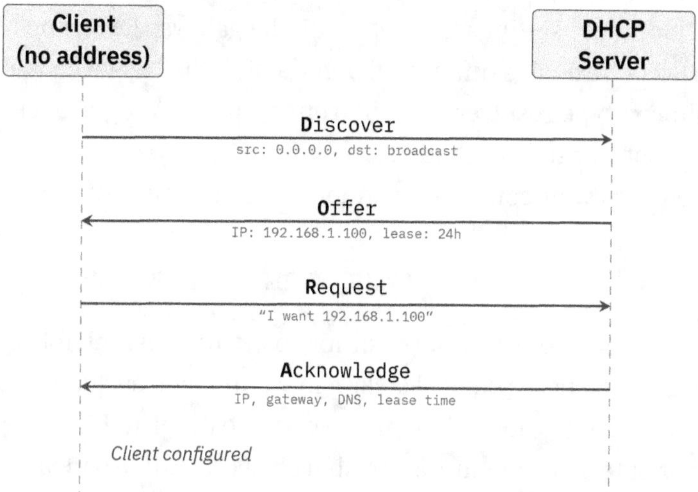

Figure 15.1: The DHCP DORA sequence. A client without an address broadcasts a Discover, receives an Offer with an available address, broadcasts a Request to claim it, and receives an Acknowledge with full configuration. The entire process takes milliseconds.

A corporate network might issue eight-hour leases. A coffee shop might use one-hour leases—short enough to recycle addresses as customers come and go. Your computer renews automatically, usually at the halfway point, before you notice anything.[190]

A lease that still has time on it keeps a machine working through trouble. The server can reboot; the network can drop for a minute and come back; the client already holds its address and its configuration, and won't need to ask for anything until renewal. All of that forgiveness assumes the other machines are playing fair.

But DHCP doesn't just hand out addresses. It configures your entire network stack. The server tells you which gateway to use for reaching the outside world. It tells you which DNS servers to query. It can specify your domain name, your time servers, your proxy settings.

Each of these settings is a lever. Pull the gateway lever, and all your traffic flows through a different machine. Pull the DNS lever, and every domain you type resolves to a different address. A rogue DHCP server doesn't just assign you a bad IP.

It rewrites your computer's understanding of the network.

15.2.3. WHY THE CLIENT CANNOT VERIFY THE SERVER

So why can't your computer simply pick the most reliable offer?

Because the base protocol lacks a mechanism to evaluate reliability. Your computer has no credentials to verify, no list of authorized servers, no certificates, no signatures, no shared secrets. It broadcasts a plea and must judge the replies without proof of who sent them.

The RFC leaves selection open. A client "may choose to wait for multiple responses," then pick from the servers that answered.[190] But waiting produces more unauthenticated offers, not evidence that any of them is legitimate.

On a network with an attacker, it's catastrophic.

The attacker's laptop can submit a plausible offer alongside the legitimate server's. If the client selects it, the attacker controls the resulting configuration.

This isn't a bug in DHCP. It's the design.

As we saw with Droms's "designated" servers, the protocol never asks whether a server is legitimate. DHCP takes the network at its word, and the network doesn't always deserve that faith.

15.3. ANYONE WITH A LAPTOP

Breaking RADIUS required cryptographic expertise, GPU clusters, and months of research. Breaking DHCP required a laptop and a cup of coffee.

Consider a scenario that plays out at tech conferences worldwide. A hotel hosts a developer conference—three thousand attendees packed into meeting rooms and hallways. The conference WiFi network requires no password. Walk in, connect, start working.

An attacker checked into the hotel and carried a laptop to a lounge overlooking the atrium. Conference attendees streamed past, badges dangling from lanyards, laptops under their arms. He ordered coffee from the bar, opened his machine, and launched a program called Yersinia.[191] Named after the bacterium that causes plague, Yersinia was a network attack tool that anyone could download. No cryptographic expertise required. No mathematics. No understanding of hash functions or collision attacks. Just a free tool and physical proximity to the victims.

Before he sent anything, he listened. Yersinia read the DHCP exchanges passing between attendees and the hotel's access points, and the whole configuration was there in the traffic: a legitimate server at 10.50.0.1, addresses handed out of the 10.50.10.0/24 subnet, two-hour leases. They were ordinary settings for a guest network with people checking in and out all day, and nothing was in place to stop a second server from answering.

The attack had two phases. First, exhaust the legitimate server's pool. Second, become the only server left.

DHCP starvation is mostly repetition. He sent Discover requests hundreds per second, each with a spoofed MAC address pretending to be a different network card, and the server read every one as another device joining the network. It offered an address to all of them, and he completed the exchange each time, taking out leases on addresses he had no intention of using. Within minutes there was nothing left in the pool. Attendees who tried to join after that got no answer at all.

Now came phase two. He ran a DHCP server on his laptop. When new attendees joined the network, their Discover broadcasts reached both the legitimate server (which had no addresses left) and his laptop (which had plenty). He responded, and the attendee accepted.

The configuration he provided looked almost legitimate. Same subnet mask. Same range of addresses. But the default gateway pointed to his laptop instead of the real gateway. The DNS servers were his as well.

Every packet the attendee sent went to his machine first. He forwarded it to the real gateway, so the connection worked normally. The attendee noticed nothing unusual—maybe the WiFi seemed slightly slow, but that's conference WiFi.

But he saw everything. Unencrypted web traffic. HTTP form submissions with usernames and passwords. Email synchronization with IMAP servers that didn't require TLS. Session cookies. API keys transmitted over HTTP during development demos. The attendees scrolled through slide decks and checked Slack. He watched their sessions populate his packet capture logs.

Attacks like this get catalogued. MITRE's ATT&CK framework lists DHCP spoofing as a standard adversary technique[192], and researchers demonstrate it at DefCon and Black Hat, showing how one laptop can compromise dozens of connections in minutes. The tools are free to download and the tutorials are on YouTube; a motivated teenager could work through one in an afternoon.

Blast-RADIUS required world-class cryptographers and months of mathematical research. Rogue DHCP required presence and patience. Blast-RADIUS demanded GPU clusters costing thousands of dollars. Rogue DHCP ran on any laptop. Blast-RADIUS exploited subtle flaws in hash functions that took decades to discover. Rogue DHCP exploited a design decision obvious since 1993: the first response wins, and anyone can respond.

The attacks work because they're trivially easy—a script can automate the entire process, and the victim's computer cooperates fully, accepting whatever configuration it receives. No passwords need to be cracked, no software flaws exploited. The system behaves exactly as specified.

Variations exist for different goals. Someone interested in surveillance routes traffic through their machine and captures it. Someone seeking credentials configures a malicious DNS server that redirects banking sites to phishing pages. Others push a proxy configuration that injects JavaScript into web pages.

The attacks combine well with techniques from other chapters. ARP spoofing (Chapter 5) lets the attacker intercept traffic without being the gateway. DNS hijacking (Chapter 7) lets them redirect specific domains. Together with rogue DHCP, attackers can control virtually every aspect of a victim's network experience.

Enterprise networks have defenses against these attacks. Consumer networks don't.

DHCP snooping is a feature available on managed network switches. When enabled, the switch tracks which ports are authorized to send DHCP server responses. Traffic from unauthorized ports is dropped. A rogue server connected to a regular network jack simply doesn't work; its responses never reach the clients.

The switch builds its knowledge from observing legitimate DHCP traffic. When a client completes a DORA exchange with an authorized server, the switch records the binding: this MAC address has this IP address, assigned by this server. The switch then enforces the binding. ARP responses that don't match the binding are blocked. IP traffic from unexpected addresses is rejected.

A corporate network with DHCP snooping enabled stops rogue server attacks cold, because the attacker's laptop can run whatever DHCP server it wants; the switch simply won't forward the packets.

But DHCP snooping requires managed switches, which cost more than consumer equipment. It demands configuration expertise. Most of all, it requires thinking about security at the network layer—and most organizations don't.

Guest WiFi networks rarely have protection. The coffee shop router cost fifty dollars. It doesn't support DHCP snooping. The hotel access points serve hundreds of guests per day; adding security would require infrastructure that doesn't exist. The conference center has a single SSID for five thousand attendees, and the IT staff is busy enough keeping the connection working at all.

802.1X authentication offers stronger protection. Before a device can communicate, it must authenticate—usually with a username and password or a certificate—and the network won't accept traffic from unknown devices. A rogue DHCP server can't attack if it can't join the network in the first place.

Enterprise environments sometimes deploy 802.1X, but consumer environments never do. The configuration burden is too high, the user experience too complex. The coffee shop just wants the WiFi to work.

This gap between enterprise protection and consumer vulnerability grows wider each year. Corporate networks deploy defense in depth: DHCP snooping, 802.1X, network segmentation, monitoring. Public networks remain undefended, relying on the good behavior of their users.

The hotel eventually added a captive portal. Attendees had to accept terms of service before getting an address. This didn't stop DHCP attacks; the portal ran after address assignment, not before. But it made guests feel safer, even though it made them no safer.

Ralph Droms, writing RFC 2131 in 1997, allowed that some installations "may include multiple, overlapping DHCP servers to enhance reliability and increase performance."[190] He meant server redundancy, not adversarial servers. The base specification includes no mechanism for distinguishing authorized servers from unauthorized ones.

Nearly three decades later, clients on airports' and conference centers' networks still receive unauthenticated configuration offers. The mechanism that solved the list problem created a different problem that remains widespread on public networks.

The internet grew out of networks where physical presence implied legitimacy. You were on the wire because you belonged there. You configured your neighbors because your neighbors expected you to. That arrangement fit 1993, when DHCP emerged, and 1997, when it was standardized.

By 2005, when public WiFi became common, it described a world that no longer existed—and the gap has only widened since. The specification hasn't changed—but the networks have.

Every time you connect to public WiFi, you broadcast a request to any server listening. You accept whatever configuration comes back first. You assume the reply is legitimate, because DHCP cannot verify. The conference badge comes with a side of blind faith.

Usually, that faith is justified—the hotel's access point responds, you get a working connection, and you browse the web and check your email and do whatever you came to do.

Sometimes, there's a laptop in the lounge, responding faster than the legitimate server. The owner looks like any other attendee, working through the conference sessions, coffee cup beside their keyboard.

Their Yersinia session runs in a minimized window. Their packet capture fills with your traffic.

You never know which connection is which—that's the point. The protocol supplies configuration without proving who supplied it.

And still, it runs.

Billions of devices wake each morning and shout into the void: "I need an address." Billions of servers answer. The exchange takes milliseconds. The system works because, on most networks, the first response comes from someone who means well.

The design that made Droms's protocol so easy to deploy also made it impossible to secure without wrapping it in something else—`802.1X`, `DHCP` snooping, enterprise monitoring. `DHCP` itself remains what it always was: a handshake between strangers who assume good intent.

The hand-kept lists are gone, and the laptops configure themselves—the pool refreshes, the leases renew. And every so often, in a conference lounge or an airport terminal, someone's laptop responds a little faster than the legitimate server.

The protocol cannot tell the difference. It was never designed to.

`DHCP` handed out addresses on faith. But addresses were only the beginning. Every day, on every network, people typed passwords into remote sessions that crossed the wire unprotected. The protocols that carried those keystrokes came from the same era of trust—and one researcher in Finland had seen enough.

CHAPTER 16

THE SECURE SHELL

SSH is a protocol for secure remote login
and other secure network services
over an insecure network.

– RFC 4251, January 2006

16.1. THE PASSWORD SNIFFER

The attack happened in early 1995.[22] Someone had placed a packet sniffer on Helsinki University of Technology's network, capturing everything–login sessions, file transfers, email, every password typed into every remote connection.

Tatu Ylönen, a cryptography researcher there, watched IT staff discover thousands of compromised passwords. The attacker had been watching for weeks, and every `Telnet` login had crossed the wire in plain text. The sniffer caught them all.

Ylönen was furious. Not at the attacker, but at the protocols. `Telnet`, `rlogin`, `rsh`–all the tools researchers used daily sent passwords without protection. Everyone knew `Telnet` was insecure. They used it anyway because nothing better existed.

Ylönen decided to build something better.

He started writing code that summer. The plan was to do what `Telnet` did—log you into a distant machine, let you run commands there—and encrypt every byte of it. Keystrokes would leave your machine as ciphertext, and the replies would come back the same way. An attacker watching the network would see nothing but noise.

He called it Secure Shell, or `SSH`. The name aimed at the thing every Unix user saw all day: the $ or # prompt waiting for a command. What changed was the wire between you and it, now unreadable to anyone watching.

The first version appeared in July 1995.[193] Ylönen released it as free software, and word spread through the academic community. Researchers at universities worldwide were dealing with the same problem Helsinki had faced. Password sniffers were appearing on networks everywhere. `SSH` was the answer they needed.

Adoption was swift. Within a year, tens of thousands of systems were running `SSH`. Ylönen started getting inquiries from companies who wanted to use it commercially. In December 1995, he founded `SSH` Communications Security to sell licenses and support.[194]

The money caused friction. Early releases of `SSH` had been free; later ones came with license terms that kept tightening, even as the source code stayed out in the open where anyone could read it. Universities and open-source projects still paid nothing, but companies now got a bill, and some of them found the number unreasonable.

By 1999, the situation had become untenable for the open-source community. The last freely usable version was `SSH` 1.2.12, released in 1995. After that, the licensing changed in ways that made many developers uncomfortable.

Theo de Raadt was building OpenBSD at the time, a fork of NetBSD focused obsessively on security. His team audited every line of code in the system, looking for vulnerabilities. They needed `SSH`—a secure operating system without secure remote access was absurd—but the licensing made the current version unusable.

De Raadt and his team decided to fork the old free version and maintain it themselves. They called it `OpenSSH`.[195]

The goal de Raadt set for the project was plain: keep a free `SSH` alive, unencumbered by restrictive licenses or patent claims, free for everyone to use. `OpenSSH` shipped with OpenBSD 2.6 on December 1, 1999.

The team started with `SSH` 1.2.12, ripped out everything they didn't need, audited what remained, and started adding features—rewriting large sections to match OpenBSD's coding standards and fixing bugs that `SSH` Communications Security had left unfixed.

Within months, `OpenSSH` supported the `SSH-2` protocol, a cleaner redesign that Ylönen's company had developed. The new protocol fixed cryptographic weaknesses in `SSH-1` and added features like improved key exchange and channel multiplexing.

A portable version, adapted to run on operating systems other than OpenBSD, appeared in late 1999. By 2000 the major Linux distributions were shipping `OpenSSH` as their default way onto a remote machine, and `Telnet` began retreating toward legacy systems and specialized uses.

`OpenSSH` now runs on nearly every Unix and Linux server in the world. Administrators reach cloud instances through it, and so do the people who configure routers and embedded hardware. All of it descends from the code one researcher wrote after a sniffer turned up on a university network.

16.2. KEYS AND HANDSHAKES

16.2.1. HOW SSH WORKS

Imagine you're making a phone call, but you're worried someone might be listening. You want to speak freely, but the line could be tapped. Worse: you're not entirely sure you dialed the right number.

SSH is the cryptographic equivalent of a secure phone line. Before you start talking, you and the other party establish a shared secret that only you two know. Then everything you say gets scrambled using that secret. Anyone listening hears only static.

But that phone analogy has a gap. When you dial, you trust the phone system to connect you to the right person. SSH has no phone company. It has to solve a harder problem: prove you're talking to who you think you're talking to, without any central authority to vouch for either side.

Three things must happen before you can type commands: encrypt the wire so eavesdroppers hear static, verify the server is who you think it is, and prove your own identity. Encryption is handled cleanly. The second part is where trouble hides.

When you type `ssh server.example.com`, your client opens a connection to port 22 on that server.[25] The first thing that happens is key exchange: both sides generate a shared secret without ever sending that secret over the wire.

The problem is that neither side can safely send the secret over the wire—and yet both sides need to agree on one.

Diffie-Hellman key exchange is what makes that possible: two parties end up holding the same secret even though an eavesdropper has read every message that passed between them. Paint is the usual way to picture it. Alice and Bob each pick a private color and stir it into a public one that everybody can see, then trade the results. Each stirs their private color into what the other sent back, and both jars come out the same shade. The eavesdropper is left with two mixed samples and no way to take them apart.

After a few messages back and forth, both sides have a key that nobody else knows. From that point on, every byte traveling between client and server is encrypted. Commands typed, output received, even the protocol control messages—all scrambled. An attacker watching the traffic sees the length of encrypted blocks and the timing of packets. Nothing else.

That's the encryption problem, solved. Now comes the harder question.

16.2.2. THE LEAP OF FAITH

Encryption protects the conversation. But it doesn't tell you who you're talking to.

When an `SSH` server starts for the first time, it generates a key pair: a private key that never leaves the server, and a public key that anyone can see. This is the server's host key: its identity, its cryptographic fingerprint.

When a client connects, the server sends its public host key. The client has a decision to make: is this the right server?

If the client has connected before, the answer is easy. `SSH` keeps a file called `known_hosts` that records every server visited and its host key. If the key matches, it's the same server as last time. If the key doesn't match, something is wrong—either the server's key changed, or someone is impersonating the server.

But what about the first connection? The server sends a host key the client has never seen. Is it legitimate?

Researchers call it "Trust On First Use," often abbreviated TOFU. The client accepts the server's identity on first contact, then alerts if it ever changes. We cannot verify that initial identity, so we take the server's word for it. If an attacker has positioned themselves between us and the real server, they could present their own host key. We'd accept it. Every subsequent connection would go through them.

SSH handles this with a prompt:

```
The authenticity of host 'server.example.com' can't be
    established.
ED25519 key fingerprint is SHA256:xvSQ2pNmG4f...
Are you sure you want to continue connecting (yes/no)?
```

Most users type "yes" without thinking. It's the only way to proceed, and who has time to manually verify key fingerprints?

TOFU. A calculated gamble that becomes permanent.

TOFU is a compromise—better than no verification at all, but weaker than a certificate authority system like TLS uses. And if the initial handshake was intercepted, all subsequent connections defer to the attacker's key.

Once you accept a key, it goes into `known_hosts`. Future connections check against that stored key. If the server's key ever changes, SSH refuses to connect and prints a stern warning:

```
@@@@@@@@@@@@@@@@@@@@@@@@@@@@@@@@@@@@@@@@@@@@@@@@@@@@@@@@@@@

@    WARNING: REMOTE HOST IDENTIFICATION HAS CHANGED!
    @
@@@@@@@@@@@@@@@@@@@@@@@@@@@@@@@@@@@@@@@@@@@@@@@@@@@@@@@@@@@

IT IS POSSIBLE THAT SOMEONE IS DOING SOMETHING NASTY!
```

The warning is intentionally alarming because a changed host key is serious. Either the server was rebuilt and got a new key, or someone is attempting an interception attack. The user has to manually remove the old key before `SSH` will connect again.

16.2.3. PROVING WHO YOU ARE

The encrypted channel is established, the remote host's identity confirmed—or at least, accepted on first use. Now you need to prove who you are. The authentication method matters here: if you've connected to the wrong server, what you hand over depends on which method you used.

`SSH` supports several authentication methods.[24] The simplest is the password: you type it, `SSH` encrypts it, and the remote host checks the result against its user database. That is already better than `Telnet`, which put the same characters on the wire for anyone to read. The catch is where the encrypted password ends up. If the machine at the other end belongs to an attacker, the encryption worked perfectly and delivered your password to them.

The stronger approach is public key authentication. You generate your own key pair: a private key that stays on your machine, protected by a passphrase, and a public key that you copy to the server. When you connect, the server challenges you to prove you have the private key—your client signs a challenge message, the server verifies the signature, and if it checks out, you're in.

The private key never crosses the network, so even if someone captures every packet, they can't extract your key. They'd have to steal the key file from your machine directly, and if you protected it with a passphrase, they'd need that too.

This is stronger than passwords—but only if you're talking to the right server. Public key authentication proves you are who you say you are, but it doesn't prove anything about who you're talking to. That's still TOFU's job.

SSH does more than remote shells—a single connection can carry multiple channels for shell sessions, file transfers, and port forwarding.[26] This power cuts both ways.

An SSH tunnel opened through a compromised server reaches straight into the internal networks a firewall was supposed to keep separate. To the monitoring tools on that link it looks like an ordinary SSH session; the contents are encrypted, which is the point, and which is also why an intruder would choose this route.

16.2.4. THE BOOTSTRAPPING PROBLEM

SSH fails differently from DHCP, whose "first response" race turns on raw speed: an attacker who answers a client faster than the legitimate server wins, and network topology decides who is faster. Speed buys an attacker nothing here. SSH's difficulty is fixing an identity in place the first time, with nothing to check it against.

SSH does have verification—the `known_hosts` file provides exactly that—but verification requires a reference point, and obtaining that reference point requires relying on something: the initial handshake, an out-of-band exchange of fingerprints, or a certificate authority.

The bootstrapping problem doesn't disappear—it just moves.

RFC 4251, published in January 2006, describes the SSH architecture[23]:

> RFC 4251 --- January 2006 --- SSH Architecture
>
> Each server host SHOULD have a host key. Hosts MAY have multiple host keys using multiple different algorithms. The server host key is used during key exchange to verify that the client is really talking to the correct server.

The word "verify" is doing heavy lifting there. Verification happens against a stored value, and that stored value was accepted on initial contact.

16.3. WHEN RANDOMNESS FAILS

The advisory the Debian security team sent on May 13, 2008, began with measured language and ended with catastrophe.[196]

The story began two years earlier, in April 2006. A Debian bug report asked that `OpenSSL`'s random-number generator be made clean under Valgrind, a tool that detects memory errors. Debian maintainer Kurt Roeckx traced the warnings to code that mixed uninitialized memory into the generator's state.[197]

Roeckx did what diligent developers do: he investigated, found the lines of code triggering the warning, and posted a query to the `openssl-dev` mailing list. "It's using uninitialized memory here," he wrote. "Is this intentional?" The responses were ambiguous, so Roeckx decided to fix it by commenting out the lines that read the uninitialized memory.

The fix was a disaster. `OpenSSL`'s generator collected entropy—genuine randomness—from whatever unpredictable sources the system offered. One of those sources was uninitialized memory, read on purpose because its contents were garbage, and those were the lines Roeckx commented out. Valgrind flagged them because reading uninitialized memory is normally a defect. In this one place it was the design.

By removing those lines, Roeckx accidentally crippled the generator. Without them, the only input the PRNG received was the process ID of the running program.

Process IDs on Linux are small numbers, ranging from 1 to 32,767 by default, so every key generated by the broken `OpenSSL` had to come from one of 32,767 possible states.

For two years, from September 2006 to May 2008, every Debian and Ubuntu system with the broken `OpenSSL` generated predictable keys. `SSH` keys. `SSL` certificates. Anything that depended on `OpenSSL`'s random number generator was affected.

Millions of `SSH` key pairs were compromised. Security researchers generated lists of all possible weak keys, and anyone could download them. With those lists, anyone could check whether a server's host key was vulnerable, or try every possible user key against a server until one worked.

System administrators worldwide scrambled to regenerate every key on every affected system. The fix itself was trivial—update `OpenSSL` and generate new keys—but discovering which keys were affected, replacing them all, and updating every `known_hosts` file and `authorized_keys` file took weeks of work.

The Debian `OpenSSL` bug (CVE-2008-0166)[198] entered Debian's archive on September 17, 2006 and was disclosed on May 13, 2008[196]—nearly two years later. With process identifiers supplying the remaining variation, Debian documented 32,767 possible random-number streams per architecture.[199] The remediation was to update `OpenSSL` and regenerate affected cryptographic keys.

The bug is hard to blame on anyone. Roeckx asked OpenSSL's own developers, and the replies settled nothing. The lines he deleted turned out to be the ones doing the real work, and the diff gave no hint of it. Nearly two years passed before anyone worked out what removing them had cost.

16.3.1. THE GITHUB EMERGENCY

Fifteen years later, SSH key management made headlines again.

On March 24, 2023, GitHub posted a security advisory.[200] Their RSA SSH host key's private component had been "briefly exposed" in a public repository—someone at GitHub had accidentally committed a file containing the private key. The exposure was brief and the file was removed quickly, but the damage was done: anyone who saw that file could impersonate GitHub's SSH servers.

GitHub rotated their RSA host key immediately, which meant every developer who had ever connected to GitHub over SSH would now see a host key mismatch warning. Millions of developers.

```
@@@@@@@@@@@@@@@@@@@@@@@@@@@@@@@@@@@@@@@@@@@@@@@@@@@@@@@@@@@

@    WARNING: REMOTE HOST IDENTIFICATION HAS CHANGED!
    @
@@@@@@@@@@@@@@@@@@@@@@@@@@@@@@@@@@@@@@@@@@@@@@@@@@@@@@@@@@@

Host key for github.com has changed and you have requested
strict checking.
```

That wall of at-signs is designed to stop users cold. But keys do sometimes need to change legitimately.

GitHub's advisory told users to update their `known_hosts` files: remove the old key, connect again, accept the new key. The instructions were correct. But each legitimate rotation teaches another cohort of developers that the alarming warning can be safe to dismiss.

The model works because host keys rarely change, and the alert gets its power from being exceptional. But every time a legitimate key rotation happens, users learn that the warning is sometimes just noise, and the next time an attacker attempts an interception attack, they might remember that time GitHub told them to dismiss the alert.

SSH replaced the exposed wire with an encrypted tunnel.

The passwords are hidden now. The sessions are authenticated. A remote administrator in Helsinki or Tokyo connects to a server in San Francisco and the conversation is private, the identity verified. Ylönen built this in a summer because the alternative was plaintext flowing over the wire for anyone to read—and he had just watched someone read it. The fix was real. It worked.

But every first connection ends with a prompt: "Are you sure you want to continue connecting (yes/no)?" Most users type "yes" without reading the fingerprint. They have no reference to check it against. They are accepting a key on faith, the way everyone accepts everything on first use.

The faith is better founded now, backed by mathematics, protected by encryption. But the Debian bug showed that the mathematics depend on their implementation, and a two-year flaw in a random number generator can hollow out every key generated during that window. GitHub showed that key rotation at scale teaches users to dismiss the warning. In July 2024, Qualys researchers found a race condition in OpenSSH that had been fixed in 2006 and reintroduced in 2021.[201] Old bugs return. The vigil never ends.

The wire is encrypted. The faith is still there.

SSH encrypted the remote shell. It replaced Telnet's cleartext with cryptography that actually worked. But encryption solved only one kind of exposure. When voice calls moved from dedicated telephone lines to the same internet that carried encrypted data, they inherited all of the network's implicit expectations. The system that made voice over IP possible accepted caller identity on faith alone.

CHAPTER 17

THE CALLER ID

SIP makes use of elements called proxy servers
to help route requests to the user's current location,
authenticate and authorize users for services,
implement provider call-routing policies,
and provide features to users.

— RFC 3261, June 2002

17.1. MAKE IT LOOK LIKE HTTP

Henning Schulzrinne wanted to make a phone call over the internet.

Not through copper wires and circuit switches that cost dollars per minute. He meant the internet, where packets were cheap and the infrastructure already existed. It was 1996, and Schulzrinne—a networking researcher who would soon join Columbia University's faculty—had been turning over the idea of internet telephony.[202]

`H.323` stood in the way.

The International Telecommunication Union had published `H.323` in November 1996 as the standard for voice and video over packet networks.[203] The protocol worked, and Intel and Microsoft were building products around it. But H.323 carried the telephone industry's genetic inheritance: binary encoding, complex state machines, committee-designed procedures. Reading an H.323 message required a decoder, and debugging required specialized tools. The protocol felt like a grudging concession that the internet existed.

Schulzrinne thought he could do better. He had been collaborating with the Multiparty Multimedia Session Control working group at the IETF, developing protocols for internet conferencing. The group had created SDP, the Session Description Protocol, which described the technical details of a multimedia session—codecs, ports, addresses—like a handwritten note specifying where to meet and what language to speak. They had created RTSP for streaming media. The pieces were in place. What was missing was the signaling layer—the part that would set up a call.

He started sketching something simpler.

Mark Handley was thinking along the same lines. A researcher at University College London, Handley had been working on the MBONE, the experimental multicast backbone that researchers used to broadcast conferences and lectures across the internet. He understood the challenges of real-time communication over packet networks. He also understood that the telecom industry's approach—careful, standardized, backward-compatible—was too slow for the internet.

Schulzrinne and Handley began collaborating in late 1996. They exchanged emails, shared drafts, argued over details. Jonathan Rosenberg, a researcher at Bell Labs, joined them. Eve Schooler at Caltech contributed ideas. The group worked outside the formal IETF process at first, developing something lightweight enough to implement quickly.

Their design principle was radical: make it look like HTTP.

HTTP delivered web pages—text-based, human-readable, stateless. A web browser sent a request with a few headers, and a server sent a response. The interaction was simple enough that you could debug it with a telnet session, typing commands by hand and reading the responses on screen. HTTP had scaled to millions of servers, proving that text protocols could be fast enough for real applications.

SIP would follow the same pattern. A phone call would start with an INVITE request, formatted almost identically to an HTTP request. The server would answer with status codes borrowed straight from HTTP: 200 OK when the callee picked up, 404 Not Found when the number didn't exist. A third code with no HTTP counterpart, 180 Ringing, reported that the phone was ringing. Headers would carry the rest—who was calling, who was being called, where to send the audio. A person could read the message and tell what was happening.

The email metaphor went further. A SIP address looked like an email address—`sip:alice@example.com`—and a user could register her current location with a server, the way email forwarding worked. Call `sip:alice@example.com` and the call went wherever Alice had registered: the phone on her desk, or a laptop open in an airport. The designers called it personal mobility, one address that followed you from device to device.

RFC 2543 appeared in March 1999. The authors were Handley, Schulzrinne, Schooler, and Rosenberg. The abstract was modest: "The Session Initiation Protocol (SIP) is an application-layer control (signaling) protocol for creating, modifying and terminating sessions with one or more participants."[204]

The document ran to 153 pages, but the core mechanism was simpler than it looked. INVITE started a session, BYE ended it, REGISTER told a server where to reach you, and OPTIONS asked what capabilities a server supported. The rest was details.

The details included a header called From.

The From header identified the caller: when Alice called Bob, her phone would include this header with her SIP address, and Bob's phone would display the information. Caller ID, internet-style.

The RFC specified what the From header should contain. It did not specify how to verify it. Requests and responses, Section 6.21 stated, "MUST contain a From general-header field, indicating the initiator of the request." Nothing required that this indication be truthful.

The design made sense in context. Email followed the same pattern—the From line was whatever the sender claimed, since SMTP didn't verify sender addresses either. Both systems relied on social accountability, legal liability, and the desire to receive replies, expecting the network infrastructure to be operated by responsible parties.

The expectation held for email until spam overwhelmed it. It would hold for SIP until voice became free.

RFC 3261 replaced RFC 2543 in June 2002.[205] The new version, authored by Rosenberg, Schulzrinne, and six collaborators, ran to 269 pages and represented three years of implementation experience. It added security sections, clarified ambiguities, and tightened requirements throughout.

The security considerations section acknowledged the problem. "SIP is not an easy protocol to secure," the authors wrote. The document went on to catalogue registration hijacking, impostor servers, tampered messages, and denial of service, along with the countermeasures—TLS for transport security, digest authentication for users, S/MIME for message encryption.

Schulzrinne and his colleagues understood the tradeoff. Adding cryptographic verification would have required a public key infrastructure for phone numbers, a certificate authority that could attest that Alice really controlled `sip:alice@example.com`. Such infrastructure didn't exist in 2002. Building it would have delayed deployment by years. The alternative was to ship a working protocol and let the security infrastructure catch up.

They shipped the protocol. The infrastructure is still catching up.

17.2. THE FROM HEADER PROBLEM

17.2.1. HOW SIP WORKS

A phone call used to need a physical path. You dialed, relays closed in a switch at the telephone company, and a circuit ran from your handset to the one you were calling. It stayed yours for the length of the conversation, copper and equipment tied up and doing nothing else. Circuit switching worked for a century.

The phone company knew who you were because you had an account and a physical line to your house. If you misbehaved, they could disconnect you.

SIP replaces circuits with messages.

A SIP call has no dedicated connection behind it. What it has is a negotiation: two phones working out how to exchange audio, using text messages that look like web requests. The audio goes somewhere else entirely, carried by RTP, the Real-time Transport Protocol.[206] SIP handles the signaling and RTP handles the media, on two separate paths, and neither one checks the other.

SIP also inherited the web's openness. If you can send the message, you can claim any identity you want.

Alice wants to call Bob. Her phone constructs an INVITE message:

```
INVITE sip:bob@example.com SIP/2.0
Via: SIP/2.0/UDP alice-phone.example.com:5060
From: Alice <sip:alice@example.com>;tag=1234
To: Bob <sip:bob@example.com>
Call-ID: xyz123@alice-phone.example.com
CSeq: 1 INVITE
Contact: <sip:alice@192.168.1.100:5060>
Content-Type: application/sdp
Content-Length: 142
```

Look at the From field: `From: Alice <sip:alice@example.com>`.

Who verified that this was actually Alice? Nobody—her phone wrote that header, and if she wanted to write `From: Your Bank <sip:security@bigbank.com>`, nothing in SIP would stop her.

The other headers mattered for routing: Via told servers where to send responses, To identified the callee, and Call-ID tracked this particular call. Below the headers, separated by a blank line, is the body—SDP, the Session Description Protocol[207]—describing where Alice wants to receive audio by offering an IP address, a port, and a codec.

The message travels to a proxy server, which looks up Bob's registered location and forwards the INVITE. Bob's phone receives it, starts ringing, and sends back `180 Ringing`. When Bob answers, his phone sends `200 OK`.

The 200 OK includes Bob's SDP answer, specifying where he'll receive audio. Alice's phone acknowledges with an ACK. The signaling is complete. Now the phones start sending RTP packets directly to each other, carrying the actual voice data.

Signaling and media travel different paths. The INVITE might traverse multiple proxy servers while the audio packets travel directly between endpoints—efficient for bandwidth, but neither path verifies who you're really talking to.

This is how Caller ID works over VoIP. When your phone rings and displays a number, that number comes from SIP headers. If the caller spoofed those headers, you see the spoofed number. The phone company might add their own headers, might verify that the caller has the right to use that number, might mark the call as unverified. Or they might pass it through unchanged.

The verification chain breaks at the first dishonest party.

In the traditional phone network, Caller ID was difficult to spoof because access to the signaling network was controlled. You needed equipment from the phone company. You needed a physical connection. The carrier could revoke your service if you abused it.

VoIP eliminated those barriers.

SIP software was free. SIP providers competed on price, and the cheapest providers asked the fewest questions. Anyone with an internet connection could send INVITE messages claiming any identity they chose. The cost was negligible. The anonymity was nearly complete.

17.2.2. WHERE VERIFICATION FAILS

The sender field isn't the only weak point.

Registration is the other half of the email metaphor. Bob might be reachable at a desk phone, a mobile app, and a laptop client all at once, and each of them registers with his SIP domain to announce where it currently is. The registrar keeps those bindings and forwards incoming calls to them.

What happens if someone else registers as Bob?

If an attacker guesses Bob's password, or compromises his account, or spoofs the registration message, they can redirect his calls to themselves. The caller thinks they're reaching Bob. They're reaching the attacker. Registration hijacking is invisible to the caller and often invisible to Bob, who simply stops receiving calls he doesn't know were made.

The media path has its own vulnerabilities.

RTP packets flow directly between endpoints, carrying the actual voice—each packet contains a timestamp, a sequence number, and compressed audio. The receiving phone trusts without checking that these packets come from the person it thinks it's talking to.

Anyone who modifies the SDP in transit can redirect the media—a caller thinks they're talking to their bank, but the audio goes to an attacker who relays it onward while listening to both sides. An interception attack at the media layer, invisible to the signaling.

SRTP, Secure RTP, encrypts the media path—if both endpoints support it and if they negotiate keys successfully.[208]

Many VoIP calls still don't use SRTP, which means calls to doctors, lawyers, and accountants may be traveling across the internet unencrypted.

17.2.3. THE ECONOMICS OF FRAUD

Traditional phone calls cost money—long-distance calls cost more, and international calls cost even more. This expense created friction, so a scam call from overseas needed to be profitable enough to justify the cost.

VoIP removed the friction.

Calls that traverse the internet cost fractions of a cent, and VoIP providers with minimal vetting offer bulk rates with no verification. Automated dialers can place thousands of calls per hour, shifting the economics from "calls are expensive" to "calls are free."

Free calls with spoofed Caller ID enabled a new industry.

Robocalls pitch fake insurance, threaten IRS audits, impersonate Microsoft support. What sells the call is the number on the screen: a local number, or your bank's, or a government agency's. You answer because it looks legitimate.

Americans received an estimated 50 billion robocalls in 2021.[209] Most displayed spoofed Caller ID.

The From header that Schulzrinne and Handley created for a research network had become a vector for fraud at industrial scale.

17.3. THE 911 CALL

The 911 call came in just after six in the evening on December 28, 2017.

A man was on the line, speaking urgently. He was at a house in Wichita, Kansas, on West McCormick Street. He had just shot his father. He was holding his mother and brother hostage. He had poured gasoline around the house. If police approached, he would set it on fire.

The Wichita Police Department dispatched officers, a SWAT team, and negotiators. They surrounded the house, established a perimeter, and prepared for an armed standoff with a killer who had nothing to lose.

Andrew Finch opened his front door.

Finch was twenty-eight years old, unarmed, and had no idea why police were pointing weapons at him. He lived in the house with his mother and niece—no one had been shot, no hostages, no gasoline. The 911 call was a lie.

An officer fired. Finch died on his porch.

The practice is called SWATting. The name comes from SWAT teams, the heavily armed police units deployed for dangerous situations. The technique is simple: call 911 with a fabricated emergency, give the victim's address, and watch the police respond with overwhelming force.

SWATting requires two things: the victim's address, and the means to make the call appear legitimate. VoIP provides the second requirement.

The call that sent police to Andrew Finch's door came from Tyler Barriss, a twenty-five-year-old in Los Angeles with a history of making fake bomb threats.[210] Barriss used a VoIP service to place the call. He spoofed the Caller ID to show a Wichita number. The 911 operator saw a local call from someone who said he was at the scene. Nothing in the technology indicated otherwise.

The address Barriss used wasn't random. He was trying to target someone else—a man named Shane Gaskill who had gotten into an argument with Casey Viner over a $1.50 bet in the video game Call of Duty. Viner gave Barriss an address for Gaskill. The address was wrong. Andrew Finch had no connection to either man. He died because of a video game dispute, a wrong address, and a signaling system that didn't verify caller identity.

Barriss pleaded guilty to 51 federal charges and was sentenced to twenty years in prison.[210] Viner pleaded guilty to conspiracy and received fifteen months.[211] But criminal prosecution, as always, came after the harm.

SWATting emerged as VoIP services became cheap and caller ID spoofing became trivial. The FBI's first federal SWATting case was prosecuted in 2007, though earlier incidents had occurred.[212] Hackers targeted security researchers, journalists, and celebrities, while gamers targeted other gamers—and the calls were specific and detailed enough to trigger armed responses.

The victims included Brian Krebs, a security journalist who had written about hackers and faced repeated SWATting attempts.[213] They included online streamers whose addresses leaked through careless social media posts, and random families whose addresses appeared in databases sold on underground forums.

Each SWATting call exploited the same gap: 911 operators relied on Caller ID. When the screen showed a local number, dispatchers believed the call originated locally, and when the caller described an emergency, they responded to it. The system was designed to save lives, and it expected that callers who provided detailed information were telling the truth.

The expectation was reasonable for landlines. It was catastrophically wrong for VoIP.

The response came slowly.

Congress passed the Truth in Caller ID Act in 2010, making it illegal to transmit misleading Caller ID information with intent to defraud, cause harm, or wrongfully obtain anything of value.[214] Prosecuting a caller who sat overseas was harder. And much of the spoofing fell outside the statute entirely—debt collectors spoofed numbers as a matter of routine, and so did political campaigns and ordinary businesses, for convenience.

The phone industry developed a technical solution. `STIR`, Secure Telephone Identity Revisited, uses digital signatures to attest that a caller has the right to use a particular number.[215] Its companion standard `SHAKEN`, Signature-based Handling of Asserted information using tokens, defines how carriers should transmit and verify these signatures, creating a chain of trust from the originating carrier to the terminating carrier.

The FCC mandated `STIR/SHAKEN` implementation by June 30, 2021 for large carriers, with smaller carriers following later.[216] What arrived was patchy. Foreign carriers didn't participate, so international calls bypassed the system entirely, and many smaller carriers obtained extensions. Attestation came in three levels—full, partial, and gateway—and partial gave less assurance than its name suggested.

Phones now showed whether a call had been verified, in whatever notation the carrier preferred: a green checkmark on AT&T, the words "Caller Verified" on T-Mobile. A call without the mark told you only that the carrier hadn't managed to check it. It was a reason for caution and not much else.

Andrew Finch's death changed something. SWATting had been filed under prank—dangerous and illegal, but held at some distance from real consequence. Prosecutors and judges stopped filing it there. A fabricated 911 call was a way to get someone killed, and the sentences started to say so.

But the underlying standard hasn't changed. `SIP` still transmits whatever the sender claims, and the email metaphor that Schulzrinne and Handley chose in 1996 still shapes how phone calls work. The premise that participants would be honest, would be accountable, would have reasons not to lie—that premise failed at scale.

Henning Schulzrinne is still at Columbia, still working on the problem.

His protocol carries billions of calls. It also carries the 50 billion robocalls that Americans received in 2021, each one pretending to be someone else. The specification he wrote made voice free and voice anonymous, and the cost of that anonymity shows up in drained bank accounts, in stolen identities, in a man dead on his porch in Wichita. `STIR/SHAKEN` adds signatures now, and some carriers verify them. International calls bypass the system. The From header is still text that anyone can write.

The calls still connect. The specification didn't fail—it succeeded completely, beyond anything its authors imagined. A protocol designed for researchers at Columbia and UCL now carries voice for the entire planet, and the openness that made it possible is the same openness that made it dangerous. Schulzrinne knew the tradeoff in 2002. The infrastructure to close it still hasn't caught up.

Voice was not the only thing moving to the internet. So was everything else—documents, commerce, conversation. The web would carry its own assumptions about identity and sessions, and those assumptions would prove no sturdier.

CHAPTER 18

THE STATELESS DANCE

The Hypertext Transfer Protocol (HTTP) is an application-level protocol with the lightness and speed necessary for distributed, collaborative, hypermedia information systems.

– RFC 1945, Tim Berners-Lee, Roy Fielding, and Henrik Frystyk Nielsen, May 1996

18.1. VAGUE BUT EXCITING

Tim Berners-Lee spent March 1989 at a desk in Building 31 at CERN, working on a problem that had nothing to do with physics. The machinery was fine: accelerators, detectors, experiments pouring out data at staggering rates. What was drowning was the knowledge.

Thousands of physicists collaborated there, arriving from universities worldwide, working for months or years, then leaving. When they left, their knowledge left with them. Where did that analysis software end up? Who wrote the detector calibration notes? What happened to the documentation for the experiment that ended in 1986?

The answers existed, scattered across computers that ran different operating systems and stored their files in formats the others could not read. CERN had VAX machines and Unix workstations and Macintoshes and IBM mainframes, and each of them kept its documents to itself.

Berners-Lee picked up a pen. He had an idea, though he was not sure anyone else would understand it.

The document he wrote was titled “Information Management: A Proposal”.[217] It ran sixteen pages and included hand-drawn diagrams, circles connected by arrows: the circles were documents and people and concepts, the arrows the links between them. Any piece of information, he proposed, could point to any other, no matter where it lived or what computer stored it. A “web” of notes with links, he called it.

His supervisor, Mike Sendall, read the proposal. In the margin, he scrawled two words: "Vague but exciting.”

It was neither an approval nor a rejection. The proposal sat on Sendall’s desk, and Berners-Lee waited.

The problem wasn’t new. Researchers had been dreaming of linked documents since 1945, when Vannevar Bush described a hypothetical “memex” machine.[218] Ted Nelson had coined “hypertext” in 1965 and spent decades on an ambitious system called Xanadu that never shipped.[219] The idea was well established, but no one had made it work simply, at scale, across real networks.

Berners-Lee’s insight was to build on what already existed. The internet was there, connecting universities and research labs. DNS was there—the naming system from Chapter 7—providing human-readable names for computers. Email showed that global communication could work. He did not need to invent a new network. He needed a new way to use the network that already existed.

In late 1990, Sendall finally gave Berners-Lee permission to work on the project. Berners-Lee bought a NeXT workstation—a sleek black cube that Steve Jobs had designed after leaving Apple—and began building. Someone taped a hand-written note to the black cube: “This machine is a server. DO NOT POWER DOWN!!” The entire World Wide Web, in late 1990, could be killed by an inattentive cleaner with a power strip.

What he built on it came in three parts, none of them large. HTML, Hypertext Markup Language, let a document carry its own structure in tags as plain as <a> for a link and <p> for a paragraph. HTTP, Hypertext Transfer Protocol, was the way one machine fetched a document from another. Last was the URL, Uniform Resource Locator, one line of text that could name any document on any machine—and without it the other two had nothing to point at.

HTTP, the protocol, is almost comically minimal. The first version had only one command: GET. A client connects to a server, asks for a document by name, and receives it back. That is the entire transaction. No login, no negotiation, no state. You ask, you receive, and then you are both strangers again.

Berners-Lee would later describe the design philosophy as ”simple things first.”[220] HTTP was supposed to be so easy that anyone could implement it. A basic server could be written in an afternoon. A basic client could be written by a graduate student learning to program. This was deliberate.

By Christmas 1990, Berners-Lee had the first browser/editor, web server, and website running at CERN.[221] The NeXT computer ran a program called WorldWideWeb—both a browser and an editor, letting users read documents, create them, and follow links to other documents.

On August 6, 1991, Berners-Lee posted a message to a Usenet newsgroup describing his project.[222] The message included an address: `info.cern.ch`. This was the first public web server, running on a NeXT computer at CERN.

The world's first website described the World Wide Web project itself—a document about how to create documents, containing links to other documents explaining how links worked. The snake ate its own tail.

The reaction was modest: a few dozen people visited the site, and a few of them set up servers of their own. By December 1991, there was a web server in the United States, at the Stanford Linear Accelerator Center. By the end of 1992, there were fifty servers worldwide. It was growing, slowly, the way things grow when no one is paying attention.

Then, in January 1993, a twenty-one-year-old student at the University of Illinois released a program called Mosaic.

Marc Andreessen and Eric Bina had built Mosaic at the National Center for Supercomputing Applications, spending nights and weekends on what they considered a side project.[223] Mosaic was a web browser, like Berners-Lee's WorldWideWeb. But Mosaic did something new: it showed images inline with text. Previous browsers required you to click on an image link and view the picture in a separate window. Mosaic put the pictures right there on the page, mixed with the words. It sounds trivial now. It was not.

Suddenly the web was colorful, visual—it looked like something you might actually want to use. Mosaic was also easier to install than previous browsers, and it ran on Windows and Macintosh, not just Unix workstations. Within months, web traffic began doubling every few weeks.

In December 1993, Matthew Gray's World Wide Web Wanderer counted 623 web sites. By June 1994, it counted 2,738; by December, 10,022.[224] Newspapers were writing stories about something called the "information superhighway." Andreessen left Illinois, moved to California, and co-founded a company called Netscape.[225] The browser wars had begun.

HTTP, the mechanism that made this possible, was still the same one Berners-Lee had sketched in 1990. Request a document, receive a document. No login required. No encryption. No way to verify that the server you were talking to was actually the server you thought it was. If you asked for a document, you meant to ask. If the server sent a document, it sent the right one.

This was a design for physicists sharing research papers at CERN—and it was about to carry the entire world's communication.

18.2. REQUEST, RESPONSE, DONE

18.2.1. HOW HTTP WORKS

Think of HTTP as a librarian at a reference desk. You hand over a slip of paper with a call number and get a book back, and that is the entire relationship. Yesterday's visit left no trace, so the librarian has no idea what you read last week or what you plan to read tomorrow. Ask, receive, and you are just another patron again.

This library, though, has no walls. You hand the librarian your request, and everyone in the building can see what you wrote. The librarian hands you the book, and everyone can see what you received. The transaction is public.

This is HTTP's request-response model. A client—your browser—sends a request to a server. The server sends back a response. Each request is independent. Each response is complete. The server maintains no memory of previous interactions. In protocol terminology, HTTP is **stateless**. In security terminology, HTTP is *cleartext*—readable by anyone who can see the traffic.

A request looks something like this:

```
GET /index.html HTTP/1.1
Host: www.example.com
User-Agent: Mozilla/5.0
Accept: text/html
```

The first line contains the **method** (GET), the path to the resource (/index.html), and the protocol version. GET means "give me this document." Other methods exist—POST for submitting data, PUT for uploading, DELETE for removal—but GET is what your browser sends every time you click a link.

The lines that follow are **headers**: the Host identifies which website you want, the User-Agent identifies your browser, the Accept header tells the server what content you can handle.

Notice what is missing. No encryption. No signature. No proof that this request came from you or that it has not been modified in transit. The bytes travel over the wire as naked text. Anyone along the path can read them.

The server responds:

```
HTTP/1.1 200 OK
Content-Type: text/html
Content-Length: 1234

<!DOCTYPE html>
<html>
...
```

The first line contains the status code. `200 OK` means everything worked. `404 Not Found` means the document does not exist. `500 Internal Server Error` means something broke on the server's end. The status codes are arranged in categories: 2xx for success, 3xx for redirection, 4xx for client errors, 5xx for server errors.

After the status line come more headers, then a blank line, then the actual content: the HTML of the webpage, or an image, or whatever you requested.

That completes the transaction: request, response, done. The server has no memory of what just happened, and the next request starts fresh.

And every byte of it—your request, the response, the content—traveled in the clear. If you requested a page while sitting in a cafe, anyone on that WiFi network with a packet sniffer could read what you asked for and what you received. HTTP assumes you do not mind.

18.2.2. THE STATELESSNESS PROBLEM

Statelessness made HTTP fast and scalable. Servers did not need to track thousands of ongoing conversations. Each request was self-contained. Load balancing was easy: any server could handle any request.

But statelessness created a problem. How do you build applications that need to remember things?

Consider a shopping cart. You add an item on one page. You navigate to another page to add a second item. You go to the checkout page. At each step, the server needs to know what is in your cart. But HTTP provides no mechanism for this. Each request is independent. The server cannot tell that the person requesting the checkout page is the same person who added items five minutes ago.

Or consider login. You authenticate on one page, then try to access your account settings—but the server has forgotten you. According to HTTP, the request for account settings comes from a stranger.

The web needed state. HTTP would not provide it.

18.2.3. THE COOKIE SOLUTION

In 1994, a Netscape engineer named Lou Montulli invented the **cookie.**[226] The mechanism was straightforward. When a server wanted to remember something about a client, it would include a special header in its response:

```
Set-Cookie: session=abc123
```

The browser would store this cookie and send it back with every subsequent request to that server:

```
Cookie: session=abc123
```

The server could recognize returning visitors now. Everything it wanted to remember about you—that you had logged in, what sat in your cart—stayed on its own side of the wire, filed under abc123. The cookie carried the key and nothing else, a name tag with a number written on it.

The solution was clever. It grafted state onto a stateless system without changing HTTP itself. Cookies became the foundation of web commerce, social media, advertising, and authentication. Every time you stay logged into a website after closing your browser, a cookie is doing the work.

But the solution had a flaw.

The cookie is a **bearer token**, like a concert wristband. Whoever has it gets access. No questions asked.

If someone steals your cookie, they become you. The server does not verify identity or check who is presenting the cookie—it simply accepts that the cookie arrived through legitimate means.

Your cookie travels over the connection naked, visible to anyone watching. On an open WiFi network, "anyone watching" means everyone.

This design choice made sense in 1994. The web was small. Networks were controlled by universities and corporations. The idea that someone might intercept your cookie seemed remote. But the web was about to grow beyond universities. The cookies would follow.

`HTTP`'s fundamental premise: the network is honest enough. When you request `http://example.com`, `HTTP` expects that the data you receive actually comes from example.com. It expects no one has intercepted the request or modified the response. It expects the path between your browser and the destination is clean.

RFC 1945, the formal specification for `HTTP/1.0` published in May 1996, is refreshingly candid about this.[227] The security considerations section notes that "the Basic authentication scheme is not a secure method of user authentication, nor does it prevent the Entity-Body from being transmitted in clear text across the physical network." The RFC does not claim `HTTP` is secure. It observes that security mechanisms could be added "to increase security."

The authors knew—they always knew. `HTTP` was built for a web where security was someone else's problem, to be handled at a different layer of the stack. The specification would move documents. Protecting those documents would require something more.

18.2.4. FASTER, NOT SAFER

The web grew a thousandfold, but the security did not grow with it. HTTP evolved, always in pursuit of speed, not safety.

HTTP/1.0[227] opened a fresh connection for every request, then closed it—clean and slow. **HTTP/1.1**[228] left the connection open so the next request could reuse it, and **HTTP/2**[229] learned to send many requests down that one connection at once. **HTTP/3**[230] went a layer further down and swapped in QUIC, which gets a connection established faster still.

Each version made the web faster. None made HTTP itself more secure.

Through every iteration, the security model stayed the same. The standard moves bytes. Protecting those bytes requires HTTPS: HTTP wrapped in TLS, which we will examine in a later chapter. Plain HTTP remains what it always was: a clear channel through which anyone can listen.

18.3. FACES IN THE SIDEBAR

18.3.1. THE COFFEE SHOP PROBLEM

Eric Butler stood before a crowd at ToorCon, a security conference in San Diego, on October 24, 2010.[231] He was about to release a Firefox extension called Firesheep, and he knew exactly what would happen next.

His motivation was clear. "Websites have a responsibility to protect the people who depend on their services," he wrote in the release post.

"They've been ignoring this responsibility for too long, and it's time for everyone to demand a more secure web."

The tool was shockingly direct: install it, open it, wait.

Firesheep put the wireless network adapter into promiscuous mode, listening to all traffic on an open WiFi network. When it saw `HTTP` traffic containing session cookies for popular websites–Facebook, Twitter, Amazon, Flickr–it extracted those cookies and displayed them in a sidebar. Each stolen session appeared as a face: the profile picture of someone you could impersonate.

Click on a face, and Firesheep injected the stolen cookie into your browser. You were logged in as that person. No password required. No hacking required. One click.

Session hijacking was not new. Security researchers had known about it for years. Academic papers described the technique in detail, and anyone with `Wireshark` and some patience could capture cookies from an open WiFi network. The vulnerability was well documented.

But no one had made it easy. No one had built a tool that a non-technical person could use, or made session hijacking as trivial as installing a browser extension. Butler did.

The scenario Butler exploited played out millions of times a day. Someone walked into a coffee shop, connected to free WiFi, checked Facebook, browsed Twitter, maybe bought something on Amazon.

Within weeks, demonstrations were happening everywhere. In November 2010, a software engineer named Gary LosHuertos sat in a Starbucks, running Firesheep. He watched as people around him logged into Facebook. He clicked their faces, "nabbed identities," and posted status updates to their accounts warning them: "Your account is exposed." The abstraction of "session hijacking" had become the reality of strangers controlling your screen.

Each of these actions created network traffic. When users logged in, their browsers sent usernames and passwords to the server. If the connection was encrypted with HTTPS, the credentials were safe. An attacker could not read encrypted traffic.

But in 2010, most websites used HTTPS only for the login page. Once you were logged in, the site would switch back to plain HTTP to save computing resources. HTTPS was considered expensive—it required more server processing power and slowed down page loads. So Facebook and Twitter and most other sites would authenticate you over HTTPS, set a session cookie, and then serve all subsequent pages over HTTP.

The cookie traveled with every request. Unencrypted. Visible to anyone on the same WiFi network.

This is where the coffee shop becomes dangerous. Open WiFi networks do not encrypt traffic between your laptop and the access point. Anyone in range can capture packets. Your unencrypted traffic moves through the air, and every device nearby can receive it.

An attacker does not need to break into anything—they just need to listen, and Firesheep made listening trivial.

18.3.2. THE DEMONSTRATION EFFECT

Butler's stated purpose was not to enable attacks. He wanted to embarrass the technology industry into fixing a problem it had known about for years.

The demonstration worked. Within hours of Firesheep's release, security journalists were testing it in coffee shops, videos appeared showing how easy it was to hijack Facebook accounts, and mainstream news organizations ran alarmed stories about WiFi security. The technology industry scrambled.

Twitter made an always-on HTTPS setting available to all users in March 2011.[232] Facebook had added the same option that January.[233] Gmail, which had already defaulted to HTTPS for webmail, extended it to all Google services. Over the following years, the web underwent a fundamental shift. HTTPS went from expensive option to expected default.

In 2015, a non-profit organization called Let's Encrypt began issuing TLS certificates for free, which took the price of a certificate out of the argument.[234] Two years later, more than half of all web traffic was encrypted. By 2020 Google reported that over ninety-five percent of browsing time on Chrome was spent on HTTPS pages, a number that has not moved much since.[235]

But encrypting the channel does not protect the server. In October 2021, a path traversal vulnerability in Apache—the same HTTP server software that has run since the web's early days—allowed attackers to read any file on affected machines.[236] The first patch introduced a second flaw.[237] Ransomware operators were exploiting both within days. The vulnerability tracking system itself is buckling (Chapter 22). The Apache HTTP Server that Tim Berners-Lee would recognize still runs on millions of machines. Still vulnerable. Still essential.

Firesheep did not reveal anything new. The vulnerability had been documented for a decade. What it did was make the vulnerability visceral. Watching your neighbor's face appear in a sidebar, one click away from impersonation, was more persuasive than any security white paper.

The web that Berners-Lee imagined was a space of linked documents, knowledge flowing freely between machines. HTTP was the language of that flow—a language without encryption, without verification, without suspicion. He built it to share physics papers at CERN. It moves the world's commerce now.

Today, a layer of encryption wraps most HTTP traffic, transforming it into HTTPS. But the encryption sits on top, and beneath it, HTTP remains what it always was: a request, a response, the conversation continuing billions of times per second. The session cookie is still a bearer token—whoever possesses it possesses the session—and the stateless core is unchanged from what Berners-Lee sketched on a NeXT workstation in 1990. The web grew from fifty servers to billions. The fundamental design did not change with it.

Berners-Lee's supervisor wrote "Vague but exciting" in the margin of a sixteen-page proposal. Thirty years later, that proposal carries the world's banking, its medical records, its political speech. Every security fix has been bolted on afterward—cookies, HTTPS, certificate pinning—because the original design assumed the network was honest enough. It was not. The bolts hold anyway.

HTTP carries everything, and most of it is encrypted now. But the encryption is not built into HTTP. It wraps around it—a separate protocol layered on top, negotiated before the first request is sent. That protocol is TLS, and its story is about what happens when the internet tries to fix a trust problem with mathematics.

CHAPTER 19

THE LOCK ICON

The primary goal of the TLS Protocol
is to provide privacy and data integrity
between two communicating applications.

— RFC 2246, TLS 1.0, January 1999

19.1. THE PADLOCK PROBLEM

It's late 1994. Taher Elgamal has a problem.[238]

The Egyptian-born cryptographer sits in Netscape's Mountain View offices, surrounded by the buzz of the technology boom. Netscape Navigator is eating the browser market. Marc Andreessen graces magazine covers. The company is racing toward an IPO that will make history.

But Elgamal isn't thinking about stock options. He's thinking about credit cards.

The web is growing faster than anyone predicted. Millions are typing URLs, clicking through pages, discovering the internet contains more than email. They want to buy things—books from Amazon, auctions on eBay, flowers, plane tickets, software.

The problem is simple: HTTP sends everything in plain text. When you type your credit card number and click submit, those sixteen digits travel like a postcard—visible to anyone watching. Your ISP can read them, every router can read them, and a student with a packet sniffer can read them.

Commerce online is impossible without privacy. And privacy online does not exist.

Elgamal knows cryptography. He invented the ElGamal signature scheme a decade earlier, based on public-key cryptography.[239]

Public-key cryptography works like a mailbox with two keys. The slot is the public key: anyone in the world can drop a letter through it, and there is no undropping one. Opening the box and reading those letters takes the private key, which stays in your pocket.

Before the 1970s, this was impossible. Now it makes secure communication possible between strangers who have never met. Elgamal knows the mathematics exist to solve the commerce problem. What doesn't exist is a practical way to deploy them at internet scale.

He assembles a small team. Their protocol would wrap HTTP in encryption and show the user nothing at all, except for a small padlock in the corner of the browser's status bar.

They call it Secure Sockets Layer—SSL for short. A socket is just the connection between a client and a server; making it secure was the hard part.

```
HTTP Request (without SSL):
GET /checkout.html HTTP/1.0
Host: www.amazon.com
Cookie: session=abc123

Credit-Card: 4111-1111-1111-1111
Expiry: 12/98
CVV: 123
```

Anyone watching the network could read this. Every router, every ISP, every curious graduate student with the right tools.

SSL 1.0 never ships. The team finds security flaws before release—a sign of careful engineering, or a worrying sign of how hard the problem is, depending on your perspective.

SSL 2.0 launched in February 1995 with Netscape Navigator 1.1. It worked—users could connect to secure servers, and the padlock appeared. E-commerce websites started advertising "SSL Secured" to reassure nervous customers. VeriSign, a company spun out of RSA Security, began selling digital certificates—the credentials that let servers prove their identity. (RSA took its name from the cryptographers Rivest, Shamir, and Adleman, who made public-key encryption practical.)

But SSL 2.0 has problems. Cryptographers find weaknesses in the key exchange. The protocol allows cipher suites so weak they can be broken in hours. An attacker can downgrade connections to pathetically weak encryption without either party knowing.

By late 1996, Netscape released SSL 3.0, a substantial redesign.[240] Paul Kocher, a cryptographer who would later become famous for breaking hardware security, co-designs the protocol.[241] The protocol is cleaner, stronger, more resistant to the attacks that plagued version 2.0.

But Netscape owns SSL. Every implementation requires their blessing. Microsoft has its own browser war to fight, and depending on a competitor's protocol feels wrong. The IETF steps in with a proposal: take SSL 3.0, change the name, make minor modifications, and publish it as an open standard.

Tim Dierks and Christopher Allen write it up. In January 1999, RFC 2246 defines Transport Layer Security version 1.0—TLS for short.[242] The differences from SSL 3.0 are minor, but the political difference is everything.

> RFC 2246 --- January 1999
>
> The TLS protocol provides communications privacy over the Internet. The protocol allows client/server applications to communicate in a way that is designed to prevent eavesdropping, tampering, or message forgery.

The lock icon became universal. Every major browser displayed it by the early 2000s, and users learned to check for it before typing a password or a card number. Banks and e-commerce sites turned it into advertising copy. "Look for the padlock," they said. "Your connection is secure."

What they don't say is what "secure" means. The padlock promised less than most users believed.

But that confusion is a problem for later. In 1999, the web finally has encryption. Money can flow, and the dot-com boom has the infrastructure it needs.

19.2. THE CRYPTO WARS

19.2.1. THE GOVERNMENT'S OBJECTION

The same year Netscape was building SSL, the U.S. government was trying to kill civilian cryptography.

In April 1993, the Clinton administration announced the Clipper Chip.[243] The plan put a government-designed encryption chip inside telephones and computers, running a strong NSA algorithm called Skipjack. The catch had a bureaucratic name: "key escrow." A copy of every encryption key would be split in half and deposited with two government agencies, and law enforcement with a court order could collect both halves and decrypt any Clipper-protected communication.

The administration presented this as a compromise. Citizens would get strong encryption, law enforcement would retain the ability to conduct wiretaps, and everyone would be happy.

Almost no one was happy.

Phil Zimmermann had seen this coming. In 1991, he released Pretty Good Privacy—PGP—a free encryption program anyone could download.[244] PGP used public-key cryptography, the same mathematics that would later power SSL. Zimmermann named it after Ralph's Pretty Good Groceries from the radio show *A Prairie Home Companion*. The understatement was deliberate—the encryption was better than pretty good.

The government investigated Zimmermann for three years. Exporting strong cryptography was illegal under arms control regulations—the same rules that governed missiles and tanks. Zimmermann faced potential prison time. "I think it's ironic," he said when the Electronic Frontier Foundation honored him in 1995, "that the thing I'm being honored for is the same thing that I might be indicted for." The investigation was eventually dropped, but not before Zimmermann became a symbol of the fight for civilian encryption.

Clipper had a technical problem too. In 1994, Matt Blaze, a young researcher at AT&T Bell Labs, published "Protocol Failure in the Escrowed Encryption Standard".[245] He had found a way around the key escrow mechanism entirely. Wiretapping depended on a component called the Law Enforcement Access Field, and its checksum was only 16 bits wide. An attacker could brute-force that checksum in about forty minutes, Blaze showed, and end up with a chip that still encrypted properly while its surveillance features went dead.

"It's good that Clipper was killed," Blaze later reflected, "and I'm glad that I helped kill it...but it was sorta killed for the wrong reasons. The bug I found wasn't why it was a bad idea." The real problem was the architecture: any key escrow system created a target that attackers would inevitably try to compromise.

A third front opened in the courts. Daniel Bernstein, a mathematics graduate student at UC Berkeley, wanted to publish an encryption algorithm he had developed. The government told him he needed an arms export license. In 1995, Bernstein sued. Four years later, the Ninth Circuit Court of Appeals ruled that source code was protected speech under the First Amendment.[246] "Cryptographers use source code," the court wrote, "to express their scientific ideas in much the same way that mathematicians use equations."

The Crypto Wars ended in a rout. By 2000, the export restrictions had been largely lifted. SSL and its successors could use strong encryption without government backdoors. The lock icon in your browser represents a victory that was far from inevitable.

But the government that funded ARPANET had tried to control the cryptography that would secure it. The same agencies that enabled the internet's creation sought to ensure they could always read its traffic. They lost that battle, but they did not stop trying.

In 2006, the National Institute of Standards and Technology published a random number generator called Dual_EC_DRBG.[247] Security researchers were suspicious from the start—the algorithm was slower than alternatives and had unusual mathematical properties. In 2007, two Microsoft researchers showed that the algorithm could contain a backdoor: anyone who knew certain secret values could predict its output.[248] The secret values, if they existed, would be known only to whoever designed the algorithm. The designer was the NSA.

In 2013, Edward Snowden's disclosures confirmed the suspicions. The NSA had paid RSA Security ten million dollars to make Dual_EC_DRBG the default in their products.[249] The agency that lost the Clipper fight had found another way in.

19.2.2. THE HANDSHAKE

We encrypt messages with a key. We send the key to the recipient so they can decrypt our messages. But if we send the key in plain text, an eavesdropper can read it. Then they can read everything we encrypt.

This is the central paradox of internet cryptography. How do two parties who have never met establish a shared secret without anyone else learning it?

The answer involves clever mathematics, but we don't need the equations. We met the trick briefly with SSH (Chapter 16); here it is in full. Imagine two people, Alice and Bob, trying to agree on a secret color over a public channel where everyone can see what they're saying.

Each picks a private color—let's say Alice chooses yellow and Bob chooses cyan—colors they can never reveal to anyone.

Now they agree on a public color, red, which everyone knows. Alice mixes her private yellow with this public red to get orange, while Bob mixes his private cyan with the same red to get purple. They exchange these mixed colors publicly.

Here's the trick: Alice takes Bob's purple and mixes in her private yellow. Bob takes Alice's orange and mixes in his private cyan. They both arrive at the same color—a muddy brown that depends on all three inputs.

An eavesdropper sees the red, the orange, and the purple. But mixing colors is easy while unmixing them is impossible. The eavesdropper cannot work backward from orange to yellow, from purple to cyan. The shared secret—that muddy brown—remains hidden.

This is Diffie-Hellman key exchange, invented in 1976[250], using paint as analogy for modular exponentiation. The real mathematics involves very large prime numbers and operations that are easy to perform but practically impossible to reverse.

TLS uses this principle, or variants of it, to establish a session key between your browser and a web server.

But key exchange alone isn't enough. The color-mixing trick proves no one can learn the secret, but it doesn't prove you're mixing colors with the right person.

19.2.3. CERTIFICATES AND CHAINS

Encryption protects the content of a conversation. But what good is encryption if we're talking to the wrong person?

This is the identity problem. When we connect to `bank.com`, we want to talk to the actual bank, not an impostor pretending to be the bank. The connection might be perfectly encrypted, but if the other end is a thief, encryption just means no one else can watch the theft in progress.

TLS solves this with certificates. A certificate is a document that binds an identity (like "bank.com") to a public key. The binding is secured by a digital signature—a cryptographic stamp that proves the certificate came from someone specific and hasn't been altered.

But who signs the certificate, and who vouches for the bank?

Certificate authorities exist to answer that question. A CA is an organization trusted to verify identities and issue certificates. Bank of America, wanting an HTTPS website, goes to a CA like DigiCert or Let's Encrypt. The CA confirms that the requester really controls `bankofamerica.com` and signs a certificate with its own private key.

The catch: how does your browser know to trust the CA?

The answer is built in. Your browser ships with a list of approved root CAs—about 150 organizations for Firefox, more for Windows. Most of these names you've never heard of. DigiNotar, Comodo, Trustwave—small companies scattered across the globe. Your browser accepts their signatures completely.

When you connect to a secure website, the server sends its certificate. The browser checks: is this certificate signed by a CA on the approved list? Is the certificate valid for this domain? Has it expired? Has it been revoked?

If all checks pass, the padlock appears.

This creates a chain of delegation: the browser accepts the root CA, which vouches for an intermediate CA, which vouches for the website. Each link depends on the one above it.

The problem emerges when a link breaks.

The system has a name: Public Key Infrastructure, or PKI. It's the reason e-commerce works. When we buy something from Amazon, the browser verifies Amazon's certificate, establishes an encrypted connection, and we can enter a credit card with reasonable confidence that only Amazon sees it.

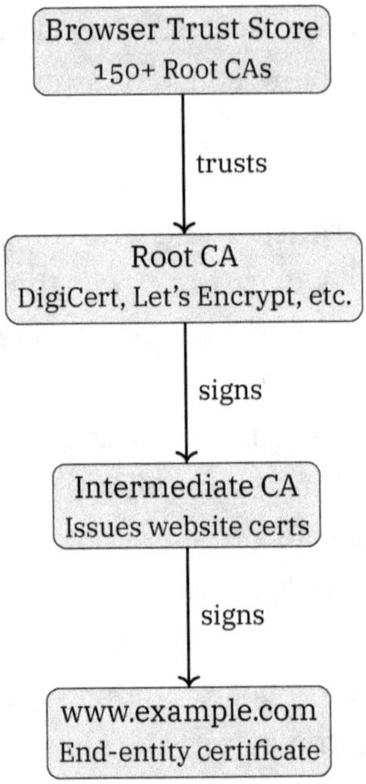

Figure 19.1: The certificate chain. Trust flows from your browser's built-in list of root CAs, through intermediate CAs, down to the website's certificate.

The weakness: every CA in your browser's certificate store can issue a certificate for *any* domain. DigiCert can issue a certificate for `google.com`. So can Let's Encrypt. So can a small CA in the Netherlands that you've never heard of. Your browser will accept any of them.

The chain is only as strong as the weakest CA, and you have no idea which one that is.

All of this—the certificate check and the key exchange—happens in a single negotiation called the handshake.

Your browser reaches out: "I want a secure connection." That opening is the ClientHello. It lists the encryption methods the browser supports—each entry on that list is a **cipher suite**, one full combination of lock types—plus a random number that makes this handshake unlike any other. The server answers with the ServerHello: one method picked from the menu, a random number of its own, and its certificate.

Now comes the moment of truth. Your browser examines the certificate. Is it signed by a CA in the trust list? Is it valid for this domain? Has it expired? Has it been revoked? The browser checks each link in the chain, from the website's certificate up through intermediate CAs to a root it recognizes.

If any check fails, the connection stops. If all checks pass, the browser proceeds—assuming the CA verified the server's identity correctly.

The key exchange comes next, and it is the color-mixing trick again. Each side keeps a private color and combines it with what the other side sent in the clear, and the two combinations turn out to be the same secret. Anyone watching the traffic sees the mixed colors go by and has no way to unmix them. Milliseconds later, browser and server share a key that was never transmitted.

Both sides confirm success by sending a message encrypted with the new key. If either can decrypt the other's confirmation, the key exchange worked—the handshake is complete. The lock icon appears.

After the handshake, every message is encrypted with this session key. Your `HTTP` requests, the server's responses, your passwords, your credit cards—all unreadable to eavesdroppers.

But notice what the browser accepted on faith: that the CA verified the server's identity correctly, that the certificate chain is legitimate, that no one has compromised any CA on the list. One corrupted link, and the whole chain breaks—but your browser would never know.

`TLS 1.3`, published in RFC 8446 in August 2018, tightened the handshake.[251,252] It cuts the exchange from two round trips to one. It removes legacy algorithms that cryptographers had proven weak. It encrypts more of the handshake itself, so eavesdroppers learn less about the connection being established.

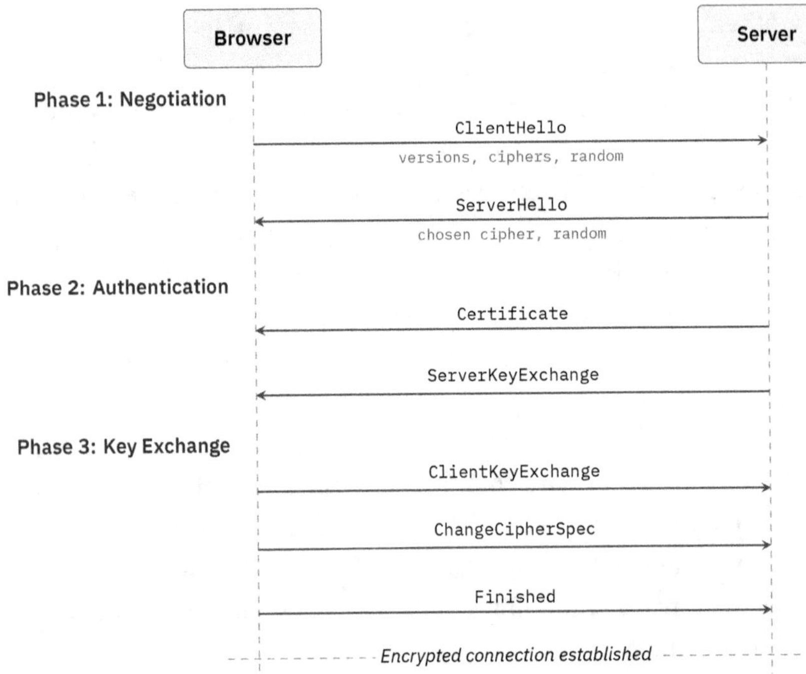

Figure 19.2: TLS 1.2 handshake. The browser and server negotiate encryption parameters (Phase 1), the server proves its identity with a certificate (Phase 2), and both sides establish a shared secret key (Phase 3). TLS 1.3 reduces this to a single round trip.

> RFC 8446 --- August 2018
>
> The primary goal of TLS is to provide a secure channel between two communicating peers; the only requirement from the underlying transport is a reliable, in-order data stream.

Eric Rescorla, who edited the `TLS 1.3` specification, spent years negotiating with browser vendors, server administrators, and cryptographers to get it right. The result is cleaner and faster than its predecessors, and **forward secrecy** is now mandatory.

Forward secrecy means each connection mixes its own session key and throws it away when the connection closes. An attacker who records today's encrypted traffic and steals the server's private key next year still cannot read those old conversations. The secret that protected them was a one-time mix of colors, and it no longer exists anywhere to be stolen.

19.2.4. WHAT THE LOCK ICON ACTUALLY MEANS

Users have been taught to look for the padlock before entering sensitive information. "If you see the lock," the advice goes, "you're safe."

This is half true at best.

The lock means the connection is encrypted—eavesdroppers cannot read the traffic—and that the server presented a valid certificate for this domain, vouched for by a certificate authority.

The lock does *not* mean the website is legitimate, the website won't steal your information, or the people running it are who they say they are. The lock only proves the connection is private. It says nothing about whether the recipient deserves your confidence.

Phishing sites routinely use `HTTPS`. They get certificates from legitimate CAs—which only verify domain control, not business legitimacy. A site called `paypa1-secure-login.com` (note the "1" instead of "l") can get a valid certificate. Your browser will show the padlock. You'll enter your PayPal password, and it will go—encrypted and secure—directly to criminals.

Security researchers call this a "false sense of security." The padlock certified privacy. Users read it as a background check on the site itself.

Modern browsers have tried to fix this confusion. By 2023, Chrome had quietly retired the lock icon.[253] But decades of "look for the lock" advice are hard to undo.

19.3. THE DUTCH FAILURE

A user in Iran opened Gmail one summer morning in August 2011. Something looked wrong. His browser—Google Chrome—displayed a warning he had never seen before. The security certificate for `mail.google.com` didn't match what the browser expected.

He posted about it on a Google help forum. Within hours, security researchers were investigating. What they found would bring down a certificate authority and expose how brittle the PKI really was.

The certificate his browser rejected came from DigiNotar, a Dutch CA, and it was technically valid: signed by DigiNotar's root key, which every major browser accepted. Chrome rejected it anyway. Google had told the browser in advance what its own certificates should look like, and this one did not match.

Someone had gotten DigiNotar to issue a fake certificate for `*.google.com`. The asterisk is a wildcard—it matches any subdomain. A certificate for `*.google.com` covers `mail.google.com`, `docs.google.com`, `www.google.com`, and every other subdomain. Organizations use wildcards for convenience: one certificate protects dozens of services. The attackers got a certificate that covered Gmail, Google Search, Google Docs—everything Google operated.

Chrome's detection relied on certificate pinning—hard-coded expectations about which certificates Google properties should present.

Certificate Transparency, the public logging system that now makes fraudulent certificates visible to anyone, did not yet exist in 2011.

The investigation moved fast. Researchers at Google and security firms started digging.[254] On August 30, days after the forum post, DigiNotar admitted it had been hacked a month earlier. Attackers had penetrated their systems in mid-July and issued more than 500 fraudulent certificates.[255]

Not just for Google—for Microsoft, Yahoo, Mozilla, the CIA, MI6, and Mossad, according to the Fox-IT investigation.

The attackers had been inside DigiNotar's systems for weeks, issuing certificates for whatever they wanted. A certificate for `*.torproject.org`—the anonymity network used by dissidents worldwide. A certificate for `windowsupdate.microsoft.com`—meaning attackers could potentially push malware as legitimate Windows updates.

Fox-IT, the Dutch forensic firm brought in to investigate, published a report on what it found.[255] DigiNotar's network had no segmentation between its parts, passwords weak enough to guess, and software left unpatched against known vulnerabilities. There was no intrusion detection either. The attackers had moved through the systems with apparent ease.

But the worst part wasn't the breach itself. The worst part was what the certificates were used for.

Fox-IT found 298,140 unique IP addresses that had contacted Google's services while the fraudulent certificate was in use; more than 99 percent were in Iran.[255] That figure counts network addresses rather than confirmed Gmail accounts, and it is not proof that every connection was intercepted. What it establishes is scale: the certificate was deployed against Iranian users in enormous numbers, potentially exposing their credentials and the contents of their sessions. Who ran the interception was never established publicly, though suspicion centered on the Iranian state. For dissidents organizing against the regime, what rode on a certificate check was their freedom and their lives.

The context matters. In 2009, millions of Iranians had taken to the streets to protest a disputed election. The Green Movement, as it became known, organized through social media—through Gmail and Facebook and Twitter. The regime crushed the protests—thousands arrested, some tortured, some killed in custody. Two years later, a fraudulent Google certificate appears to have been used to monitor a large population of users connecting from Iranian networks.

Hans Hoogstraaten, who led the Fox-IT investigation, was blunt about the stakes: "People got killed for having a different opinion".[256] The failure of one small Dutch company was connected, however indirectly, to the suppression of a political movement. The attackers had stolen something more useful than data: the authority to be believed.

The attackers left traces. In a text file on DigiNotar's servers, someone wrote in Persian: "There is no God but Allah." Another signature appeared in the code: "I am Comodo Hacker." The same claim had appeared in an earlier attack on Comodo, another certificate authority, in March 2011. The same individual—or the same unit—had compromised two separate CAs within months of each other.

On September 3, 2011, every major browser revoked DigiNotar's root certificate. Overnight, every website that used a DigiNotar certificate became invalid. The Dutch government, which had used DigiNotar for citizen-facing services, scrambled to get new certificates.

Three weeks later, DigiNotar filed for bankruptcy.[257] A certificate authority—accepted by every browser on the planet—was destroyed in less than a month.

19.3.1. THE OPENSSL BUG

The DigiNotar breach showed that CAs could be compromised. A bug discovered three years later showed that TLS itself had hidden weaknesses—not in the protocol design, but in its most common implementation.

On April 7, 2014, security researchers from Google and Codenomicon disclosed a bug they called Heartbleed.[258,259] The name came from the TLS "heartbeat" extension, a keep-alive feature that let clients and servers confirm the connection was still active.

The heartbeat works simply: a client sends a message saying "echo this back to me," and the remote host copies the specified data and returns it as proof of life.

The bug was in the copy.

A heartbeat message includes two fields: the data to echo and the length of that data. A legitimate message might say "Here are 16 bytes of data—echo them back," and the receiving machine dutifully reads those 16 bytes and returns them.

But OpenSSL, the software library that handles TLS for most of the internet's servers, didn't check whether the stated length matched the actual data. An attacker could send a message saying: "Here is 1 byte of data. Echo back 64,000 bytes."

The server would obediently read 1 byte of the attacker's data, then copy 63,999 bytes of whatever happened to be next to it in memory. And what was in memory? Potentially, anything. Other users' session cookies, private encryption keys, passwords, usernames, credit card numbers. Whatever had recently passed through the server's TLS processing.

```
Heartbeat Request:
  Data: "X"
  Claimed Length: 65535 bytes

Heartbeat Response:
  Data: "X" + [65534 bytes of server memory]
```

The leaked memory could include private SSL keys, session tokens, usernames, passwords, and other users' requests.

The buggy code was committed in December 2011 and shipped in released software on March 14, 2012, with OpenSSL 1.0.1. For over two years, anyone who knew about the bug could have silently stolen data from the roughly 17% of the web's secure servers that Netcraft found vulnerable.

Bruce Schneier, the security expert, was blunt: "Catastrophic is the right word. On the scale of 1 to 10, this is an 11".[260]

The cleanup was miserable. Every server running a vulnerable OpenSSL had to be patched, and every private key on those servers treated as already stolen. That meant revoking and reissuing certificates by the million. Users were told to change their passwords everywhere, but not until the sites they used had patched.

The bug was a missing bounds check: two lines that would have compared the claimed length against the data actually sent, and that had never been written. Adding them took minutes. The two years before that were the problem.

19.3.2. THE CONTINUING TENSION

TLS works—e-commerce exists, banks operate online, and we send passwords and credit cards through encrypted channels where, the overwhelming majority of the time, only the intended recipient sees them.

But the architecture assumes that verification can be delegated. That a small number of organizations—CAs that most users have never heard of—can vouch for the identity of every server. That those organizations will maintain perfect security, forever.

DigiNotar demonstrated the cost of a single CA failure, while Heartbleed showed that even correct protocols can be undermined by implementation bugs.

The padlock remains, though browsers display it less prominently now. Security depends on delegation, and delegation can fail. Concentrated authority creates single points of failure.

We built a system where 150 organizations can vouch for any website and assumed it would hold. Usually it does—but when a small Dutch company gets hacked, dissidents on the other side of the world pay the price.

The padlock is disappearing from browsers.

Encryption won, and winning is what killed the icon. Chrome stopped displaying the lock in September 2023, on the reasoning that HTTPS was now the default rather than the exception, and Firefox and Safari followed. By 2024, over 95% of pages loaded in Chrome traveled over HTTPS.[261] Let's Encrypt alone secures more than half a billion websites.[262] Thirty years of "look for the lock" ended because the lock had stopped marking anything unusual. Governments contested what Taher Elgamal assembled in a Netscape office in 1994. Export law limited it, and early users rejected it. Today it runs invisibly beneath nearly every web transaction on the planet.

You notice TLS only when it breaks. A certificate error stops a page load and warns you away from a site you meant to visit. Success looks like nothing at all: the key is mixed, the encrypted page arrives, and there is no moment to point at. Billions of times a day the protocol does its work and vanishes. Elgamal and Dierks were building toward that disappearance, even if they never described it in those words.

The CA system still has weaknesses. The 150 root certificates in your browser represent 150 organizations you have never vetted. One failure—DigiNotar proved this—can weaponize trust against the people it was built to protect. Certificate Transparency records publicly trusted TLS certificates in append-only logs, so unauthorized issuance becomes detectable. Chrome requires publicly trusted TLS certificates issued after April 30, 2018, to support CT in order to validate.[263,264] CAA records let domain owners restrict which CAs may issue for their names.[265] The bargain holds, mostly. The lock is gone from the address bar. The encryption it represented is not.

TLS solved one problem: eavesdroppers could no longer read the conversation. But the conversation still had to reach you, and reaching you increasingly meant traveling through the air. The coffee shop WiFi that Eric Butler exploited with Firesheep, the hotel network where business travelers checked email, the airport lounge where executives negotiated deals—all of them broadcast radio waves that anyone with an antenna could receive. TLS encrypted what traveled over those airwaves. It could not prevent someone from capturing them.

Encrypting the air would prove even harder than encrypting the wire.

==================================

CHAPTER 20

WAVES OF TRUST

==================================

WEP is intended to provide data confidentiality
that is subjectively equivalent
to the confidentiality of a wired LAN
that does not employ cryptographic techniques
to enhance privacy.

— IEEE 802.11 Standard, 1997

20.1. THE CABLE WAS THE PROBLEM

Vic Hayes watched technicians snake Ethernet through the ceiling tiles of a Dutch warehouse in 1988.[266] NCR Corporation wanted to connect its cash registers to a central computer. That meant running wire to every checkout lane—an installation that took weeks. Every time the layout changed, every time a new register was added, the technicians came back with spools of cable and ceiling ladders. Hayes, a lanky engineer at NCR's Utrecht facility, stood watching and thinking there had to be a better way.

Radio was not new to networking. HAM operators had been experimenting with packet radio since the 1970s, and the military ran encrypted wireless links, but those applications needed expensive equipment and licensed spectrum. You could not just walk into a warehouse and start broadcasting. Hayes wanted wireless that was cheap and unlicensed, something anyone could deploy in place of the cable.

The obstacles were large. Radio frequencies belonged to governments. To transmit without a license, you needed spectrum regulators had left open for anyone. In the United States, the FCC had designated bands for "industrial, scientific, and medical" applications—the ISM bands. Your microwave oven operates there. So do garage door openers. The ISM bands were a radio free-for-all: anyone could transmit, everyone tolerated interference.

Hayes started building prototypes in 1988. He was born in Surabaya in the Dutch East Indies, trained as an electrical engineer at the Hogeschool van Amsterdam, and joined NCR in 1974. His team worked out of a cramped lab in Utrecht, soldering transceivers and writing driver software for the 2.4 GHz ISM band, chosen because no government claimed exclusive rights to it. By 1990 NCR had wireless networking hardware that worked. It ran at about one megabit per second and the range topped out at a hundred meters under ideal conditions, but cash registers could talk to servers without a single cable between them.

The technology was useless without a standard. NCR's wireless would not talk to anyone else's wireless. Every vendor had its own frequencies, its own encoding, its own packet formats. Proxim sold one wireless product, Motorola sold another, and Symbol Technologies had its own approach. If you bought from one vendor, you were locked in. For wireless networking to become ubiquitous, companies would have to agree on a common way to do it.

Hayes took on the standardization effort himself. In 1990, the Institute of Electrical and Electronics Engineers formed a working group to develop a wireless local area network standard.[267] Hayes became its chairman. The group was designated `802.11`, following the IEEE's numbering scheme for networking standards: `802.3` was Ethernet, `802.5` was Token Ring, and `802.11` would be wireless. The number was bureaucratic, but the ambition was sweeping: a single standard that would let any device talk to any access point, from any manufacturer, anywhere in the world.

The committee meetings were contentious. AT&T, which had acquired NCR by this point, favored one approach and Proxim favored another. Lucent, Symbol Technologies, and Apple each turned up with their own preferences about frequency bands, modulation schemes, and collision avoidance. The representatives sat in conference rooms in hotels near airports, arguing about technical minutiae while their companies' patent portfolios hung over every decision. Hayes spent seven years mediating and compromising, and now and then he forced a vote when consensus looked hopeless. He also fought a parallel battle with European regulators. The goal was harmonized spectrum: 83.5 MHz in the 2.4 GHz band and 475 MHz in the 5 GHz band, the same allocations on both sides of the Atlantic, so that a device built for Europe would work in America and vice versa.

```
IEEE 802.11 Project Authorization Request --- 1990

The IEEE 802.11 Working Group shall develop a wireless
LAN Medium Access Control (MAC) and Physical Layer (PHY)
specification... compatible with existing 802 networks...
The standard shall support multiple physical layers.
```

The hardest problem was security. Radio signals do not stop at walls. Anyone within range can hear the traffic: a competitor in a van outside your building, a bored teenager in the next apartment, a spy in the embassy across the street. If you replace the Ethernet cable, you must replace the physical security that cable provided. Someone has to tap a wire to eavesdrop on Ethernet. With wireless, they need only an antenna and patience.

The committee knew encryption was necessary. They also knew it was problematic. In 1997, when the `802.11` standard was finalized[268], the United States regulated cryptography as a munition.[269] The State Department limited exports to 40-bit keys—weak enough to crack in hours. The `802.11` committee faced the same dilemma that had constrained `SSL` designers a few years earlier (Chapter 19): build strong encryption that could not ship internationally, or weak encryption that would fail.

The committee designed what they called Wired Equivalent Privacy, or WEP. The name set the bar: privacy "equivalent" to a wired network. In practice that meant good enough to keep a casual eavesdropper out, and no real barrier to a determined attacker with physical access. They were not trying to build the strongest possible encryption. They were putting a lock on the door, not a vault.

They chose deployment over security. WEP's 40-bit version became the default for international markets.

WEP used the `RC4` stream cipher, a fast algorithm that could run on the weak processors in networking hardware. `RC4` was popular in the 1990s: it required minimal memory, computed quickly, and had been designed by Ron Rivest of `RSA` fame. RSA Data Security initially kept the design secret; an anonymous 1994 post to the Cypherpunks mailing list disclosed it publicly.[270] WEP combined a shared key with a 24-bit initialization vector to generate a keystream—a sequence of random-looking bytes. That keystream was XORed with the plaintext to produce ciphertext. XOR is a simple bitwise operation: apply it twice and you get back the original. Standard stuff, for 1997.

The committee made choices that would prove fatal. A 24-bit initialization vector gave only about 17 million possible values, which a busy network would exhaust in hours, and the key scheduling was weak, leaking information about the secret key itself. Nothing in the design changed keys automatically; rotating your network password meant visiting every device and typing in a new one. In 1997, with export regulations limiting what they could ship and hardware limiting what they could compute, WEP seemed good enough.

Hayes called wireless "the final step" in the networking puzzle. He imagined laptops roaming freely through office buildings, connecting to the network from anywhere. He imagined homes without Cat5 cables running along baseboards. He imagined airports and coffee shops where travelers could check email without hunting for a phone jack. For his work chairing the `802.11` committee through seven years of contentious standardization, the industry would later call him "the father of WiFi." In 2007, the IEEE awarded him the Charles Proteus Steinmetz Award. In 2012, the American Computer Museum gave him the George R. Stibitz Computer and Communications Pioneer Award.

All of this came true—so did the security problems the committee had underestimated.

20.2. BREAKING THE AIR

20.2.1. THE SHARED SECRET PROBLEM

You open your laptop at a cafe and type the WiFi password from the chalkboard. Thirty feet away, someone else types the same password, and a third person by the window does the same. You all know the secret, so you are all inside.

That password is the only wall.

If the key travels over the air unencrypted, anyone listening can capture it. WiFi solves this with cryptographic key derivation: both your device and the access point know the password, so they can derive encryption keys without transmitting the password itself. An eavesdropper sees the encrypted negotiation but cannot work backward to the underlying secret. Two parties agree on a key while a third party watches the entire conversation and learns nothing useful.

The problem is that everyone who knows the password can do the same math. The password on the chalkboard is not protecting you from the person by the window. It protects both of you from people who do not know the password—and only if the encryption works.

The question is whether it does.

20.2.2. WEP: HOW TO BREAK ENCRYPTION

WEP failed spectacularly. To understand why, we need to understand how stream ciphers work—and how WEP got them wrong.

A stream cipher encrypts data bit by bit, generating a pseudorandom keystream—a sequence of random-looking bits—from a key and an initialization vector. XOR the plaintext with the keystream and you get ciphertext; XOR is reversible, so apply it twice and you are back where you started. The receiver, knowing the key and IV, generates the same keystream and recovers the plaintext.

The security rests on one rule: never reuse the same keystream.

If two messages are encrypted with identical keystreams, an attacker holding both ciphertexts can XOR them together; the keystreams cancel and what is left is the XOR of the two plaintexts. Recovering the originals from there is straightforward, especially when the messages have predictable structure like HTTP headers or email formats. The encryption is simply gone.

Figure 20.1: A WEP packet. The IV is transmitted in the clear. With only 24 bits, IV collisions are guaranteed on busy networks – and each collision leaks information about the key.

WEP's IV is only 24 bits long—just 16.7 million possible values. On a busy network transmitting 1,000 packets per second, all possible IVs are exhausted in about four and a half hours. After that, IVs start repeating, keystreams start repeating, and the encryption is broken. And it gets worse.

In 2001, three cryptographers—Scott Fluhrer, Itsik Mantin, and Adi Shamir—published a paper at the Selected Areas in Cryptography workshop showing that some IVs were worse than others.[271] They called it "Weaknesses in the Key Scheduling Algorithm of RC4." The title was understated. The implications were not.

A "weak IV" is an initialization vector that leaks clues about the secret key, and WEP fed the IV into the RC4 cipher in a way that let the clues through. The first bytes out of the cipher were not quite random; their statistics leaned toward the key. Anyone who captured enough packets with weak IVs could recover the key one byte at a time, without guessing at any of it.

The result was devastating: collect a few million packets—a few hours of traffic on a typical network—and the key falls out. Security researchers immediately built tools to automate the process, with AirSnort appearing first, then weplab, then `aircrack`, each generation faster than the last.

In 2007, three German researchers at Darmstadt University of Technology—Erik Tews, Ralf-Philipp Weinmann, and Andrei Pyshkin—made the original attack look primitive.[272] Their paper was titled "Breaking 104 bit WEP in less than 60 seconds," and it delivered what the title promised. The Pyshkin-Tews-Weinmann attack needed 40,000 packets for even odds of recovering the key and 85,000 for near-certainty, down from millions. Replaying captured ARP requests forced the network to generate packets on demand instead of waiting for traffic, and a WEP key came out in under a minute. The attack went into `aircrack-ng` and became the default method.

```
$ aircrack-ng capture.cap
Opening capture.cap
Read 68291 packets.

   #  BSSID              ESSID         Encryption

   1  00:14:BF:3B:96:41  LINKSYS       WEP (47281 IVs)

Choosing first network as target.

                         KEY FOUND! [ 41:42:43:44:45 ]
      Decrypted correctly: 100%
```

Tools like `aircrack-ng` automated the process. Breaking WEP became something a teenager could do with a laptop and a few minutes of patience. "Wired Equivalent Privacy" provided privacy equivalent to shouting your data across a crowded room.

By 2002, the `802.11` committee knew WEP was dying. The attacks were public and administrators were panicking, but replacement was not simple. Millions of devices were already in the field—access points, laptops, PDAs, industrial equipment—and every one of them expected WEP. A clean break would turn all of them into scrap.

The WiFi Alliance released `WPA` in 2003 as an emergency measure.[273] `WPA` kept the `RC4` cipher but wrapped it in `TKIP`, the Temporal Key Integrity Protocol. `TKIP` extended the IV to 48 bits, eliminating IV exhaustion. It generated a unique key for every packet. It added integrity checking to detect tampering.

But `RC4` was weak, and researchers kept finding attacks that `TKIP`'s patches could only partly contain.

The real fix came in 2004 with `WPA2`[274], which replaced `RC4` entirely with `AES`—the cipher NIST had selected after a five-year international competition. `AES` was stronger, well-analyzed, and designed to resist the statistical attacks that killed WEP. `WPA2` was what WEP should have been from the start.

`WPA2` is what most networks use today, and the encryption is solid. But WiFi security involves more than encryption—it involves key management, and key management is where `WPA2` still has problems.

20.2.3. THE FOUR-WAY HANDSHAKE

How do two strangers agree on a secret key while someone else is listening? `WPA2` solves this problem every time you connect to a network. Your laptop and the access point both know the password. From that password, they derive encryption keys—fresh ones, unique to this session—without transmitting the password itself. An attacker watching the entire exchange learns nothing.

Protocol	Encryption	Key Size	Status
WEP	RC4	40/104 bits	Broken
WPA	RC4/TKIP	128 bits	Deprecated
WPA2	AES/CCMP	128/256 bits	Standard
WPA3	AES/GCMP	128/256 bits	Recommended

Table 20.1: WiFi security protocol evolution. WEP shipped in 1997; practical attacks broke it from 2001, and by 2007 it fell in under a minute.

The solution is a four-message exchange called the handshake. Watch how confidence builds—and where it could break.

Both sides start by computing a master key from the password. They run it through 4,096 rounds of hashing, deliberately slow to punish anyone trying to guess passwords by brute force. This master key never changes; it is the foundation. But you cannot encrypt traffic with the master key directly. If you did, every session would use the same encryption, and an attacker who broke one session would break them all.

So they derive a session key by mixing fresh random numbers from both sides—called nonces, used only once—with the master key and the hardware addresses of both devices. The result is a unique session key, different every time you connect.

The handshake unfolds in four steps. First, the access point sends its random number. Your device generates its own random number, computes the session key, and sends its number back along with a cryptographic proof that it knows the password. The access point, now having both random numbers, computes the same session key and sends the shared broadcast key. Your device acknowledges.

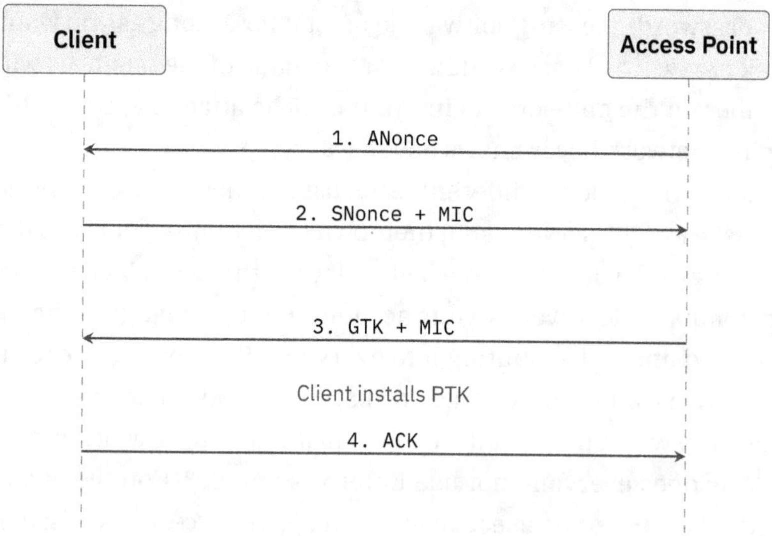

Figure 20.2: The WPA2 four-way handshake. Both sides derive the same PTK from the PMK and exchanged nonces.

After message three, your device installs the session key and starts encrypting. Both sides end up with identical keys, derived from fresh random values. An eavesdropper who captured all four messages still cannot decrypt anything. Without the password, the math does not work.

The handshake has to handle errors. Wireless is unreliable. Packets get lost. What happens if message four does not arrive?

`WPA2` has two modes. Personal mode uses a pre-shared key—the password you type when joining the network—and everyone who knows it can connect. That is why you use it at home, why most coffee shops use it, why small businesses use it. One password, shared among all users.

Personal mode has a weakness: if you know the password and capture the four-way handshake, you can derive the session key and decrypt traffic. Worse, you can take the captured handshake home and run password-guessing software against it for as long as you want. A weak password—"password123," or the name of the business with a number on the end—cracks in minutes. The attack happens offline, and the network never knows anyone is trying.

Enterprise mode is different: each user authenticates individually against a `RADIUS` server using their own credentials—your username and password, your employee badge, your certificate. When you leave the company, IT revokes your account without changing the WiFi password and redistributing it to everyone. Someone who captures Enterprise traffic cannot crack a shared password because there is none; they would need to attack individual credentials, which is harder.

Why does everyone not use Enterprise mode? Complexity. You need a `RADIUS` server, user account management, certificate issuance, and access point configuration—routine for a corporation with an IT department, but beyond a neighborhood cafe.

So the world runs on Personal mode, with all its weaknesses.

20.2.4. THE SHARED AIR

The password is the perimeter. Everyone who has it is inside, and the arrangement holds only as long as it stays with the people it was given to.

For home networks, the model works well enough—you share the password with family and guests. For businesses, it is less ideal since every employee knows the password, and when someone leaves, you should change it. For public networks, the model breaks down entirely: open networks have no encryption at all, and "secured" networks often post the password on a sign above the counter.

For twenty years after WEP's collapse, `WPA2` held this line. Security researchers probed it, looking for weaknesses. They found some: dictionary attacks against weak passwords, attacks on `TKIP` that worked under specific conditions. But the core of `WPA2—AES` encryption with the four-way handshake—seemed solid.

Then, in 2017, a Belgian researcher found a hole in the handshake itself.

20.3. WARDRIVING IN MARSHALLS

In the summer of 2005, Albert Gonzalez sat in a car outside a Marshalls store in Miami[275,276], armed with a laptop, a directional antenna, and patience. Through the windshield he could see shoppers coming and going, hunting for bargains on discount clothing. Inside, cash registers were processing credit card transactions—and the store's wireless network was running WEP.

Gonzalez was twenty-four years old, thin, with the wired intensity of someone who spent too much time staring at screens. He had learned about credit card theft the hard way. The Secret Service arrested him in 2003 for running a website that trafficked in stolen credit cards, and he cut a deal—inform on other carders, stay out of prison. For two years he worked both sides, feeding his handlers information on former associates while quietly building his own criminal operation. The Secret Service thought they had turned him. They were wrong.

TJX Companies owned Marshalls, along with T.J. Maxx, HomeGoods, and several other retail chains.[277] Their stores processed millions of credit card transactions every month. And in 2005, their wireless security was stuck in 1997. While security researchers had been warning about WEP for years, while corporations with experienced IT departments had long since upgraded, TJX was still protecting its networks with broken encryption.

The WEP key fell quickly. Gonzalez's crew collected packets, ran `aircrack`, and within minutes had access to the network. From the parking lot they could watch traffic moving between the cash registers and the store's servers: credit card numbers, expiration dates, CVV codes, everything a carder needed. WEP was doing exactly what the committee had settled for in 1997.

But Gonzalez wanted more than one store's traffic—he wanted the entire company.

TJX's corporate systems sat in Framingham, Massachusetts, and from the store network his team could see connections reaching them. The internal network was more secure than the store-level WiFi, though not secure enough: the store networks that processed credit cards ran into the same network that handled inventory and logistics. SQL injection and weak access controls carried the crew deeper, onto internal servers where they installed packet sniffers to capture card data moving between point-of-sale terminals and the company's central processing systems. By early 2006 they had reached the systems that processed card transactions for thousands of stores across the country.

The breach continued for a year and a half. Gonzalez and his crew siphoned credit card numbers from TJX's databases, tens of millions of them. They sold the data to buyers in Eastern Europe who specialized in fraud. They encoded stolen numbers onto blank magnetic-stripe cards and used them to withdraw cash from ATMs. They bought electronics and gift cards, converting stolen data into untraceable goods. A single WEP vulnerability in a Marshalls parking lot had become the entry point for one of history's largest data breaches.

In July 2005, Gonzalez's team cracked WEP at a Marshalls store in Miami. By late 2005, they had access to TJX's corporate network. Throughout 2006, they exfiltrated credit card data continuously. TJX detected suspicious activity in December 2006 and disclosed the breach in January 2007. By March, the full scale of the breach became clear. Gonzalez was arrested in May 2008 for a different breach and sentenced to twenty years in federal prison in March 2010.[278]

TJX reported at least 45.6 million compromised credit and debit card numbers.[277] The company later put its cumulative pre-tax intrusion-related expense at $171.5 million through January 30, 2010.[279] Banks reissued millions of cards, and customers got letters telling them to watch their accounts for fraudulent charges. Credit monitoring became the standard consolation offered to breach victims, and still is.

The attackers had not exploited a software bug. They had not used a zero-day vulnerability. They had simply taken advantage of a protocol that the security community had known was broken for years. WEP was still protecting financial transactions in 2005 because upgrading was inconvenient, expensive, and—until someone actually exploited it—seemingly unnecessary. The gap between "known to be broken" and "actually broken into" was eighteen months of stolen credit cards.

20.3.1. KRACK: THE HANDSHAKE BETRAYED

TJX was a failure of deployment: using broken security when better alternatives existed. A decade later, a Belgian researcher would demonstrate that even the better alternatives had problems.

Mathy Vanhoef was a postdoctoral researcher at KU Leuven, working on WiFi security in Frank Piessens's imec-DistriNet research group. His office was in the university's computer science building in Leuven, a medieval city east of Brussels. He spent his days reading specifications, writing proof-of-concept code, and looking for flaws that might have been overlooked. In 2016, he began analyzing the `WPA2` handshake—the very mechanism that was supposed to have replaced WEP's broken security.

The IEEE `802.11i` specification ran to hundreds of pages. Vanhoef read it the way a cryptographer does, hunting for the assumptions underneath the instructions. For its main purpose—deriving session keys without transmitting the password—the four-way handshake was well designed. What caught his attention was buried in the error handling, in the gap between intent and implementation.

The handshake has a reliability mechanism because radio is lossy and acknowledgments vanish. If the client sends message four but the access point does not receive it, the access point retransmits message three. The client is supposed to handle this gracefully—acknowledge again and continue. The protocol designers had thought about this and built in error handling.

Vanhoef realized that handling retransmissions was dangerous. When the client receives message three, it installs the session key and resets its nonce counter—the number that increments with each packet to ensure unique encryption. If an attacker forces message three to be retransmitted, the client reinstalls the key and resets the nonce. The same key. The same nonce values. Used again.

Nonce reuse in encryption is catastrophic: with the same key and nonce, you get the same keystream, and if you XOR two ciphertexts encrypted with the same keystream, the keystreams cancel out—the same failure mode that killed WEP, now appearing in its successor.

An attacker who could trigger key reinstallation could collect traffic encrypted with repeated nonce values, XOR the ciphertexts together, and recover plaintext. With enough traffic, they could inject packets and, in some cases, take over the connection entirely. The mechanism designed to handle lost packets became the vulnerability.

The attack required the attacker to be positioned between the client and the access point. This meant cloning the target access point on a different channel and forcing the client to connect to the attacker's copy.

From there, the attacker could selectively block and replay handshake messages, triggering key reinstallation at will.

Vanhoef called the attack KRACK: Key Reinstallation Attack.[280]

On October 16, 2017, Vanhoef publicly disclosed the attack; the formal paper was presented at the ACM Conference on Computer and Communications Security in November.[281] The paper, "Key Reinstallation Attacks: Forcing Nonce Reuse in WPA2," earned the conference's Real-World Impact Award. Vanhoef had coordinated with major vendors for months before the announcement, giving them time to prepare patches. US-CERT issued ten CVE numbers spanning CVE-2017-13077 to CVE-2017-13088—one for each variant of the attack.

When the news went public, the response was immediate. Every WiFi device in the world—every laptop, phone, tablet, IoT sensor, smart thermostat, WiFi-connected camera—was vulnerable. The attack worked against `WPA2`-Personal and `WPA2`-Enterprise alike, on Linux, Android, Windows, macOS, and iOS. Some implementations were worse than others. Android 6.0 and certain Linux distributions, due to a quirk in their wpa_supplicant software, installed an all-zeros key on reinstallation. The encryption became entirely worthless. The bug was in how the client software interpreted the retransmission—it zeroed out key memory before reinstalling, and if the key had not arrived yet, it installed zeros.

Patches rolled out within days. Microsoft, Apple, and Google pushed updates, the WiFi Alliance issued guidance, and network administrators scheduled emergency maintenance windows. Exploiting KRACK still required being within WiFi range, so it could not be run from across the internet; you had to be in the parking lot. What unsettled people was the location of the bug. `WPA2` had been considered secure for over a decade, and the weakness turned out to be in its key management rather than its cryptography. The fault lay in the state machine that

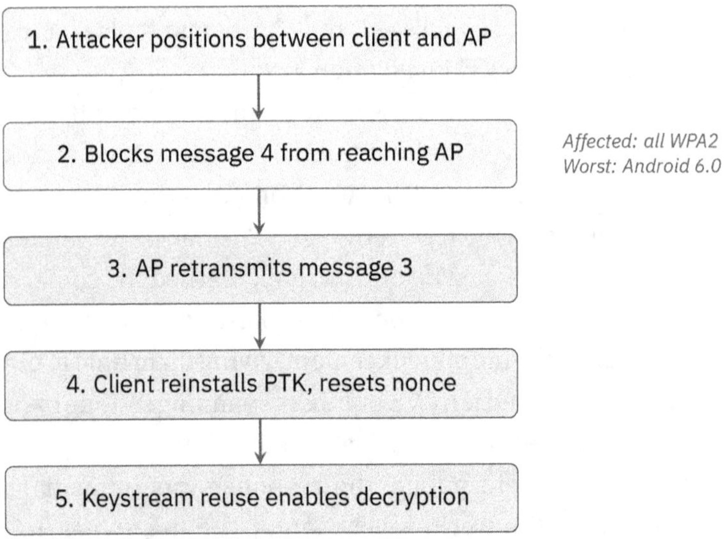

Figure 20.3: KRACK attack exploits the WPA2 four-way handshake state machine. By blocking the client's acknowledgment (message 4), the attacker forces the access point to retransmit message 3, causing the client to reinstall an already-used encryption key — and reset the nonce counter to zero.

managed the handshake, in how software kept track of what step it was on.

WPA3, finalized in 2018[282], addresses KRACK and other weaknesses by replacing the four-way handshake with SAE, or Simultaneous Authentication of Equals[283]. The name carries the difference: both sides prove they know the password at the same time, instead of the access point challenging the client. SAE also provides forward secrecy and resists offline dictionary attacks, so an attacker who captures a handshake and later learns the password still cannot decrypt the traffic it protected. Adoption has been slow. WPA2 devices outnumber WPA3 devices by a wide margin, and many access points still have to support older clients.

Vanhoef was not finished. In 2019, he broke WPA3 with an attack called Dragonblood[284], exploiting flaws in the SAE handshake within months of its release. In 2021, his FragAttacks research[285] revealed something worse: bugs in the original 1997 802.11 specification—design flaws from the very first standard—had persisted through every revision for twenty-four years, unnoticed.

20.3.2. THE ENCRYPTED AIR

Wireless signals respect no perimeter. Anyone within range receives your traffic. The only protection is encryption, and encryption is only as good as its implementation. Each generation of WiFi security has been an attempt to patch a fundamental problem: radio waves go everywhere, and mathematics has to stop everyone who should not be listening.

From Vic Hayes's dream of wireless freedom to Albert Gonzalez's parking lot laptop, faith in the airwaves is faith in mathematics, and mathematics has to be flawless. The cables were never this complicated.

Vic Hayes wanted to eliminate the cable. He succeeded on a scale no one on the committee predicted. The wireless network that started in a Dutch warehouse now blankets the planet, reaching coffee shops, airports, hospitals, and homes, connecting billions of devices that have never touched a wire.

The encryption keeps breaking. WEP was flawed from the start; WPA2 held for over a decade before KRACK opened its handshake, and WPA3 needed patches of its own within a year. The math struggles to keep up because the air will not be contained. Radio waves pass through walls and across property lines, into parking lots where somebody is sitting with a laptop and an antenna.

The waves never stop. They carry everything still.

Copper, fiber, glass, and now the open air—by now the signal travels every way there is. Which is the thing worth stopping to consider: all of it is running at once, everywhere, all the time. Even the network carrying these words to you.

INTERLUDE: RIGHT NOW

Right now, as your eyes move across this page, about 4.2 million emails are changing hands every second, and a million DNS queries are resolving. In the time it took you to read that sentence, 1.2 million TLS handshakes completed and fifteen thousand BGP route updates rippled across the global routing table.[1]

Every one of those events is an act of faith. The mail server accepts the sender's claim; the resolver believes the answer it gets; the browser walks the certificate chain; the router honors the announcement from next door. Each transaction assumes the other party is telling the truth, and most of the time—most emails, most lookups, most certificates, most routes—the assumption holds.

Most.

The design choices of 1969, of 1982, of 1993 are not history. They are executing, this second, on servers manufactured last year, in data

[1] Statistics in this interlude are order-of-magnitude estimates derived from industry reports: the email rate is derived from the Radicati Group's estimate of 361.6 billion messages sent or received per day in 2024[286], DNS query rates from Cloudflare and NS1 analyses[287,288], TLS adoption from Google's Transparency Report[261], and BGP routing data from the CIDR Report and APNIC.[174,289]

centers that did not exist when the specifications were written. The email system Jon Postel designed for colleagues who would never lie carries more than 350 billion messages a day. The phone book Paul Mockapetris sketched for a few thousand hosts answers trillions of queries between one midnight and the next. The routing system that runs on operators telling each other the truth holds a million routes across nearly eighty thousand networks, any one of which could lie.

And it works. Not perfectly, and never for free—the chapters behind you counted the cost breach by breach, from the Morris Worm to DigiNotar—but the system has outlived every betrayal so far. The betrayals are the exceptions. Most people, on any given day, do not attack. The patches accumulate, the defenses improve, the traffic flows.

The internet is not secure. It never was. It was built by people who knew each other, and that trust is now encoded in systems serving five and a half billion strangers[290]: specifications written for four nodes of colleagues, carrying the traffic of half the planet.

Engineers have a phrase for systems that fail well: **graceful degradation**. A well-designed system does not collapse when a component breaks. It limps, reduced but functional, buying time for humans to notice and repair.

The internet is the largest graceful degradation in history. Something is always failing—a root server under attack, a leaked route, a certificate that should never have been issued, a cache quietly poisoned—and the watchers are behind. Thousands of newly reported vulnerabilities wait for someone to analyze them, and one hundred forty-three national CERTs try to keep pace with threats that cross borders in milliseconds.[2] And still the mail arrives and the pages load. Not because a central authority is holding it together—there is none—but because millions of people maintain the routers and the servers and the cables, and answer the incident tickets, and write the patches.

The internet runs on borrowed time, and the loan keeps getting extended.

None of this is an abstraction. The device in your hands depends on it; so does the screen before your eyes, and the wire—or the air—connecting you to these words. Your resolver believed an answer. Your browser walked a chain of certificates back to a root it has never questioned. Your packets took routes you will never see, honored by routers you will never own. You're soaking in it.

The chapters ahead are harder. The attackers are no longer graduate students; they are supply chains and nation-states, and what they target is the infrastructure that keeps water moving and lights on. The premises will be violated at scales the builders never imagined. The machine, so far, keeps running.

As you turn this page, it is running still—and you are part of it.

---

[2] Institutional statistics from the NIST NVD dashboard[291], CISA workforce reports[292], CVE Program funding announcements[293], and FIRST CERT directory.[294]

PART IV

THE RECKONING

CHAPTER 21

THE NEXT GENERATION

This protocol recommendation includes a simplified header
with a hierarchical address structure...
The protocol also includes packet-level authentication and encryption...

—RFC 1752, The Recommendation for the IP Next Generation Protocol, January 1995

21.1. THE WAIST OF THE HOURGLASS

In a borrowed office at Xerox PARC, Steve Deering was plotting a line that curved the wrong way.

It was the early 1990s, and Deering had built his reputation on IP multicast—a way to send one packet to many destinations at once—first in his doctoral work at Stanford, then at PARC.[295] But the graph in front of him had nothing to do with multicast. It counted addresses. The internet was doubling every year, and every machine that joined needed a number of its own. He extended the curve forward and watched it hit a wall.

The wall was a specific number: 4,294,967,296.

That is how many distinct addresses Internet Protocol version 4—IPv4—can name. Every device on a network needs a unique address, for the same reason a house needs a street number: without one, nothing sent to it arrives. IPv4 wrote those addresses as 32-bit numbers. Counted out, 32 bits come to about four billion. Vint Cerf and Bob Kahn had settled on that width in the 1970s, when the whole planet held a few million computers and most of them would never touch a network. Four billion was a joke told against the future. Two decades on it had stopped being funny. Deering was among the first to draw the curve forward and say the year out loud: sometime in the next decade, the internet would run out of room.

Frank Solensky had reached the same conclusion, and in August 1990 he brought it to a room. He was an engineer, and the occasion was the eighteenth meeting of the Internet Engineering Task Force in Vancouver, where he stood up and presented the arithmetic.[296] The Class B address blocks—the useful mid-sized ones—could be gone as early as 1994. The room did the math with him. The internet had been built on the assumption that it would never need this many numbers, and that assumption had four years left.

The obvious fixes were patches: reclaim unused blocks, ration what remained, tighten the rules. Deering wanted to do something that no one had done since the network began. He wanted to replace the foundation.

IPv4 had grown barnacles over fifteen years: optional header fields nobody used, a checksum every router had to recompute, fragmentation rules that caused more trouble than they cured. Around 1992 he began sketching the thing that would scrape all of it off—a new protocol underneath everything, down at the layer every other layer stands on.

Simple Internet Protocol, he called it. The name survived a merger with a competing design and came out one letter longer, SIPP, Simple Internet Protocol Plus, and the adjective was the promise. A header stripped back to essentials would be fast because it was plain.

There was a fight over how big the new address should be. This is the part the legend usually skips. Deering's early SIPP used 64-bit addresses—twice IPv4, and, as the white paper put it, "well matched to the new generation of 64-bit processors."[297] Others wanted variable-length addresses to interoperate with the competing OSI world; others still wanted to keep it small. The number that survived was not a lone visionary's leap but a negotiated settlement. When the IETF's IP-next-generation directors wrote up their recommendation in January 1995, they recorded it in the language of the committee: "a clear majority view emerged that the use of 16 byte fixed length addresses was the best compromise."[298] Sixteen bytes. 128 bits. Even the number chosen to last forever was reached by rough consensus.

And there was one more thing the new protocol would carry that the old one never had: security. The original internet had no encryption and no way to prove a packet came from where it claimed. SIPP folded in IPsec, a set of protocols to authenticate and encrypt at the network layer. Every implementation would be required to support it. Security would be part of the floor, not a product you bought and bolted on.

The IETF ran a contest—SIPP against two rivals, TUBA and CATNIP—and in the summer of 1994, SIPP won, with changes. They renamed it IPv6, skipping version 5, which had already been spent on an experimental streaming protocol that never spread. In December 1995, Deering and Bob Hinden published the first specification as RFC 1883.[299] It read like a statement of faith. IPv6 would end the address famine and leave the routers less to do, and it would secure the network from the ground up. All the world had to do was upgrade every device on Earth.

Deering knew where the difficulty actually lay, and it was not in the specification. He had already designed the mechanisms for getting from one internet to the other—ways to run them side by side, tunneling IPv6 through IPv4 and translating at the seams. Twelve years earlier, on the first day of 1983, the entire ARPANET had switched from its old protocol to TCP/IP in a single coordinated moment its engineers called Flag Day. It was the last time anyone could break everything at once. Afterward the network was too large to reboot, which left Deering offering the world a new floor for a building that could never be evacuated. He guessed the job might take a decade.

He was optimistic by a factor of three.

What actually happened was a hack. Network Address Translation—NAT—let an entire household or company hide behind a single public IPv4 address, thousands of devices sharing one number. It cost something. Every connection that had to cross a NAT picked up delay and complication, and the internet's founding principle, that any machine could speak directly to any other, quietly stopped being true. Network operators took the trade anyway, because NAT was free and it worked. And while it worked, the address crisis that was supposed to force the migration kept sliding into next year. By the late 1990s IPv6 existed and almost no one ran it.

In October 1998, Deering stood in front of a room of network engineers in Austin and drew a picture of the thing he loved.[300] The internet, he said, was shaped like an hourglass. At the top, an ever-widening spread of applications; at the bottom, an ever-widening spread of physical networks; and in the narrow middle, one thin waist through which everything had to pass—the Internet Protocol itself. "The IP layer," he told them, "is the only layer small enough for me to get my arms around." The thin waist was the whole trick. Because everything agreed on that one layer, anything could run over anything.

The next slide had two bulbs where the waist should have been. IPv4 and IPv6 sat side by side, refusing to merge, and Deering had titled it "Mid-Life Crisis." He expected a long doubled coexistence rather than a clean replacement, two internets stacked in the place where there was supposed to be one. The slide was a warning. It covered the next thirty years.

Jim Roskind had a smaller problem and a shorter fuse. The web was too slow.

It was 2012, and Roskind was a principal engineer at Google who had spent a career chasing latency. He had helped build the Netscape browser in the 1990s and tuned performance at company after company. He was staring at charts that would not improve, and the reason was structural. TCP carries almost every web page, and it opens each connection with a handshake: the client says hello, the server says hello back, the client confirms. Three packets before a single byte of content moves. Encrypt the connection and the TLS handshake adds two more round trips. On a phone with a hundred milliseconds of lag, that is half a second of the user staring at nothing.

He wanted those round trips gone, and he knew what stood in the way, because he had watched other people try. TCP lived in the operating systems of billions of machines, and inside the routers and firewalls and middleboxes strung between them. All of those read its headers and expected them to look the way they always had. Changing it meant moving the whole world at once. That is what a Flag Day is, and there would never be another one. IPv6 sat there as the proof: the better protocol, designed by the field's best engineers, stalled for two decades because it asked the network for permission.

So Roskind decided not to ask.

TCP had a plainer neighbor. UDP did no handshake and promised no delivery; a UDP packet was a destination and a payload, and middleboxes waved those through without a second look. A whole new transport could ride on top of that, carrying the intelligence—reliability, encryption, congestion control—inside itself, which put the entire protocol in the hands of whoever shipped it. And it could ship inside a browser that updates itself every six weeks instead of an operating-system update that takes ten years to reach everyone. Roskind's design document was blunt about why he built on UDP rather than something more elegant: "middleboxes and firewalls would typically block or dramatically degrade any transport based on formats other than TCP or UDP," so "we will not even consider revolutionary protocols."[301]

He called it QUIC, later backronymed to Quick UDP Internet Connections. By June 2013, Google was quietly testing it on a slice of Chrome users talking to Google's servers.[302] It folded the connection handshake and the encryption handshake into one, so an encrypted connection opened in a single round trip instead of three or four. For a returning visitor it could open in zero—the first packet already carrying the request. When it worked, it worked measurably: a later study of the internet-scale deployment found QUIC cut Google Search latency by 8 percent on desktop and rebuffering on YouTube by roughly 18 percent.[303]

Deering had tried to move the thin waist of the hourglass, and it would not budge. Roskind left it exactly where it was, built his new protocol in the wide glass above, and dressed it up as ordinary traffic on the way through the narrow middle. The question underneath both projects was the same: how to change an internet that can no longer be rebooted. Deering asked the world for permission and was still waiting thirty years later. Roskind shipped in a browser.

Both answers created new ways to break in.

21.2. TWO INTERNETS, ONE WIRE

After twenty chapters, the stack is familiar: physical links carry signals, IP routes packets across the globe, TCP and UDP carry them the last step to a program. The question here is narrower and harder: what it costs to change one of those layers while five billion people are standing on it.

21.2.1. IPV6: CHANGING THE FLOOR

The address grew from 32 bits to 128. An IPv4 address like `192.168.1.1` is one of four billion, shared out among the whole world. An IPv6 address like `2001:0db8:85a3::8a2e:0370:7334` is drawn from a pool of 340 undecillion—340 followed by thirty-six zeros, a number you can write out but not hold in your head. Sensors, implants, machines not yet imagined: the space will hold them. It is less a bigger number than a decision never to count again.

The header got simpler on purpose. An IPv4 header could run anywhere from 20 to 60 bytes depending on what had been stuffed into it; the IPv6 base header is a fixed 40. A router no longer recomputes a checksum at every hop or fragments packets in transit, and the grab-bag of options is gone. It reads the same 40 bytes and moves on. Anything unusual goes into optional extension headers, chained one behind another after the base, which is where the design planted a seed we will watch grow. A router or firewall is supposed to walk that chain and examine what it finds. But "supposed to" is not "must," and a chain of headers a device does not fully understand is a chain it can be tricked by. The simplicity at the front was paid for out the back.

Security was supposed to come with all this, and `IPsec` was mandatory. The first specifications said so, and as late as 2006 RFC 4294 still insisted that the security architecture "MUST be supported" on every node.[304] Read that as a description rather than a requirement and the ambition is enormous: every packet on Earth authenticated and encrypted, its source impossible to forge, its contents unreadable in transit. It would all happen down at the network layer. It never happened. The cryptography was the part that worked. What did not work was getting two endpoints to agree on keys before either could say a word. The machinery for that was awkward enough that operators rarely set it up. And by then the middle of the network had quietly become a workplace. Firewalls inspected traffic there. `NAT` boxes rewrote addresses, load balancers read packets to pick a server, and encryption at that layer would have put all of them out of a job.

Operators kept the machinery. In 2011 the IETF admitted defeat and rewrote the rule: RFC 6434 downgraded `IPsec` to a "SHOULD."[305] A suggestion is a thing you can decline, and the world declined it. `IPv6` shipped with a vast address space and a clean header, and the security stayed in the document.

21.2.2. QUIC: HIDING IN PLAIN SIGHT

`QUIC` took the opposite lesson from the same history. If security that lives at the network layer needs the whole network's cooperation—and the whole network will never cooperate—then do not live there. Live in the application, where you control both ends, and make cooperation unnecessary by making the network unable to interfere.

The mechanism that makes this work sounds like a privacy feature. It is an engineering one. `QUIC` encrypts not just the contents of a packet but almost all of its own header—the control information a middlebox would need to understand what `QUIC` is doing.

> Jim Roskind --- QUIC Design Document, 2012
>
> "The only way to prevent middleboxes from maligning a new protocol built atop UDP or TCP…is to encrypt as much of the payload and control structure as feasible."

The reasoning goes back to why `IPv6` was so hard to move. Middleboxes ossify: they learn the shape of a protocol, freeze around it, and break whatever deviates, which is why `TCP` can never really change. `QUIC`'s answer is to show them almost nothing, on the theory that what a middlebox cannot read it cannot calcify around. The IETF later wrote down the short list of properties a `QUIC` packet must expose on the wire and left everything else encrypted, so the protocol could keep changing without the network having a say.[306] Speed comes out of that decision. So does resistance to interference, and so does the protocol's ability to change from inside the application.

It also gets a side effect the designers understood perfectly: a network that cannot read `QUIC` to interfere with it also cannot read `QUIC` to protect anyone using it. Your ISP goes blind. So does everyone else watching the wire, whatever their reason for watching.

`IPv6` assumed the network would eventually adopt what was better, and waited. `QUIC` assumed the network would never change, and hid from it.

`IPv6` did not wait politely offstage while the world debated adoption. Every modern operating system—every copy of Windows since Vista, every Mac, every phone—ships with `IPv6` switched on and, given the choice, prefers it. On a network the administrator believes is IPv4-only, the machines are already speaking IPv6, asking anyone who will listen how to configure themselves. Every network in the world is quietly running two internets. Most administrators have configured only one.

21.3. THE INTERNET NOBODY TURNED ON

In early 2018, Dirk-jan Mollema, a penetration tester at the Dutch security firm Fox-IT, sat down on a client's corporate network with a plan that should not have worked. The company ran IPv4. Its firewalls filtered IPv4 and its monitoring watched IPv4; its administrators would have told you, correctly, that they had never deployed IPv6. Mollema was about to take over its Windows domain by speaking a language they were sure nobody on the network spoke.[307]

The trick was that the network was speaking it already. As Mollema put it plainly, "all Windows versions since Windows Vista...have IPv6 enabled and prefer it over IPv4." Every Windows machine in the building was periodically broadcasting a request for IPv6 configuration—a DHCPv6 solicitation—into a void that had never answered. Mollema answered. His tool, `mitm6`, replied to each request, handed the machines an IPv6 address, and named itself their DNS server. Because the machines preferred IPv6, they preferred his answers. In one move he had become the network's phonebook without touching its real one.

From there the dominoes fell in seconds. As the network's DNS, Mollema answered a query every Windows machine makes on its own—the lookup for WPAD, the Web Proxy Auto-Discovery address—and pointed it at a proxy he controlled. When a machine's software dutifully authenticated to that proxy, it handed over a Windows credential handshake, which a companion tool relayed, live, to the company's Active Directory server. A relayed credential is a valid credential. Minutes after plugging in, Mollema could create accounts and read the directory that governed every login in the building. When he stopped the tool, the phantom internet evaporated, leaving the administrators exactly where they started: certain they did not run `IPv6`.

The attack did not exploit a bug in `IPv6`. It exploited the fact that `IPv6` was on when everyone believed it was off—the seam between the two internets Deering had drawn on his "Mid-Life Crisis" slide twenty years before.

`mitm6` was one attack along that seam, and the seam runs the whole length of the transition. Neighbor Discovery, the `IPv6` mechanism that lets a machine configure itself by trusting Router Advertisements on the local wire, inherited the oldest weakness in networking: it believes whoever speaks first. Marc Heuse's THC-IPv6 toolkit includes a program that floods a segment with forged advertisements. Windows machines trust each one. They grind to a halt trying to obey them all.[308] It is the same lie `ARP` spoofing told in the earliest chapters of this book, moved into a newer protocol.

Transition tunnels made it worse. `Teredo` and mechanisms like it carried `IPv6` inside `IPv4` packets, straight through firewalls that inspected only `IPv4`, opening a door in a wall the administrators thought was solid.[309] Then there were the extension headers, the complexity `IPv6` had pushed out the back of its clean front header. They turned out to be exactly the parsing minefield the design implied. In 2012 the researcher Antonios Atlasis showed at Black Hat that crafted chains of extension headers slipped past firewalls and intrusion detectors that could not agree on how to read them.[310] All of it ran unwatched, on networks whose defenders were guarding the other internet.

QUIC's trouble is the mirror image of IPv6's, and it comes from the same source as its strength. Opacity does not choose sides. The encryption that keeps a middlebox from meddling also keeps a corporate firewall from inspecting for malware, and leaves an intrusion detector with a connection it cannot read at all. To QUIC a defender and a meddler are the same shape. Some enterprises answered the only way available to them and blocked QUIC outright: filtering UDP on port 443 forces the browser back onto TCP, where the inspection tools can still see. Vendors now publish that blocking as routine security guidance.[311] The protocol built to slip through networks gets stopped by policy instead.

And its fastest feature carries its own hazard. The zero-round-trip mode that lets a returning visitor send a request in the very first packet also lets an attacker capture that packet and send it again. The standard says so in plain words—0-RTT data "can be replayed by an attacker," so it must never carry an instruction that would do harm if it ran twice.[312] The warning is printed in the specification. Applications ignore warnings.

IPv6 and QUIC reached the same flaw from opposite directions. IPv6 tried to change the foundation and left a seam, decades long, where the old internet and the new one overlap—and attackers live in the seam. QUIC refused to touch the foundation, sealed itself off above it, and locked the people paid to watch the network outside along with everyone else. Neither could do the clean thing and simply replace what came before. That has not been possible since 1983. The internet is something you build on top of now, and every new layer is one more place to hide.

The addresses will not run out.

The crisis Deering charted at PARC arrived on schedule. In February 2011 the last great blocks of IPv4 were handed out and the registries began rationing. The internet did not stop. NAT had bought the time, and IPv6 spent the next fifteen years slowly coming into use. In April 2026, for the first time, more than half the traffic reaching Google came over IPv6.[313] The protocol Deering began sketching in 1992 is the majority now—thirty-four years late, running on devices he could not have pictured. It outlived the very address famine that was meant to force it into existence within a decade.

He had feared the thin waist of the hourglass was being lost, split into two bulbs that would never merge. He was right. It was split, and it stayed split, and the network kept passing traffic through the doubled middle anyway—two internets braided together on the same wire, plus a transport protocol hiding inside another one, the whole improbable stack negotiating itself into working order billions of times a second. The words on this page may have reached you over IPv6, wrapped in a QUIC packet, and you would have no way of knowing. That was always the design.

And yet the attackers had already moved on. While the engineers spent three decades securing the protocols one seam and one handshake at a time, someone found a shorter path—one that skips the specifications entirely. Do not break the internet's protocols. Compromise the source of its software, and let the infrastructure deliver the payload itself.

CHAPTER 22

THE CONVERGENCE

We are witnessing an attack
by a nation with top-tier offensive capabilities.

— Kevin Mandia, FireEye CEO, December 8, 2020

22.1. THE FIRM THAT GOT ROBBED

On December 8, 2020, the company that catches other companies' hackers announced that it had been hacked.

FireEye was not an ordinary victim. For years its investigators had been the people you called after the worst had already happened. They traced nation-state intrusions and wrote the field manuals other responders followed. They also kept a private arsenal of red-team tools, built to break into their own clients' networks so the clients could learn where they were weak. Now someone had walked off with that arsenal. Kevin Mandia, the CEO, told the world it was a government. "This was not a drive-by shooting on the information highway," he said a few days later. "This was a sniper round from somebody a mile away from your house."[314]

The obvious question was how. FireEye's analysts turned the question on themselves, and the answer did not come from any of the places they were paid to watch. The attackers had not cracked a password, forged a certificate, or slipped through a firewall. They had come in through an update.

Five days later, on December 13, FireEye named the source, and it was a piece of software almost no one outside a server room had ever heard of: SolarWinds Orion, a network-monitoring platform.[126] The same day, the first federal victims surfaced—the Treasury Department, the Commerce Department—and the government ordered every civilian agency to pull Orion off its networks by noon the next day.[127] FireEye ran Orion. So did the Pentagon, the State Department, the nuclear-weapons agency, and a long list of the companies that build the internet. Every one of them had installed a routine software update, signed and verified, that carried a back door inside it.

This is a trust none of the previous chapters touched. DNS tries to verify the answer; TLS tries to verify the server; BGP at least pretends to verify the route. None of them checks the software already running on your own computer. That trust—that the program is what it says it is, that the update came from the vendor and no one touched it on the way—sits underneath all the others, and there is no handshake for it. You just believe.

Ten years earlier, a different kind of code had shown what was possible—and how hard the last step used to be.

In 2010, a worm called Stuxnet tore apart roughly a thousand of the nine thousand centrifuges spinning uranium at Iran's Natanz enrichment plant.[315] It was, by every later account, a joint American and Israeli operation, and it did something militaries had only theorized:

software reached across the world and destroyed physical machinery. But Natanz was air-gapped—no wire connected it to the internet—and so the weapon faced a problem no amount of code could solve. Someone had to carry it across the gap by hand. A 2024 Dutch investigation identified the man as Erik van Sabben, an engineer recruited by Dutch intelligence, who reportedly walked the malware into the facility inside the equipment he was there to install.[316,317] He died in a motorcycle crash months later, at thirty-six.

That was the state of the art in 2010: to cross one trusted boundary, a superpower needed a human being willing to risk his life. Stuxnet is remembered as the first true digital weapon, but the lesson buried inside it is quieter. The hard part was never writing the code. The hard part was delivery. What SolarWinds proved, a decade on, is that the delivery problem had solved itself. No agent, no USB drive, no air gap crossed by hand. The attackers poisoned one update at one vendor, and eighteen thousand organizations reached out and carried it across their own boundaries, automatically, believing the whole time that they were doing routine maintenance. The trusted software supply chain is an air gap that opens itself.

22.2. THE TRUST WITH NO PROTOCOL

Everything this book has described stacks into a single tower. When you open a web page, the request falls through every layer of it—and every layer takes the one beneath it on faith.

For decades the reassuring idea was defense in depth: one layer fails and the next one catches it. A poisoned DNS answer would run into certificate checking at TLS, and a hijacked route would still land

Table 22.1: The Trust Stack

Layer	Protocol	Trust Assumption
Application	HTTP/HTTPS (Ch. 18)	Server is legitimate
Security	TLS (Ch. 19)	CAs are trustworthy
Resolution	DNS (Ch. 7)	Responses aren't poisoned
Transport	TCP (Ch. 4)	Handshake equals identity
Network	IP (Ch. 4)	Source addresses are honest
Link	ARP/Ethernet (Ch. 5)	Neighbors don't lie

on an encrypted connection. Stack enough independent barriers, the theory went, and no single failure gets all the way through.

The SolarWinds attackers did not fail at any layer. They stood outside the stack. Every barrier in that table checks something about the party at the far end of the wire, and the attackers were not at the far end of the wire—they were already inside the building, running as trusted software the defenders had installed themselves. TLS encrypts the pipe between two machines; it cannot tell you the machine on your own desk is honest. That is the gap the whole tower is built over, and nothing in it looks down.

What fills the gap is the software supply chain, and the supply chain runs on transitive trust. You rely on your vendor. Your vendor relies on its build system. The build system relies on the developers' laptops, and the laptops on an operating system, and the code on a hundred open-source libraries pulled in automatically, each maintained by someone you will never meet.

Eight dependencies for a trivial program, and each is a decision to trust. You did not install most of them; the ones you installed installed the rest. One stolen credential or one malicious pull request, and the poison arrives through the same channel as every honest update: signed, verified, routine.

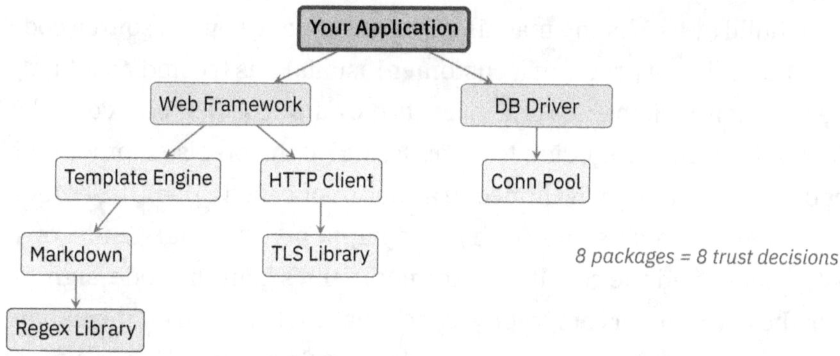

Figure 22.1: Software dependency tree. Each package represents a trust decision you inherit.

The last twist is the cruelest, and SolarWinds Orion sat exactly on it. A monitoring tool cannot watch a network without the keys to all of it—credentials for every server and router and device it is meant to observe. Compromise the tool and every door opens at once, while the guard hired to watch them goes blind. The attackers came in through the security camera.

22.3. ANATOMY OF A SIGNED LIE

The break-in had begun more than a year before FireEye noticed anything. In September 2019—and by the company's own later admission, perhaps months earlier still—the attackers quietly let themselves into SolarWinds' development environment and did nothing loud.[318] They studied how Orion was built. Then they planted a tool that CrowdStrike investigators would later name SUNSPOT, whose only purpose was to sit inside the build process and wait.[319]

A build system is the machine that turns a developer's source code into the finished program a customer installs. It is trusted absolutely, because it is invisible: no one inspects the output of their own compiler. SUNSPOT waited for Orion to compile, and at the precise moment the code passed through, it slipped in a back door called SUNBURST—then let the build finish as if nothing had happened.[320] SolarWinds' own systems signed the result with the company's genuine code-signing certificate. Every cryptographic check that could be run on the update passed, because the update really was from SolarWinds. It was simply also a weapon.

The poisoned versions shipped between March and June 2020. Roughly eighteen thousand organizations downloaded and installed them.[321] The list read like a directory of everything that matters: the Treasury, Commerce, State, Homeland Security, and Energy departments—including the National Nuclear Security Administration—alongside Microsoft, Intel, Cisco, and hundreds of other agencies and Fortune 500 firms.[127] The United States would formally attribute the operation, in April 2021, to APT29, or Cozy Bear—the hacking arm of Russia's SVR foreign intelligence service.[322]

What makes the attack worth studying is the patience. SUNBURST did not fire when it landed. It sat dormant for up to two weeks, verifying it had not been dropped into a researcher's sandbox, and only then reached out to its controllers—through domain names its own code generated, disguised as the ordinary telemetry Orion sends home anyway.[323] Of those eighteen thousand, the attackers went deeper into fewer than a hundred. They looked at each victim's domains and network, decided whether the risk was worth it, and ignored anything that was merely a company. They wanted governments and the firms that armed them.

The tradecraft, once they committed, was the work of professionals who understood the defenders better than the defenders understood themselves. Their traffic ran through servers in the victim's own country so it would look local. They mimicked the behavior of legitimate administrators, avoided the actions that write to logs, and stayed away from any machine running security software that might recognize them.

Testifying before the House in February 2021, Mandia did not reach for understatement. "So this was the varsity team on offense," he said. If a company had locked its doors and its windows, this was "the special ops robbing the house, not some average criminal just trying to shake the doorknobs."[324] Microsoft's president, Brad Smith, went further, calling it on television "the largest and most sophisticated attack the world has ever seen," and estimating that more than a thousand engineers had worked on it.[325]

At the same hearing came a smaller, more human note. Investigators had earlier found that an update server at the company had been left behind a password—`solarwinds123`—the sort a bored teenager would crack. It was not how SUNBURST got in, but it captured the distance between the two sides. "I've got a stronger password than `solarwinds123`," Representative Katie Porter told a former SolarWinds chief, "to stop my kids from watching too much YouTube on their iPad."[326] The company said an intern had set it. On one side, the varsity team, a thousand engineers, a foreign intelligence service. On the other, the ordinary human sloppiness that the whole edifice of trust quietly runs on.

The company's official account of all this, filed with the SEC on December 14, was written in a different language entirely. The update, it said, "could potentially allow an attacker to compromise the server on which the Orion products run."[321] The gap between "varsity team" and "could potentially" is the gap between what a breach is and what a corporation is willing to say it is.

Everything converged in this one attack. Every trust assumption we have traced was present in SolarWinds, and the attackers broke none of them. They became the signed code that TLS faithfully delivered, the trusted update the monitoring tool obediently ran. They did not defeat the stack. They wore it.

The official response, when it came, was an admission dressed as a policy. In May 2021 the White House issued an executive order: vendors that sell to the government must ship a software bill of materials, an ingredient label for code. The order also pushed "zero trust," an architecture whose founding premise is that nothing on the network, no user and no program, is trusted by default.[327] It is sensible. But the old arrangement—rely on your vendors, accept your updates, trust your tools—had been the architecture of the internet since the beginning, and it no longer held.

There is one more supply chain, and it is the one that tells everyone else what to fear.

Since 1999, a nonprofit called MITRE has run the Common Vulnerabilities and Exposures program, which assigns every known security flaw a single identifier. A defender in Ohio and a vendor in Berlin can be certain they are talking about the same bug. It is the shared language underneath every patch. In April 2025, its funding nearly stopped. The government contract that pays for it was set to lapse on the sixteenth, and the Cybersecurity and Infrastructure Security Agency—CISA—renewed it only the night before, hours from the deadline.[328] Jen Easterly, who had run CISA until that January, said losing the program would be "like tearing out the card catalog from every library at once."[329]

The near-miss was not an isolated accident. By that summer roughly a thousand people had left CISA, cutting the agency by nearly a third.[292] The backlog of vulnerabilities waiting to be analyzed at the national database climbed past twenty-seven thousand. In April 2026 the government gave up on keeping current and restricted full analysis to flaws already being exploited or present in federal software.[330] The institution meant to catalog the danger could no longer keep pace with it.

The irony has a shape. SolarWinds was a supply-chain attack on code; the vulnerability catalog is a supply chain of knowledge about attacks. Both depend on the same fragile assumption: that somewhere, someone is funded and staffed and awake, maintaining the infrastructure everyone else takes for granted. And the vendor at the center of it all never quite left the story: seven SolarWinds flaws now sit in the government's catalog of actively exploited bugs—including, in one product, a password hard-coded straight into the source.[331] Four years after SUNBURST, the company whose name became a synonym for supply-chain catastrophe had repeated the elementary mistake of `solarwinds123`.

The infrastructure was never designed for this.

The routing protocols were built for a research network. The certificate system was built for selling books. The monitoring tools were built to keep servers running, not to survive an adversary who would target them precisely because everyone trusted them. No one sat down and designed a system that could carry billions of people through nation-state campaigns and ransomware and poisoned updates. What we have is the sum of ten thousand reasonable decisions, each sound on the day it was made, each now holding up weight its authors never imagined.

And it holds because people keep showing up. A router drops its session at three in the morning, and someone is awake to patch it. Somebody answers the incident ticket on a Sunday. A back door does not ship because a maintainer reads the pull request line by line and sees what is sitting in it. The maintainers are underpaid and mostly invisible, and they did not design the cathedral or get their names carved anywhere on it. They are the crew that keeps it standing, watching for cracks and deciding each morning that the work is worth doing.

The catalog keeps cataloging. The IETF still meets, still argues, still reaches rough consensus and ships running code. The protocols built for a room full of colleagues now carry the traffic of five billion strangers—and the strangers, almost all of them, almost all the time, do not attack. That is the whole secret, and it has to be enough.

SUNBURST took a state intelligence service, a compromised build system, and nine months of patience. The last agreement in this book had no defenses to breach at all—no signatures, no certificates, nothing but thirty years of everyone choosing to keep it.

CHAPTER 23

THE HONOR SYSTEM

The Robots Exclusion Protocol
is not a substitute for valid content security measures.
Listing paths in the robots.txt file exposes them publicly
and thus makes the paths discoverable.

— RFC 9309, Martijn Koster et al., 2022

23.1. KOSTER'S PROPOSAL

The newest trust assumption to fail is the oldest in spirit. No exploits required. No code signing to forge. Just a plain text file that says "please don't"—and a world that stopped listening.

Martijn Koster stared at his server logs and watched his machine die.

It was September 1993. Something was crawling through his website at Nexor in Nottingham, England. The requests came in bursts, one per second, following hyperlinks with mechanical persistence. Koster's Perl-based web server couldn't keep up. Response times climbed. Other users waited. The logs showed the same pattern: a program from MIT, methodically downloading every page it could find.

The program was called the World Wide Web Wanderer. Matthew Gray, an undergraduate physics student at MIT, had created the web's first autonomous crawler to answer a simple question: how big was the web?[332] The Wanderer visited sites, recorded pages, and followed links. Its published counts identified 130 websites in June 1993 and 623 that December.[224]

The Wanderer wasn't malicious, and its data was valuable. But early versions had a flaw: they didn't know when to stop. The Wanderer returned to the same sites again and again, re-requesting pages it had already catalogued. Gray's curiosity was overwhelming Koster's infrastructure.

Koster wasn't alone. Across the young web, server administrators were discovering the same problem. The Wanderer had company: WebCrawler, the World Wide Web Worm, JumpStation, and a growing population of automated agents that followed links without asking permission. Among the programs hammering Koster's server was one run by Charles Stross, a programmer already writing the science fiction that would later make him famous. Each crawler served a purpose; each consumed resources. And server operators couldn't refuse.

Koster understood the problem better than most: besides running a web server, he was building an early search engine. ALIWEB, which he announced in November 1993[333], took a different approach: instead of visiting every site automatically, it asked webmasters to submit descriptions of their content, and it indexed only what they chose to share.

The approach was elegant but doomed. Webmasters didn't want to maintain submission files. They wanted to be discovered automatically. The crawlers won because crawlers did the work. But ALIWEB's philosophy stuck with Koster: webmasters should have some control over what robots accessed.

In February 1994, Koster—who had been collecting information about active robots and their behavior—posted a proposal to the www-talk mailing list. Early drafts bore a blunter name, `RobotsNotWanted.txt`, a nod to Stross's runaway crawler, before he settled on "A Standard for Robot Exclusion."

The idea: place a text file at the root of your website, under a predictable name. Call it `robots.txt`. List the areas you don't want robots to access. Any well-behaved crawler would check for the file before visiting and respect what it found.

The format was deliberately minimal:

```
User-agent: *
Disallow: /cgi-bin/
Disallow: /private/
Disallow: /tmp/
```

Anyone with a text editor could create one. Any programmer could parse it. No special software, no protocol extensions, no authentication.

Koster's approach mirrored Steve Crocker's RFC 1 twenty-five years earlier. Both men faced the same problem: coordinating a community without central authority. Crocker, the graduate student in Chapter 1, had titled his document "Request for Comments" rather than "Specification" because he didn't want to seem presumptuous. Koster called his proposal "a convention, not a standard" for the same reason. Both built infrastructure that outlasted the community that created it.

The responses came quickly. The web in 1994 was small enough that most of the people building it had met at conferences, or knew someone who had. Tim Berners-Lee, the web's inventor, participated in the discussion. So did Brian Pinkerton, creator of WebCrawler, and other crawler authors who recognized that their programs were causing problems.

By June 1994, Koster published the finished document.[334] Not a standard in any formal sense—no working group had debated it, no committee had approved it. Just a proposal that solved a problem everyone shared.

The crawler authors adopted it—they had no reason not to. Respecting `robots.txt` cost almost nothing; ignoring it earned blocked IP addresses and angry emails. A crawler that deliberately violated it would be named and shamed.

By July, most active robots supported the convention or had promised to. WebCrawler checked for `robots.txt`, Lycos checked, and AltaVista, when it launched in December 1995[335], checked from the beginning. Google would check too.

Koster had created something rare: a protocol with zero enforcement that would govern the relationship between websites and automated agents for nearly three decades. No one was forced to respect `robots.txt`. Everyone chose to.

The web grew past hundreds of thousands of sites by 1996 and into the millions by 2000. Search engines became essential infrastructure somewhere in there, helped along by Google's PageRank, which ranked a page by the links pointing at it and turned search from a curiosity into a necessity. Through all of it, `robots.txt` endured.

It held because the incentives aligned. Search engines needed good relationships with the sites they indexed; publishers needed search to drive traffic. Everyone had something to lose by breaking the agreement.

Attempts to formalize `robots.txt` as a proper internet standard came and went—proposals circulated through the Internet Engineering Task Force in 1996, again in 2007, again in 2019, but none achieved consensus. The convention worked fine without a standard.

The standard finally arrived in 2022, twenty-eight years after Koster's proposal, when `robots.txt` became RFC 9309.[336] Koster was listed as first author, joined by three engineers from Google. The document formalized what everyone already knew: the syntax, the semantics, the expected behavior.

But by the time the standard was published, the social contract was already dissolving.

23.2. POLITE REQUESTS

23.2.1. HOW ROBOTS.TXT WORKS

Think of `robots.txt` as a sign on your front lawn that says "Please don't walk on the grass." Polite people respect it. Nothing stops anyone from ignoring it. The request works only because most people are polite.

When a crawler visits your website, it first requests a specific file: `/robots.txt`, located at the root. If the file exists, the crawler reads it, and if it contains instructions, the crawler follows them.

Nothing in the protocol forces it to. Nothing verifies its identity. The crawler announces who it is; you believe it, or you don't, and either way you can't stop it from looking.

The format is simple enough that anyone can read it—and that's the problem. Each entry names a crawler and lists paths it shouldn't access:

```
User-agent: Googlebot
Disallow: /admin/
Disallow: /private/
Disallow: /tmp/

User-agent: *
Disallow: /cgi-bin/
```

The asterisk is a wildcard, meaning "all crawlers." Specific entries override the wildcard. In this example, Google's crawler is blocked from `/admin/`, `/private/`, and `/tmp/`. All other crawlers are blocked only from `/cgi-bin/`.

What if you want to allow one file in a blocked directory? RFC 9309 added an Allow directive:

```
User-agent: *
Disallow: /directory/
Allow: /directory/public.html
```

This blocks everything under `/directory/` except `public.html`—the most specific rule wins, and Allow takes precedence when specificity is equal.

The logic presumes a crawler parsing your file in good faith. Nothing enforces that. A crawler can impersonate Googlebot or pose as a browser, and most servers never check. The file is advisory—a preference, not a permission.

Worse: the `robots.txt` file itself is public. Listing `/secret-project/` in your Disallow rules advertises that `/secret-project/` exists. You've drawn a map and labeled the treasure.

Courts have sometimes considered `robots.txt` when evaluating unauthorized access claims, but the file creates no enforceable rights. RFC 9309 is blunt about this: the protocol cannot replace actual security.

Like SMTP, the email protocol from Chapter 6, `robots.txt` accepts an unverified header—the User-Agent string here, the From address there. Both were designed for neighborhoods where lying carried social costs, and both broke when the neighborhood became the world.

The good faith survived anyway. Scrapers that ignored `robots.txt`, or lied about their identity, were around the whole time, but Google, Bing, Yahoo, and DuckDuckGo read the file and obeyed it. Their businesses depended on staying welcome.

Publishers had a second defense, one that worked page by page rather than directory by directory:

```
<meta name="robots" content="noindex, nofollow">
```

The robots META tag sits inside a page's HTML, where `noindex` means "don't remember this page exists" and `nofollow` means "don't follow links from here to anywhere else." Publishers who wanted belt-and-suspenders protection would use both: `robots.txt` to block crawling at the gate, META tags to catch anything that slipped through.

Neither mechanism has teeth. The tag is a whisper in the ear of a machine that may not be listening.

By 2020, Googlebot handled most of the web's indexing. The specialty crawlers worked underneath it, run by SEO tools and archive services and academic researchers. Every one of them identified itself in a User-Agent string—a text label included with every HTTP request—and the crawlers that wanted to be treated as legitimate used their real names. Googlebot announced itself as Googlebot, Bingbot as Bingbot, and publishers who wanted indexing let them through.

The arrangement held because the stakes were manageable—indexing cost a publisher something, but not much, and no search engine would risk its reputation over one site's content.

Then the stakes changed.

23.3. THE MACHINES STOPPED ASKING

Training GPT-3 required about 300 billion tokens of text. GPT-4 likely required far more. No one knows the exact numbers—OpenAI hasn't published them. But training a large language model demands a corpus of human writing larger than any ever assembled. The obvious source was the web itself.

The web in 2020 contained over a billion websites and trillions of pages. Much was freely accessible. Much was protected by `robots.txt`. For decades, the distinction had been clear: if you blocked a crawler, it wouldn't access your content.

AI companies had different priorities.

The training data for early language models came from Common Crawl[337], a nonprofit foundation that had been archiving the web since 2008. Common Crawl operated CCBot, a crawler that respected `robots.txt`, and made its archives freely available. The corpus was vast but imperfect, shaped by whatever sites CCBot could access.

OpenAI, Anthropic, Google, and others scraped the web directly. They built custom crawlers and assembled training sets bigger than anything that had come before. Some of this scraping respected `robots.txt`; some didn't. The details remain murky because the companies didn't disclose them.

By the time publishers realized what was happening, the moment had passed. The training data had been collected. The models had been trained. ChatGPT launched in November 2022[338] and became the fastest-growing consumer application in history.[339] The content that powered it was already inside.

OpenAI eventually named its crawler—GPTBot—and told publishers how to block it:[340]

```
User-agent: GPTBot
Disallow: /
```

The response was immediate. Within weeks, Amazon, The New York Times, CNN, and Wikihow had blocked the crawler. By November, roughly a quarter of the top 1,000 websites had opted out—a share that would climb past a third over the following year. The trust was draining away in real time.

But opting out of future crawling couldn't undo past crawling. GPT-4 had shipped; ChatGPT was live. OpenAI was handing out locks after the house had been emptied.

Google followed with Google-Extended[341], a standalone `robots.txt` product token rather than a separate crawler identity. Publishers could use it to restrict Google's use of crawled content for Gemini while still allowing Googlebot for search indexing. Anthropic documented its crawlers. Meta announced Meta-ExternalAgent. Each company created its own opt-out mechanism.

Publishers scrambled to keep up. Every company's crawler identity or `robots.txt` product token had to be blocked by name, in its own directive group, and the roll call kept growing: GPTBot, Google-Extended, CCBot, ClaudeBot, anthropic-ai, Claude-Web, PerplexityBot, Bytespider, Meta-ExternalAgent. Koster had designed the file to be simple. It was becoming a catalog of denial.

The New York Times had invested heavily in digital journalism. Its reporting required months of investigation, teams of reporters, legal review, fact-checking. The resulting articles sat behind a paywall, generating subscription revenue that funded the next investigation.

In December 2023, the Times sued OpenAI and Microsoft for copyright infringement.[342] The lawsuit alleged that OpenAI had used Times content without permission, that ChatGPT could reproduce substantial portions of articles verbatim, and that AI products let users bypass the paywall.

The filing included examples. Prompts caused ChatGPT to output paragraphs matching Times articles word for word. Responses reproduced investigative journalism, recipes, opinion columns. The model had memorized parts of its training data—and some of that data was copyrighted content.

The Times had blocked GPTBot, but the training data was already inside the model.

OpenAI's defense centered on fair use. Like Google's book-scanning project before it, the company argued, AI training was a new kind of use that copyright law should accommodate. Training a model wasn't copying in the traditional sense: a model learns patterns rather than storing text, and the output transforms the input past recognition.

The case remains unresolved. In 2025, the court largely rejected OpenAI's motion to dismiss, and the core copyright claims went forward. Similar suits piled up behind it: authors who found book excerpts in training data, artists whose work had trained image generators, publishers whose archives had been scraped.

The legal questions are genuinely difficult: Does training constitute copying? Nobody can even agree on what "reproduce" means when the output emerges from billions of parameters rather than a stored file.

But the `robots.txt` question is simpler: publishers said no, and AI companies scraped anyway.

In June 2024, journalists at WIRED[343] and independent researcher Robb Knight[344] exposed something worse. Perplexity AI, a search startup valued at roughly three billion dollars, was circumventing `robots.txt`.

The pattern was easy enough to see once someone looked. Publishers had blocked PerplexityBot in their `robots.txt` files, and their content kept appearing in Perplexity's responses regardless. The requests fetching it carried standard browser User-Agent strings, claiming to be Chrome on Windows rather than any kind of bot, and they reached content that PerplexityBot was blocked from.

Perplexity's published crawler addresses were easy to block. An unlisted machine on a commercial cloud fetched the pages anyway. The sign on the lawn had not come down. Based on the investigation's findings, Perplexity had simply arrived dressed as someone the sign did not apply to.

Cloudflare, which sits in front of millions of websites, de-listed Perplexity as a verified bot, published a blog post documenting the violations, and updated its systems to detect the stealth crawlers.[345]

Perplexity's CEO responded[346]: "The Robots Exclusion Protocol is not a legal framework." He was right. It never was. That was the whole point.

A handshake among colleagues, nothing more. The AI gold rush ended the era of handshakes: training data became worth billions of dollars, and first-mover advantage in language models translated to market dominance.

RFC 9309 contains a section called "Security Considerations." It's brief. The protocol, it notes, provides no access control. Listing paths in the file makes them publicly discoverable. The mechanism is advisory only.

The section doesn't mention AI. It was written before the training data wars, before the lawsuits, before the collapse of the social contract it documents. RFC 9309 describes a protocol built on voluntary compliance at the moment compliance was becoming optional.

What changed wasn't the technology. The syntax of `robots.txt` in 2024 is nearly identical to Koster's 1994 proposal. What changed was the value of the content. When crawling a site meant indexing it for search, the value was modest and shared—publishers got traffic, search engines got content, and each side needed the other to come back tomorrow. That mutual dependence was the whole enforcement mechanism. A search engine that ignored the rules got blocked; a publisher that blocked everyone vanished from search. Neither could afford to defect.

Training a model dissolves that symmetry. An AI company needs the content once. Train on it, and the model holds it forever—embedded, transformed, unreachable, with no traffic to send back and no reason to return. There is nothing left to withhold, so there is nothing left to bargain with. The honor system had always run on mutual need. AI kept the need and discarded the mutual.

New protocols are emerging. TDMRep[347], the Text and Data Mining Reservation Protocol, lets publishers express rights reservations in machine-readable form. In Europe, the AI Act now requires providers of general-purpose models to identify and honor those rights reservations.[348]

None solve the fundamental problem. Technical opt-outs work only when everyone respects them; legal frameworks work only when courts can reach across borders. The web still has no central authority.

And the money now runs one way: the companies doing the scraping are worth hundreds of billions, while the journalism they harvest is funded by the very readers the scraping draws away.

Martijn Koster, the Dutch engineer who proposed `robots.txt` from his office in Nottingham, saw it become RFC 9309 in 2022: a formal standard for a social norm that had governed the web for a generation.

The web was built on trust. `robots.txt` is that trust made visible, a plain text file that works only because everyone agrees it should. For twenty-eight years, they agreed. The honor system held.

Then the AI companies came, and asking stopped working.

The lawsuits grind on. Rate limiting, fingerprinting, blocked IP ranges: the web fights back with what it has, haltingly and imperfectly. And some crawlers keep obeying. Googlebot respects the rules, and the infrastructure of search—billions of pages indexed, trillions of links followed—rests on a convention Koster wrote thirty years ago.

Most websites still have a `robots.txt` file. They still specify which crawlers are welcome. They still believe—despite everything—that declaring their preferences matters.

You are reading these words because someone wrote them. The writing took time, research, care. Somewhere, right now, a crawler is deciding whether to index this page. Somewhere, a model is being trained on text scraped from a site that asked not to be scraped. The outcome—multiplied across billions of pages, trillions of requests—will shape what the web becomes.

Every protocol in this book was designed by people who knew each other. They expected their users to be colleagues. Those expectations became vulnerabilities when strangers arrived. You are not a stranger to this moment. You are inside it.

The honor system is breaking. What replaces it depends on choices being made now—by engineers, by courts, by companies, by us.

Martijn Koster put a sign on his lawn in 1994. The sign still stands. Whether it means anything is the question this book cannot answer.

That's up to you.

EPILOGUE: LO AND BEHOLD

That question is not only yours.

To understand what we're choosing, return to where it started.

Boelter Hall is still there, on the UCLA campus. Room 3420 is an ordinary laboratory now, indistinguishable from a hundred others in the building. The IMP is gone, shipped to the Smithsonian decades ago. The Model 33 Teletype is gone. The cables that once connected this room to Menlo Park are gone.

Steve Crocker was a UCLA graduate student when he wrote RFC 1, organized the Network Working Group, and started the RFC series.[4,349] The network he helped build now struggles with problems that did not exist in 1969. No single person holds formal authority over the internet's technical direction. No one ever has.

In October 1969, Charley Kline sat in this room and typed `L-O-G`.[350] The system crashed after two letters. The first message on the ARPANET was `LO`.

The graduate students were solving a practical problem: how to share expensive computers across research labs. The assumptions they made—trust the sender, believe the address, accept the packet—were right for the problem they faced. Fifty-five years later, a text file asking crawlers to stay away would fail for the same reason: it assumed everyone was playing by the same rules.

Because anyone could participate, anyone did. The network grew from four nodes to five billion users. The colleagues who fit around a conference table became anonymous strangers, state actors, criminal syndicates. The intimacy that made openness safe disappeared—but the openness remained.

And yet.

The costs are real, and they keep mounting.

The Morris Worm choked the network in 1988.[10] DigiNotar's compromised certificates enabled surveillance of Iranian dissidents.[351] SolarWinds delivered malware through the software supply chain itself.[126] And now the AI training data wars—content scraped from sites that asked not to be scraped.

Business email compromise drains billions of dollars a year.[352] Ransomware encrypts hospitals. Botnets control millions of infected machines.

The systems expected cooperation. The attackers declined.

The watchers are falling behind. NIST's vulnerability database carries a backlog of records it has not analyzed and a longer queue it has no plans to reach.[291] The costs accumulate faster than anyone can count them.

But the gains are real too.

Global communication, instant and nearly free. Wikipedia, built by volunteers who will never meet. Dissidents coordinating across borders, and video calls with grandchildren on another continent.

The Arab Spring organized on social media. So did the riots. Linux began as a Finnish student's hobby project;[353] the open development model that let strangers build an operating system together also served malware distribution networks.

A network that demanded verification at every step could not have grown this way. The World Wide Web emerged from a physics lab because Tim Berners-Lee could build it without asking permission.[217] Permission was never required. That was the point. That was also the problem.

While you read these words, the internet is running.

You type a URL and press enter, and a chain of strangers goes to work. You have walked every step of it in these chapters. The resolver takes a stranger's word for an address. The handshake Cerf and Kahn designed completes somewhere for the billionth time today.[36,38] A certificate chain settles on a root you never chose, and a router hands your packets to a neighbor it has simply decided to believe. It ran again just now, in milliseconds, and you are still soaking in it.

Crocker, Cerf and Kahn, Postel, Mockapetris, Berners-Lee: they never sat in a room together and designed a system. They built pieces, and the pieces fit—not perfectly, not securely, but well enough. A cathedral, built by architects who never met.

Then there is the scaffolding. CERT in 1988, responding to the Morris Worm. CVE in 1999, naming the vulnerabilities. CISA in 2018, defending federal networks, and national CERTs in more than a hundred countries. These were repairs, retrofitted onto a structure never meant to bear this load. The cathedral stands.

The premises were wrong, and it keeps working anyway.

The ratio holds. Honest traffic still outnumbers the malicious, valid certificates outnumber the forged, accurate lookups outnumber the poisoned. We keep extending the loan.

It is late in Lagos. A university student sits before a laptop, screen bright in the darkness. She is building a mobile payment system for market vendors who lack bank accounts. The established players ignored this problem. She did not.

She does not know the full history—Crocker's legal pad, Postel's robustness principle, RFC 1. She does not know the protocols carrying her API calls were built for four nodes and a handful of trusted operators.

None of that matters to her. She knows the network is there, and she knows it works. She is building something on it.

In Bangalore, a teenager writes code that will run on the servers of a company that does not exist yet. In São Paulo, a developer patches a library that ten thousand other projects depend on. In Berlin, in Seoul, in Cairo, in a hundred cities, people extend the network. They have no reason to doubt it will hold.

Each of them is pulling on a chain that runs back through every patch and every specification, through Postel's cluttered office, all the way to Boelter Hall. The premises come with it. So do the exposures.

Jon Postel died in 1998, at fifty-five, of complications from heart surgery, and no one knew exactly what his job had entailed.[354,355] The robustness principle lives on, and so do its consequences.

The network is still open, right now, as you hold this book.

We cannot go back. The community of researchers who knew each other's faces ended when the network outgrew any one person's comprehension. We cannot uninvent the vulnerabilities or unlearn the exploits.

In 1992, at the twenty-fourth IETF meeting, an MIT researcher named David Clark stood before his colleagues and articulated the philosophy that had guided them from the beginning[7]:

> ```
> David Clark --- IETF 24 --- July 1992
>
> We reject: kings, presidents and voting.
> We believe in: rough consensus and running code.
> ```

Clark was not proposing a new rule. He was naming what the room already believed: no central authority anywhere in sight, just engineers arguing until most of them agreed and then writing code to prove it worked.

That philosophy created the network, and it created the weaknesses.

We carry forward what that community created. The habit of documenting decisions in RFCs. The principle that anyone can participate if their ideas work. The expectation—still operative, still dangerous, still generative—that most participants mean well.

Rough consensus built the internet. Rough consensus broke it. Nearly ten thousand RFCs later, the process remains: someone writes a document, others respond, and if most agree it works, it becomes the standard. Thousands of contributors have joined the conversation Crocker started.

RFC 1 ended with an admission[4]:

> ```
> RFC 1 --- April 7, 1969 --- Steve Crocker
>
> I present here some of the tentative agreements reached
> and some of the open questions encountered. Very little of
> what is here is firm and reactions are expected.
> ```

Reactions are still expected.

The graduate students in 1969 could not have known what they were starting. The builders today cannot know where it is going.

The threats are not waiting. By the end of 2023, American investigators had traced a Chinese state campaign—Volt Typhoon, as Microsoft had named it—into power grids, water systems, and transportation networks.[356] It was not there to spy. It was waiting, holding access in reserve for a conflict that may never come.

Salt Typhoon, disclosed in late 2024, targeted telecommunications. By December 27, the White House had confirmed that nine U.S. telecommunications companies were compromised.[357] The hackers also gained access to information associated with systems used for court-authorized wiretaps.[358] The infrastructure the government built to enable surveillance had been turned against it.

The attacks proved something the early engineers never imagined: the standards they built for colleagues would become the battlefield where nations compete. Attackers are still exploiting the openness those engineers built in, more than fifty years after the first RFC was written.

The network bent, but it did not break.

Lo and behold. It still works.

AUTHOR'S NOTE

This is a book about trust: who the internet was built to trust, and what happened when it started trusting the whole world. So I owe you some of my own.

I did not learn these protocols from textbooks. I learned them the way most people my age did who ended up here—by poking at things I did not own, reading RFCs I barely understood, and occasionally breaking something I then had to explain. My name is on a handful of CVEs, the first from 2002. I have spent the twenty-odd years since building and breaking systems for a living. I love this machine, and I have seen exactly how fragile it is. Both feelings are in this book.

I also used AI to help write it. Claude Code, Anthropic's agentic command-line tool, assisted with research, drafting, and revision—every query routed through the same protocols this book describes, resolved by `DNS`, carried by `TCP`, encrypted by `TLS`, and trusted, at every hop, on faith. The irony is the point.

Where I quote RFCs, transcripts, and people, the words are theirs, drawn from the public record. Where I am uncertain, I have tried to say so.

—MJB, 2026

ACKNOWLEDGMENTS

A book about a network built by strangers is, fittingly, indebted to a great many of them.

The first debt is to the engineers whose work fills these pages. They wrote their protocols in the open, argued in public, and left a record so complete that a stranger could reconstruct their reasoning fifty years later. That openness is the reason this book could be written at all. Steve Crocker still answers questions with the same patience he showed in RFC 1; the tradition he started has outlived nearly everyone who shaped it, and it carried the research here.

This book rests on public archives that too few people thank. The RFC Editor has preserved every one of these documents, from RFC 1 to the nine thousand that followed, and kept them free to read. The CVE program, CISA, and the incident responders who publish their findings turned decades of breaches into a record anyone can study. The Internet Archive held the pages that would otherwise have vanished between the writing and the reading.

The tools were themselves the argument. This book was made with open-source software—LaTeX and its package ecosystem, and the type designers whose work gives these pages a voice—the same spirit of freely shared work that the protocols were built on.

To the early readers who caught errors while the ink was still wet, and to my family, who tolerated a household organized around a fifty-year-old apology: thank you. Any errors that remain are mine alone—and, in the spirit of the subject, corrections are expected. They can be sent by way of `builttheinternet.com`.

TIMELINE OF INTERNET HISTORY

This section consolidates key events from the history of internet protocols.

ARPANET 1969

April 7	Steve Crocker writes RFC 1 at UCLA
September 2	First IMP delivered to UCLA
October 29	First ARPANET message sent (“LO”)
November 21	SRI node operational
December	UC Santa Barbara and Utah join

TELNET TIMELINE

- **1971** — RFC 97: "A First Cut at a Proposed Telnet Protocol"
- **1983** — RFC 854/855: Formal Telnet standard published
- **1986** — Clifford Stoll begins tracking the Hannover Hacker
- **1987** — German police search Hess's Hannover apartment (June)
- **1989** — Hess arrested (March); *The Cuckoo's Egg* published
- **1990** — Hess convicted of espionage (February 15)
- **1995** — Tatu Ylönen releases SSH as secure replacement
- **2006** — IETF publishes core SSH protocol suite as RFCs 4251-4254[23–26]

FTP EVOLUTION

- **1971** — RFC 114: Bhushan's original File Transfer Protocol[29]
- **1971** — RFC 172: Expanded FTP with restart and status commands[30]
- **1980** — RFC 765: FTP restructured for TCP/IP environment[359]
- **1985** — RFC 959: Definitive FTP specification (still current)[31]
- **1995** — Hobbit publishes FTP bounce attack[33]
- **1997** — RFC 2228: FTP security extensions proposed[360]

TCP/IP TIMELINE

- **1973** — Cerf and Kahn sketch TCP/IP at the Cabana Hyatt, Palo Alto
- **May 1974** — "A Protocol for Packet Network Intercommunication" published
- **September 1981** — RFC 791 (IP) and RFC 793 (TCP) published
- **January 1983** — Flag Day: ARPANET switches from NCP to TCP/IP
- **December 1994** — Mitnick attacks Shimomura using IP spoofing
- **May 1996** — RFC 1948 proposes cryptographic sequence numbers

ARP & ICMP TIMELINE

- **1981** — RFC 792: ICMP published by Jon Postel
- **1982** — RFC 826: ARP published by David Plummer
- **1996** — Ping of Death attack discovered
- **1997** — Smurf attack tool (smurf.c) released
- **1998** — First major Smurf attacks documented
- **1999** — RFC 2644: Disable directed broadcasts
- **2000** — dsniff package makes ARP spoofing trivial
- **2004** — RFC 3704: Ingress filtering (BCP 84) updated

EMAIL TIMELINE

1971 — Ray Tomlinson invents network email, chooses @

1973 — 75% of ARPANET traffic is email

1978 — First spam: Gary Thuerk's DEC advertisement

1982 — RFC 821 (SMTP) and RFC 822 (message format) published

1996 — "Phishing" term first used on Usenet

2014 — SPF published as RFC 7208[65]

2015 — DMARC published as RFC 7489[67]

DNS TIMELINE

1973 — HOSTS.TXT maintained by NIC

1983 — Mockapetris publishes RFC 882/883 (DNS concept)

1985 — First TLDs established: .com, .edu, .gov, .mil, .org

1987 — RFC 1034/1035: definitive DNS specification

1989 — Last HOSTS.TXT distribution

1999 — DNSSEC first standardized (RFC 2535)[82]

2008 — Kaminsky discloses cache poisoning attack

2010 — Root zone signed with DNSSEC

NTP TIMELINE

- **1979** — Mills begins work on network time synchronization
- **1983** — RFC 868: Simple Time Protocol
- **1985** — RFC 958: First NTP specification
- **1992** — RFC 1305: NTPv3 (the definitive specification)
- **2010** — RFC 5905: NTPv4 published
- **2014** — NTP amplification attacks reach nearly 400 Gbps[96]
- **2020** — RFC 8915: Network Time Security (NTS)
- **2024** — David Mills dies at age 85

THE NETWORK ANYONE COULD JOIN

- **Late 1979** — Truscott and Ellis create Usenet at Duke[104]
- **January 1980** — Usenet presented at USENIX conference[105]
- **February 1986** — RFC 977 standardizes NNTP[107]
- **1987** — "Big Seven" newsgroup reorganization[106]
- **September 1993** — AOL offers Usenet; Eternal September begins[112]
- **April 1994** — Green Card spam demonstrates commercial abuse[109]
- **May 2010** — Duke University shuts down its Usenet servers[116]

KERBEROS DEVELOPMENT

- **1983** — Project Athena begins at MIT
- **1988** — Kerberos v4 released for production use
- **1993** — RFC 1510 standardizes Kerberos v5[122]
- **2000** — Microsoft adopts Kerberos for Windows domain authentication
- **2005** — RFC 4120 updates the specification[123]
- **2011** — mimikatz reveals Windows credential vulnerabilities[124]

FROM CHAT TO BOTNETS

- **August 1988** — Oikarinen creates IRC at University of Oulu
- **1989** — First servers outside Scandinavia (MIT)
- **1990** — EFnet forms as first major IRC network
- **January 1991** — Gulf War updates spread via IRC
- **May 1993** — RFC 1459 standardizes the protocol[134]
- **2000** — GTBot proves IRC can control malware
- **February 2000** — Mafiaboy attacks take down major sites[140]
- **October 2010** — BredoLab botnet (30M machines) taken down[142]

NETWORK MANAGEMENT'S SECURITY GAP

- **November 1987** — RFC 1028 introduces SGMP[145]
- **May 1990** — RFC 1157 defines SNMP with community strings[146]
- **January 1996** — SNMPv2c keeps community-based security[148]
- **December 2002** — RFC 3411 introduces SNMPv3 with real authentication[149,150]
- **2014** — US-CERT lists SNMPv2 GETBULK as a UDP amplification vector[153]
- **October 2016** — Mirai botnet uses default credentials for IoT attack[151,361]

BGP TIMELINE

- **1989** — RFC 1105: BGP-1 designed on napkins in Austin, Texas
- **1995** — RFC 1771: BGP-4 with classless addressing
- **2006** — RFC 4271 replaces RFC 1771 as the BGP-4 Draft Standard[163]
- **2008** — Pakistan/YouTube hijack reveals global vulnerability
- **2012** — RPKI (Resource Public Key Infrastructure) standardized
- **2024** — Approximately 50% of routes have ROAs; many networks don't validate

THE LONG FUSE

- **1991** — Livingston develops RADIUS in response to Merit's requirements[176]
- **1997** — RFC 2138 standardizes RADIUS[178]
- **June 2000** — RFC 2865 updates the specification[179]
- **2004** — Shandong University demonstrates MD5 collision attacks[182]
- **2007** — Marc Stevens shows chosen-prefix MD5 collisions[183]
- **July 2024** — Blast-RADIUS (CVE-2024-3596) disclosed[180]

FROM STATIC TO DYNAMIC CONFIGURATION

- **September 1985** — RFC 951 defines BOOTP for diskless workstations[188]
- **October 1993** — RFC 1531 introduces DHCP with dynamic allocation[187]
- **1995** — Windows 95 ships with DHCP client support
- **March 1997** — RFC 2131 revises DHCP[190]
- **Late 1990s** — Home routers adopt DHCP by default

SSH DEVELOPMENT TIMELINE

- **Spring 1995** — Password-sniffing attack at Helsinki University[22]
- **July 1995** — Tatu Ylönen releases SSH 1.0[193]
- **December 1995** — SSH Communications Security founded[194]
- **December 1999** — OpenSSH 1.2.2 ships with OpenBSD 2.6[195]
- **June 2000** — OpenSSH 2.0 adds SSH-2 protocol support
- **January 2006** — RFCs 4251-4254 publish the core SSH protocol suite[23–26]

VOIP'S TRUST PROBLEM

- **1996** — Schulzrinne and Handley begin developing SIP
- **March 1999** — RFC 2543 publishes the first SIP specification[204]
- **June 2002** — RFC 3261 replaces original with enhanced security sections[205]
- **2007** — First federal SWATting case prosecuted[212]
- **2010** — Congress passes Truth in Caller ID Act[214]
- **December 2017** — Andrew Finch killed in SWATting incident[362]
- **June 2021** — FCC mandates STIR/SHAKEN for major carriers[216]

WEB TIMELINE

1989 — Berners-Lee writes "Information Management: A Proposal"

1990 — First web server and browser at CERN

1991 — Web announced publicly on Usenet

1993 — Mosaic browser released; web explosion begins

1994 — Netscape founded; cookies invented

1996 — RFC 1945: HTTP/1.0

1999 — RFC 2616: HTTP/1.1

2010 — Firesheep demonstrates session hijacking

2015--2016 — Let's Encrypt launches; HTTP/2 published

2022 — RFC 9114: HTTP/3 over QUIC

TLS TIMELINE

1994 — Netscape develops SSL; version 1.0 never released

1995 — SSL 2.0 ships with Netscape Navigator 1.1

1996 — SSL 3.0 addresses critical weaknesses

1999 — RFC 2246: TLS 1.0 (SSL becomes open standard)

2006 — RFC 4346: TLS 1.1

2008 — RFC 5246: TLS 1.2

2011 — DigiNotar CA compromise; 300k Iranians affected

2014 — Heartbleed bug disclosed; OpenSSL patched

2015--2016 — Let's Encrypt launches free certificates

2018 — RFC 8446: TLS 1.3 with mandatory forward secrecy

THE CRYPTO WARS

1991 — Phil Zimmermann releases PGP; investigation begins

1993 — Clinton administration announces Clipper Chip

1994 — Matt Blaze publishes Clipper vulnerability

1995 — Daniel Bernstein sues over export restrictions

1996 — Zimmermann investigation dropped; Clipper defunct

1999 — Ninth Circuit: code is protected speech

2000 — Export restrictions on cryptography largely lifted

WIFI SECURITY TIMELINE

- **1990** — IEEE 802.11 working group formed; Vic Hayes chairs
- **1997** — IEEE 802.11 standard finalized with WEP
- **2001** — Fluhrer-Mantin-Shamir paper breaks WEP
- **2003** — WPA (TKIP) released as emergency fix
- **2004** — IEEE 802.11i (WPA2) with AES/CCMP
- **2005** — TJX breach begins via WEP vulnerability
- **2017** — KRACK attack breaks WPA2 handshake
- **2018** — WPA3 with SAE handshake finalized
- **2021** — FragAttacks reveals 1997 bugs in all WiFi

IPV6 & QUIC TIMELINE

1990 — Frank Solensky warns of IPv4 address exhaustion

1992 — Steve Deering begins designing SIPP

1995 — RFC 1883: IPv6 specification published

2011 — IANA exhausts IPv4 address pool

2012 — World IPv6 Launch; Google begins QUIC development

2015 — RFC 7526 deprecates 6to4 tunneling

2021 — RFC 9000: QUIC standardized

2022 — RFC 9114: HTTP/3 over QUIC

2024 — IPv6 carries 50% of Google traffic

SUPPLY CHAIN ATTACKS

2010 — Stuxnet: first known nation-state supply chain attack (industrial controllers)[363]

2017 — NotPetya: Ukrainian tax software M.E.Doc used to distribute wiper malware[364]

2020 — SolarWinds/SUNBURST: 18,000 organizations receive backdoored updates[321]

2021 — Codecov: CI/CD tool modified to steal credentials[365]

2021 — Kaseya: MSP software used to deploy ransomware to customers[366]

ROBOTS.TXT TIMELINE

1993 — Matthew Gray's Wanderer creates web crawling problem

1994 — Martijn Koster proposes robots.txt convention

1995 — Major search engines adopt the standard

2008 — Common Crawl begins archiving the web

2022 — RFC 9309: robots.txt becomes formal standard

2022 — ChatGPT launches; AI training controversy begins

2023 — Publishers block GPTBot en masse

2023 — New York Times sues OpenAI

2024 — Perplexity caught circumventing robots.txt

REFERENCES

[1] Leonard Kleinrock. *The Day the Infant Internet Uttered its First Words*. UCLA Connection Lab. [Kleinrock's account of the first ARPANET message, October 29, 1969]. 2019.

[2] Katie Hafner and Matthew Lyon. *Where Wizards Stay Up Late: The Origins of the Internet*. First paperback edition. Simon & Schuster, 1998.

[3] Steve Crocker. *How the Internet Got Its Rules*. The New York Times. [Op-ed on the 40th anniversary of RFC 1]. Apr. 2009.

[4] Steve Crocker. *Host Software*. RFC 1. UCLA, Apr. 1969.

[5] Steve Crocker. *Documentation Conventions*. RFC 3. UCLA, Apr. 1969.

[6] Peter J. Denning. The ARPANET after Twenty Years. *American Scientist* **77**. (1989). [Historical account noting 15 nodes in 1971, 37 nodes in 1973], 530–534.

[7] David D. Clark. A Cloudy Crystal Ball: Visions of the Future. *Proceedings of the Twenty-Fourth Internet Engineering Task Force*. [Plenary presentation at IETF 24, July 13–17, 1992. Origin of the phrase "rough consensus and running code."]. Cambridge, MA, July 1992.

[8] United States General Accounting Office. *Computer Security: Virus Highlights Need for Improved Internet Management*. Report GAO/IMTEC-89-57. GAO, June 1989.

[9] Federal Bureau of Investigation. *The Morris Worm: 30 Years Since First Major Attack on the Internet*. FBI News. Nov. 2018.

[10] Eugene H. Spafford. The Internet Worm: Crisis and Aftermath. *Communications of the ACM* **32**. (June 1989), 678–687.

[11] Mark W. Eichin and Jon A. Rochlis. With Microscope and Tweezers: An Analysis of the Internet Virus

of November 1988. *Proceedings of the IEEE Symposium on Security and Privacy* (1989), 326–343.

[12] John Markoff. Student Testifies His Error Jammed Computer Network. *The New York Times* (Jan. 1990). [Trial testimony; includes Graham quote: "I said, 'You idiot.' It was such a good idea and he just blew it, I was so mad."], A19.

[13] Software Engineering Institute. *Fostering Growth in Professional Cyber Incident Management.* [History of Innovation entry for 1988]. Carnegie Mellon University. 2026.

[14] Georgia Killcrece et al. *State of the Practice of Computer Security Incident Response Teams (CSIRTs).* Technical Report CMU/SEI-2003-TR-001. Software Engineering Institute, Carnegie Mellon University, Oct. 2003.

[15] United States Court of Appeals, Second Circuit. *United States v. Morris, 928 F.2d 504.* [Appeal upholding Morris worm conviction under Computer Fraud and Abuse Act]. Mar. 1991.

[16] John T. Melvin and Richard W. Watson. *First Cut at a Proposed Telnet Protocol.* RFC 97. SRI-ARC, Feb. 1971.

[17] Jon Postel and Joyce Reynolds. *Telnet Protocol Specification.* RFC 854. USC/Information Sciences Institute, May 1983.

[18] Clifford Stoll. Stalking the Wily Hacker. *Communications of the ACM* **31**. (May 1988). [Technical account of the Lawrence Berkeley Lab intrusion investigation, published before The Cuckoo's Egg], 484–497.

[19] Clifford Stoll. *The Cuckoo's Egg: Tracking a Spy Through the Maze of Computer Espionage.* Doubleday, 1989.

[20] Guinness World Records. *First incident of cyber-espionage.* Guinness World Records. [Documents Markus Hess arrest on 29 June 1987 and conviction on 15 February 1990]. 2020.

[21] Der Spiegel. *KGB-Hacker Markus Hess verurteilt.* Der Spiegel. [German news coverage of Hess conviction]. 1990.

[22] Tatu Ylönen. *SSH (Secure Shell) Remote Login Program.* comp.security.unix announcement. [Original SSH release announcement]. July 1995.

[23] Tatu Ylonen and Chris Lonvick. *The Secure Shell (SSH) Protocol Architecture.* RFC 4251. SSH Communications Security, Cisco Systems, Jan. 2006.

[24] Tatu Ylonen and Chris Lonvick. *The Secure Shell (SSH) Authentication Protocol.* RFC 4252. SSH Communications Security, Cisco Systems, Jan. 2006.

[25] Tatu Ylonen and Chris Lonvick. *The Secure Shell (SSH) Transport Layer Protocol.* RFC 4253. IETF, Jan. 2006.

[26] Tatu Ylonen and Chris Lonvick. *The Secure Shell (SSH) Connection Protocol.* RFC 4254. SSH Communications Security, Cisco Systems, Jan. 2006.

[27] hrbrmstr and Orbie. *2026-01-14: The Day the telnet Died.* GreyNoise Labs Grimoire. [Analysis of a 59% sustained drop in non-spoofable Telnet sessions observed by the GreyNoise Global Observation Grid]. Feb. 2026.

[28] *CVE-2026-24061: GNU Inetutils telnetd Authentication Bypass.* [CVSS 9.8 CRITICAL. Authentication bypass via argument injection in USER environment variable. Vulnerability present since 2015. Added to CISA KEV January 26, 2026]. 2026.

[29] Abhay K. Bhushan. *File Transfer Protocol.* RFC 114. MIT Project MAC, Apr. 1971.

[30] Abhay Bhushan et al. *The File Transfer Protocol.* RFC 172. MIT/Project MAC, June 1971.

[31] Jon Postel and Joyce Reynolds. *File Transfer Protocol.* RFC 959. USC/Information Sciences Institute, Oct. 1985.

[32] U.S. Department of Justice. *Federal Law Enforcement Targets International Internet Piracy Syndicates.* DOJ Press Release. [Operation Buccaneer targeting warez groups using FTP]. Dec. 2001.

[33] Hobbit. *The FTP Bounce Attack.* Bugtraq mailing list. [Security advisory describing FTP PORT command abuse]. July 1995.

[34] Mozilla Security Team. *Stopping FTP Support in Firefox 90.* Mozilla Security Blog. [Announcement of FTP protocol removal from Firefox]. July 2021.

[35] Vinton G. Cerf. *Oral History of Vint Cerf.* Computer History Museum. [Interviewed by David Hochfelder]. Nov. 2007.

[36] Vinton G. Cerf and Robert E. Kahn. A Protocol for Packet Network Intercommunication. *IEEE Transactions on Communications* **22**. (May 1974), 637–648.

[37] Jon Postel. *Internet Protocol.* RFC 791. USC/Information Sciences Institute, Sept. 1981.

[38] Jon Postel. *Transmission Control Protocol.* RFC 793. USC/Information Sciences Institute, Sept. 1981.

[39] Jon Postel. *NCP/TCP Transition Plan.* RFC 801. [Plan for ARPANET transition from NCP to TCP/IP on January 1, 1983 (Flag Day)]. USC/Information Sciences Institute, Nov. 1981.

[40] James L. Pelkey, Andrew L. Russell, and

Loring G. Robbins. *TCP/IP and XNS 1981–1983*. Circuits, Packets, and Protocols: Entrepreneurs and Computer Communications, 1968–1988 (online edition), Section 11.8. [Documents Dan Lynch's 500 "I survived the TCP transition, 1/1/83" pins]. 2022.

[41] Robert T. Morris. *A Weakness in the 4.2BSD Unix TCP/IP Software*. Computing Science Technical Report 117. AT&T Bell Laboratories, Feb. 1985.

[42] Jerome H. Saltzer, David P. Reed, and David D. Clark. End-to-End Arguments in System Design. *ACM Transactions on Computer Systems* **2**. (Nov. 1984), 277–288.

[43] Tsutomu Shimomura and John Markoff. *Takedown: The Pursuit and Capture of Kevin Mitnick, America's Most Wanted Computer Outlaw—By the Man Who Did It*. Hyperion, 1996.

[44] Steven M. Bellovin. Security Problems in the TCP/IP Protocol Suite. *ACM SIGCOMM Computer Communication Review* **19**. (Apr. 1989), 32–48.

[45] Steve Bellovin. *Defending Against Sequence Number Attacks*. RFC 1948. AT&T Bell Laboratories, May 1996.

[46] IEEE. *Ethernet Local Area Network (LAN), 1973-1985*. Engineering and Technology History Wiki. [DIX Blue Book specification published September 30, 1980]. 2023.

[47] David C. Plummer. *An Ethernet Address Resolution Protocol: Or Converting Network Protocol Addresses to 48.bit Ethernet Address for Transmission on Ethernet Hardware*. RFC 826. MIT Laboratory for Computer Science, Nov. 1982.

[48] Jon Postel. *Internet Control Message Protocol*. RFC 792. USC/Information Sciences Institute, Sept. 1981.

[49] University of Minnesota News Service. *U of M Computers Experience Denial-of-Service Attack*. [Contemporaneous university release describing the March 17 attack, nearly two and a half hours of disruption, and the resulting network traffic jam]. Mar. 1998.

[50] CERT/CC. *CERT Advisory CA-1998-01: Smurf IP Denial-of-Service Attacks*. CERT Advisory. 1998.

[51] TFreak. *'smurf' multi-broadcast icmp attack*. Bugtraq mailing list. [Original smurf.c release and documentation]. Oct. 1997.

[52] CERT/CC. *CERT Advisory CA-1996-26: Denial-of-Service Attack via ping*. CERT Advisory. [First documentation of the Ping of Death vulnerability]. Dec. 1996.

[53] Dug Song. *dsniff*. monkey.org. [Network auditing tools including

arpspoof for ARP cache poisoning]. 2000.

[54] Daniel Senie. *Changing the Default for Directed Broadcasts in Routers*. RFC 2644. [BCP 34: Recommends disabling directed broadcasts to mitigate Smurf attacks]. Amaranth Networks Inc., Aug. 1999.

[55] Paul Ferguson and Daniel Senie. *Network Ingress Filtering: Defeating Denial of Service Attacks which employ IP Source Address Spoofing*. RFC 2827. [BCP 38: Original network ingress filtering recommendation]. Cisco Systems, Amaranth Networks Inc., May 2000.

[56] Raymond Tomlinson. *Oral History of Raymond (Ray) Tomlinson*. Computer History Museum, interview by Marc Weber and Gardner Hendrie. [CHM reference X5409.2009; Tomlinson's first-person account of creating network email]. June 2009.

[57] Craig Partridge. The Technical Development of Internet Email. *IEEE Annals of the History of Computing* **30**. (2008), 3–29.

[58] Jon Postel. *Simple Mail Transfer Protocol*. RFC 821. USC/Information Sciences Institute, Aug. 1982.

[59] David H. Crocker. *Standard for the Format of ARPA Internet Text Messages*. RFC 822. University of Delaware, Aug. 1982.

[60] Brad Templeton. *Reaction to the DEC Spam of 1978*. Templetons.com. [History of the first spam email]. 2005.

[61] Phishing.org. *History of Phishing*. Phishing.org. [First recorded mention of phishing on alt.online-service.america-online Usenet newsgroup, January 2, 1996]. 2023.

[62] Federal Bureau of Investigation. *Internet Crime Report 2021*. Internet Crime Complaint Center. 2022.

[63] Federal Bureau of Investigation. *Internet Crime Report 2022*. Internet Crime Complaint Center. 2023.

[64] U.S. Department of Justice. *Lithuanian Man Sentenced to 5 Years in Prison for Theft of Over $100 Million in Fraudulent Business Email Compromise Scheme*. DOJ Press Release. Dec. 2019.

[65] Scott Kitterman. *Sender Policy Framework (SPF) for Authorizing Use of Domains in Email, Version 1*. RFC 7208. IETF, Apr. 2014.

[66] Dave Crocker, Tony Hansen, and Murray S. Kucherawy. *DomainKeys Identified Mail (DKIM) Signatures*. RFC 6376. IETF, Sept. 2011.

[67] Murray Kucherawy and Elizabeth Zwicky. *Domain-based Message Authentication, Reporting, and Conformance (DMARC)*. RFC 7489. IETF, Mar. 2015.

[68] Elizabeth J. Feinler. *Oral History of Elizabeth (Jake) Feinler*. Computer History Museum. [CHM Reference number: X5671.2010]. Mar. 2010.

[69] M.D. Kudlick. *Host Names On-Line*. RFC 608. SRI-ARC, Jan. 1974.

[70] Paul Mockapetris. *Internet Hall of Fame Inductee*. Internet Society. 2012.

[71] Paul Mockapetris. *Domain Names - Concepts and Facilities*. RFC 882. [Obsoleted by RFC 1034]. USC/Information Sciences Institute, Nov. 1983.

[72] Paul Mockapetris. *Domain Names - Implementation and Specification*. RFC 883. [Obsoleted by RFC 1035]. USC/Information Sciences Institute, Nov. 1983.

[73] Paul Mockapetris. *Domain Names - Concepts and Facilities*. RFC 1034. USC/Information Sciences Institute, Nov. 1987.

[74] Paul Mockapetris. *Domain Names: Implementation Specification*. RFC 1035. USC/Information Sciences Institute, Nov. 1987.

[75] ICANN. *There Are Not 13 Root Servers*. ICANN Blog. [Explains that 13 root server addresses map to hundreds of physical servers via anycast]. Nov. 2007.

[76] Kim Zetter. *Dan Kaminsky, Internet Security Savior, Dies at 42*. The New York Times. Apr. 2021.

[77] MITRE Corporation. *CVE-2008-1447: DNS Cache Poisoning Vulnerability*. CVE. 2008.

[78] Erica Naone. The Flaw at the Heart of the Internet. *MIT Technology Review* (Oct. 2008). [In-depth account of Kaminsky DNS discovery and coordinated disclosure].

[79] CERT Coordination Center. *VU#800113: Multiple DNS implementations vulnerable to cache poisoning*. CERT Vulnerability Note. [Advisory on Kaminsky DNS cache poisoning vulnerability]. July 2008.

[80] Matasano Security. *Kaminsky DNS Flaw Details Leaked*. Security advisory. [Matasano accidentally confirmed Halvar Flake's hypothesis on July 21, 2008; post removed within five minutes but already mirrored]. July 2008.

[81] Dan Kaminsky. It's the End of the Cache as We Know It. *Black Hat Briefings*. [Presentation on DNS cache poisoning vulnerability]. Las Vegas, NV, 2008.

[82] Donald Eastlake 3rd. *Domain Name System Security Extensions*. RFC 2535. [First comprehensive DNSSEC specification; obsoleted by RFC 4033-4035]. IBM, Mar. 1999.

[83] Roy Arends et al. *DNS Security Introduction and Requirements*. RFC 4033. IETF, Mar. 2005.

[84] IANA. *Root Zone Now Signed*. IANA News. [Root zone signed with DNSSEC on July 15, 2010]. July 2010.

[85] APNIC. *DNSSEC World Map*. APNIC Statistics. [Approximately 30% of DNS queries validated with DNSSEC globally]. 2024.

[86] ISC. *CVE-2025-40780: Cache poisoning due to weak PRNG in BIND 9*. Internet Systems Consortium Security Advisory. [CVSS 8.6 HIGH. Affects BIND 9.16.0-9.16.50, 9.18.0-9.18.39, 9.20.0-9.20.13, 9.21.0-9.21.12. Cache poisoning vulnerability exploiting weak pseudo-random number generation, same class as Kaminsky's 2008 attack]. Oct. 2025.

[87] David L. Mills. A Brief History of NTP Time: Confessions of an Internet Timekeeper. *ACM SIGCOMM Computer Communication Review* **33**. (2003). [Mills's own account of NTP history from 1977 onwards], 9–22.

[88] Jon Postel and Ken Harrenstien. *Time Protocol*. RFC 868. USC/Information Sciences Institute, SRI, May 1983.

[89] David L. Mills. *Network Time Protocol (NTP)*. RFC 958. University of Delaware, Sept. 1985.

[90] Harrison Smith. *David Mills, the internet's 'father time,' dies at 85*. The Washington Post. Jan. 2024.

[91] David L. Mills. *Network Time Protocol (Version 3) Specification, Implementation and Analysis*. RFC 1305. University of Delaware, Mar. 1992.

[92] David L. Mills et al. *Network Time Protocol Version 4: Protocol and Algorithms Specification*. RFC 5905. University of Delaware, June 2010.

[93] Matthew Prince. The DDoS That Knocked Spamhaus Offline (And How We Mitigated It). *Cloudflare Blog* (Mar. 2013).

[94] Brian Krebs. *The New Normal: 200-400 Gbps DDoS Attacks*. Krebs on Security. Feb. 2014.

[95] John Graham-Cumming. *Technical Details Behind a 400Gbps NTP Amplification DDoS Attack*. Cloudflare Blog. 2014.

[96] Matthew Prince. *Technical Details Behind a 400Gbps NTP Amplification DDoS Attack*. Cloudflare Blog. [Analysis of February 2014 400 Gbps NTP amplification attack]. Feb. 2014.

[97] MITRE. *CVE-2013-5211: NTP monlist Amplification Vulnerability*. Common Vulnerabilities and Exposures. [NTP monlist command allows 556x traffic amplification]. 2013.

[98] US-CERT. *NTP Amplification Attacks Using CVE-2013-5211*. US-CERT Alert TA14-013A. Jan. 2014.

[99] Aanchal Malhotra et al. Attacking the Network Time Protocol. *Network and Distributed System Security (NDSS) Symposium.* [Kiss-o'-Death (KoD) attack research from Boston University]. San Diego, CA, 2016.

[100] Daniel Franke et al. *Network Time Security for the Network Time Protocol.* RFC 8915. IETF, Sept. 2020.

[101] Joe Hernandez. *How a power outage in Colorado caused U.S. official time to be 4.8 microseconds off.* NPR. [NIST Boulder power outage December 17–21, 2025: windstorm caused 4-day power outage affecting atomic ensemble time scale]. Dec. 2025.

[102] Simon Sharwood. *NIST warns of NTP inaccuracy after blackouts across Colorado.* The Register. [Analysis of NIST Boulder power outage impact on UTC(NIST) and NTP timeservers]. Dec. 2025.

[103] Steve Bellovin. *Re: The List again :-).* Usenet History Discussion. [Contains quote about shell scripts and protocol variants]. 1997.

[104] Steven M. Bellovin. *Netnews: The Origin Story.* Department of Computer Science, Columbia University. [Historical account by one of Usenet's creators]. 2010.

[105] Steve Bellovin. *The Early History of Usenet, Part VI: The Public Announcement.* [Detailed account of January 1980 USENIX presentation in Boulder]. Nov. 2019.

[106] Usenet Big-8 Management Board. *The Great Renaming (1987).* Usenet historical reference page. [Reorganization of Usenet newsgroups into the Big Seven hierarchies: comp, misc, news, rec, sci, soc, and talk]. 1987.

[107] Brian Kantor and Phil Lapsley. *Network News Transfer Protocol.* RFC 977. University of California San Diego, University of California Berkeley, Feb. 1986.

[108] Vinod Maku, Ken Murchison, and Stan Barber. *Network News Transfer Protocol (NNTP) Extension for Authentication.* RFC 4643. Internet Engineering Task Force, Oct. 2006.

[109] Brad Templeton. *Reaction to the First Major Spam.* templetons.com. [Documentation of Canter and Siegel's green card spam]. 1994.

[110] Laurence A. Canter and Martha S. Siegel. *How to Make a Fortune on the Information Superhighway: Everyone's Guerrilla Guide to Marketing on the Internet and Other On-Line Services.* [Written by the perpetrators of the Green Card spam]. HarperCollins, 1994.

[111] Arnt Gulbrandsen. *Canter & Siegel: What actually happened.* Personal website. [First-person account of

creating the cancelbot to combat Canter & Siegel spam in June 1994]. 1994.

[112] Dave Fischer. *Re: What's the longest-running thread?* Usenet: alt.folklore.computers. [First use of term "September that never ended" (January 26, 1994)]. Jan. 1994.

[113] Juhoon Kim et al. Today's Usenet Usage: NNTP Traffic Characterization. *2010 IEEE Conference on Computer Communications Workshops (INFOCOM WKSHPS)*. [Analyzed NNTP traffic from 20,000+ residential DSL customers at a European ISP. Found yEnc-encoded binaries accounted for more than 99% of bytes transferred.]. IEEE, 2010, pp. 1–6.

[114] America Online. *AOL Discontinues Usenet Access*. AOL. [AOL discontinued Usenet access on June 25, 2005]. June 2005.

[115] New York Attorney General. *Internet Service Providers Agree to Block Access to Child Pornography*. NY Attorney General Press Release. [Verizon, Time Warner Cable, and Sprint agreed to block Usenet access; AOL had already discontinued in 2005]. June 2008.

[116] Duke University. *A Piece of Internet History*. [Announcement of Duke's Usenet server shutdown on May 20, 2010]. May 2010.

[117] MIT News. *Looking back at Project Athena*. MIT News. [35th anniversary retrospective on Project Athena]. Nov. 2018.

[118] Jennifer G. Steiner, Clifford Neuman, and Jeffrey I. Schiller. Kerberos: An Authentication Service for Open Network Systems. *USENIX Winter Conference*. [First published description of Kerberos protocol]. Dallas, TX, Feb. 1988, pp. 191–202.

[119] Jason Garman. *Kerberos: The Definitive Guide*. [Historical and technical account, including the January 24, 1989 public release of Kerberos 4]. O'Reilly Media, Aug. 2003.

[120] B. Clifford Neuman and Theodore Ts'o. Kerberos: An Authentication Service for Computer Networks. *IEEE Communications Magazine* **32**. (Sept. 1994). [Comprehensive overview of Kerberos v4 and v5], 33–38.

[121] Microsoft. *Security Support Provider Interface Architecture*. Microsoft Learn. [Documents Kerberos as the default authentication protocol for Windows domain services since Windows 2000]. 2025.

[122] John Kohl and B. Clifford Neuman. *The Kerberos Network Authentication Service (V5)*. RFC 1510. DEC, USC/ISI, Sept. 1993.

[123] Clifford Neuman et al. *The Kerberos Network Authentication Service (V5)*. RFC 4120. USC-ISI, MIT, July 2005.

[124] Benjamin Delpy. *mimikatz*. GitHub. [Windows credential extraction tool, first released May 2011 to demonstrate WDigest credential storage vulnerability]. May 2011.

[125] MITRE ATT&CK. *Steal or Forge Kerberos Tickets: Golden Ticket*. MITRE ATT&CK. [T1558.001: Golden Ticket technique reference]. 2024.

[126] FireEye. *Highly Evasive Attacker Leverages SolarWinds Supply Chain to Compromise Multiple Global Victims With SUNBURST Backdoor*. FireEye Threat Research. Dec. 2020.

[127] Cybersecurity and Infrastructure Security Agency. *Emergency Directive 21-01: Mitigate SolarWinds Orion Code Compromise*. CISA. Dec. 2020.

[128] Shaked Reiner. *Golden SAML: Newly Discovered Attack Technique Forges Authentication to Cloud Apps*. CyberArk Blog. [First documentation of Golden SAML attack technique]. Nov. 2017.

[129] Sygnia. *Detection And Hunting Of Golden SAML Attack*. Sygnia Threat Reports. [SolarWinds was first use of Golden SAML in the wild]. July 2021.

[130] National Security Agency. *Detecting Abuse of Authentication Mechanisms*. NSA Cybersecurity Advisory U/OO/198854-20. [Advisory on detecting forged SAML tokens in SolarWinds-related attacks]. Dec. 2020.

[131] B. Clifford Neuman. *Faculty Profile*. [Director of USC Center for Computer Systems Security, co-designer of Kerberos]. USC Viterbi School of Engineering. 2024.

[132] Jarkko Oikarinen. *IRC History*. IRC.org. [Oikarinen's own account: "The birthday of IRC was in August 1988"]. 1988.

[133] Daniel Stenberg. *History of IRC (Internet Relay Chat)*. daniel.haxx.se. [Comprehensive IRC history compiled by cURL creator Daniel "bagder" Stenberg]. 2023.

[134] Jarkko Oikarinen and Darren Reed. *Internet Relay Chat Protocol*. RFC 1459. University of Oulu, May 1993.

[135] Greg "wumpus" Lindahl. *EFnet Formation*. IRC history archives. ["Eris refused to remove that line, so I formed EFnet. It wasn't much of a fight."]. Aug. 1990.

[136] Multiple IRC users. *IRC logs from the beginning of the Gulf War*. Archived at ibiblio.org. [Real-time IRC coverage from January 16, 1991, with eyewitness reports

from Israel and Finland]. Jan. 1991.

[137] Paul Barford and Vinod Yegneswaran. An Inside Look at Botnets. *Malware Detection*. Vol. 27. Advances in Information Security. [Academic analysis of botnet source code]. Springer, 2006, pp. 171–191.

[138] Symantec Security Response. *W32.Sdbot*. Symantec Threat Database. [First major C++ IRC botnet with publicly available source code]. 2002.

[139] Sophos. *Agobot author arrested in Germany*. Sophos News. [Axel Gembe arrested on May 7, 2004 in Waldshut, Germany]. May 2004.

[140] Federal Bureau of Investigation. *Mafiaboy pleads guilty*. Archived FBI press release. [Contemporaneous official account of the fifteen-year-old's guilty pleas for February 2000 DDoS attacks]. Jan. 2001.

[141] Kaspersky Lab. *Workings of 30 Million Strong Bredolab Botnet Laid Bare*. Kaspersky Press Release. [Botnet owner made up to $139,000 per month from renting the botnet]. Oct. 2010.

[142] Jeremy Kirk. *Did Dutch Police Break the Law Taking Down a Botnet?* Computerworld. [Contemporaneous report that Dutch police took control of 143 servers used by BredoLab and that a suspected operator was arrested in Armenia]. Oct. 2010.

[143] John Leyden. *Armenia jails Bredolab botmaster for 4 years*. The Register. [Georgy Avanesov sentenced to 4 years for creating BredoLab]. May 2012.

[144] The Register. *Freenode IRC staff resign en masse, unhappy about new management*. The Register. [14 volunteer staff members resigned following "hostile takeover" by Andrew Lee]. May 2021.

[145] Jeffrey Davin et al. *Simple Gateway Monitoring Protocol*. RFC 1028. Proteon, University of Tennessee, NYSERNet, Rensselaer Polytechnic Institute, Nov. 1987.

[146] Jeffrey Case et al. *Simple Network Management Protocol (SNMP)*. RFC 1157. SNMP Research, Performance Systems International, MIT, May 1990.

[147] Jeffrey Case et al. *Protocol Operations for Version 2 of the Simple Network Management Protocol (SNMPv2)*. RFC 1905. SNMP Research, Cisco Systems, Dover Beach Consulting, International Network Services, Jan. 1996.

[148] Jeffrey Case et al. *Introduction to Community-based SNMPv2*. RFC 1901. SNMP Research, Cisco Systems, Dover Beach Consulting, International Network Services, Jan. 1996.

[149] David Harrington, Randy Presuhn, and Bert Wijnen. *An Architecture for Describing Simple Network Management Protocol (SNMP) Management Frameworks*. RFC 3411. Enterasys Networks, BMC Software, Lucent Technologies, Dec. 2002.

[150] Ulf Blumenthal and Bert Wijnen. *User-based Security Model (USM) for version 3 of the Simple Network Management Protocol (SNMPv3)*. RFC 3414. Lucent Technologies, Dec. 2002.

[151] Cloudflare. *Inside Mirai the Infamous IoT Botnet: A Retrospective Analysis*. Cloudflare Blog. [Detailed analysis of Mirai botnet and October 21, 2016 Dyn DDoS attack]. 2017.

[152] Rapid7. *Disclosures: Exposure of Critical Information Via SNMP Public Community String*. Rapid7 Blog. [Research on SNMP public community string vulnerabilities]. May 2014.

[153] US-CERT. *UDP-Based Amplification Attacks*. [Lists a bandwidth amplification factor of 6.3 for SNMPv2 GetBulk requests; last revised December 18, 2019]. Cybersecurity and Infrastructure Security Agency. Feb. 2014.

[154] Cybersecurity and Infrastructure Security Agency. *Reducing the Risk of SNMP Abuse*. CISA Alert. [US-CERT advisory on SNMP security best practices]. June 2017.

[155] SNMP Research. *Company History*. SNMP Research. [History of SNMP Research founded by Jeff Case at University of Tennessee]. 2024.

[156] Trend Micro Research. *Operation Zero Disco: SNMP Vulnerability Exploitation Campaign*. [Documented CVE-2025-20352 exploitation campaign targeting Cisco SNMP subsystems. Cisco estimated nearly 2 million devices running vulnerable software.]. Oct. 2025.

[157] Internet Society. *Kirk Lougheed: Internet Hall of Fame Inductee*. Internet Hall of Fame. 2012.

[158] Kirk Lougheed and Yakov Rekhter. *Border Gateway Protocol (BGP)*. RFC 1105. IETF, June 1989.

[159] Computer History Museum. *The Two-Napkin Protocol*. Computer History Museum Blog. [History of BGP's creation at the 12th IETF meeting in Austin, January 1989]. Mar. 2015.

[160] Kirk Lougheed and Yakov Rekhter. *Border Gateway Protocol (BGP)*. RFC 1163. [BGP-2]. IETF, June 1990.

[161] Kirk Lougheed and Yakov Rekhter. *Border Gateway Protocol 3 (BGP-3)*. RFC 1267. [BGP-3]. IETF, Oct. 1991.

[162] Yakov Rekhter and Tony Li. *A Border Gateway Protocol 4 (BGP-4)*. RFC 1771. [Original BGP-4

specification with CIDR support]. IETF, Mar. 1995.

[163] Yakov Rekhter, Tony Li, and Susan Hares. *A Border Gateway Protocol 4 (BGP-4)*. RFC 4271. IETF, Jan. 2006.

[164] RIPE NCC. *YouTube Hijacking: A RIPE NCC RIS Case Study*. RIPE NCC News. [Analysis of the Pakistan Telecom/YouTube BGP hijack, February 24, 2008]. Feb. 2008.

[165] Matt Lepinski and Stephen Kent. *An Infrastructure to Support Secure Internet Routing*. RFC 6480. BBN Technologies, Feb. 2012.

[166] MANRS. *RPKI ROV Deployment Reaches Major Milestone*. MANRS Blog. [Announcement that 50% of IPv4 routes are covered by ROAs]. May 2024.

[167] Doug Madory. *BGP Hijack of Twitter by Russian ISP*. Kentik Blog. [Analysis of March 28, 2022 Twitter BGP hijack by RTComm.RU]. Mar. 2022.

[168] Internet Society. *What Happened? The Amazon Route 53 BGP Hijack to Take Over Ethereum Cryptocurrency Wallets*. Internet Society Blog. [Analysis of April 24, 2018 cryptocurrency theft via BGP hijack]. Apr. 2018.

[169] MANRS. *Large European Routing Leak Sends Traffic Through China Telecom*. MANRS Blog. [Analysis of June 6, 2019 BGP route leak affecting European mobile traffic]. June 2019.

[170] Doug Madory. *Digging into the Orange España Hack*. Kentik Blog. [Analysis of the January 3, 2024 RIPE NCC account compromise, invalid ROA creation, and resulting RPKI-driven outage]. Jan. 2024.

[171] Mandiant. *APT1: Exposing One of China's Cyber Espionage Units*. Mandiant Intelligence Report. [First public attribution of Chinese state-sponsored hacking to a specific PLA unit]. Feb. 2013.

[172] U.S. Department of Justice. *U.S. Charges Five Chinese Military Hackers for Cyber Espionage Against U.S. Corporations and a Labor Organization for Commercial Advantage*. DOJ Press Release. May 2014.

[173] Chris C. Demchak and Yuval Shavitt. China's Maxim – Leave No Access Point Unexploited: The Hidden Story of China Telecom's BGP Hijacking. *Military Cyber Affairs* **3**., 7 (2018).

[174] CIDR Report. *BGP Table Statistics*. CIDR Report. [Daily BGP routing table statistics; approximately 1,000,000 IPv4 prefixes and 78,000 ASNs as of late 2024]. 2024.

[175] Jay Hipps. Lucent Acquires Livingston Enterprises. *Hacienda Online* **5**. (Dec. 1997).

[Contemporaneous trade article from the Hacienda Business Park newsletter, Pleasanton, California].

[176] John Vollbrecht. *The Beginnings and History of RADIUS*. Interlink Networks white paper. [Vollbrecht managed Merit Network's MichNet engineering group and drafted the 1991 request for proposals that led to RADIUS]. 2006.

[177] Merit Network. *History*. Merit Network, Inc. [Merit Network founded 1966 in Ann Arbor by the University of Michigan, Michigan State University, and Wayne State University]. 2024.

[178] Carl Rigney et al. *Remote Authentication Dial In User Service (RADIUS)*. RFC 2138. [Original IETF standardization of RADIUS. Obsoleted by RFC 2865]. Livingston Enterprises, Merit Network, Daydreamer, Apr. 1997.

[179] Carl Rigney et al. *Remote Authentication Dial In User Service (RADIUS)*. RFC 2865. Livingston Enterprises, Ascend Communications, Merit Network, Daydreamer, June 2000.

[180] Sharon Goldberg et al. RADIUS/UDP Considered Harmful. *33rd USENIX Security Symposium*. [Blast-RADIUS attack (CVE-2024-3596). Disclosed July 9, 2024]. Philadelphia, PA, Aug. 2024.

[181] MITRE. *CVE-2024-3596: RADIUS Protocol Forgery Vulnerability*. Common Vulnerabilities and Exposures. [CVSS 7.5, affects all RADIUS implementations using MD5]. 2024.

[182] Xiaoyun Wang et al. Collisions for Hash Functions MD4, MD5, HAVAL-128 and RIPEMD. *CRYPTO 2004 Rump Session*. [First practical MD5 collision attack from Shandong University]. Santa Barbara, CA, Aug. 2004.

[183] Marc Stevens, Arjen Lenstra, and Benne de Weger. Chosen-Prefix Collisions for MD5 and Colliding X.509 Certificates for Different Identities. *Advances in Cryptology – EUROCRYPT 2007*. Vol. 4515. Lecture Notes in Computer Science. [Demonstrated chosen-prefix collision attacks on MD5]. Berlin, Heidelberg: Springer, 2007, pp. 1–22.

[184] FreeRADIUS Project. *About FreeRADIUS*. FreeRADIUS. [FreeRADIUS founded June 1999 by Miquel van Smoorenburg and Alan DeKok]. 2024.

[185] Stefan Winter et al. *Transport Layer Security (TLS) Encryption for RADIUS*. RFC 6614. [RadSec: RADIUS over TLS]. RESTENA, OSC, Cisco Systems, May 2012.

[186] Craig Helmuth and Mike Reid. *Duplicate ethernet addresses!* Usenet: comp.dcom.lans.ethernet. [Thread on diagnosing two hosts that share one address; a reply describes "20+ PCs fighting over three ethernet addresses"]. Apr. 1992.

[187] Ralph Droms. *Dynamic Host Configuration Protocol*. RFC 1531. [Obsoleted by RFC 1541, then RFC 2131]. Bucknell University, Oct. 1993.

[188] Bill Croft and John Gilmore. *Bootstrap Protocol*. RFC 951. Stanford University, Sun Microsystems, Sept. 1985.

[189] Ralph Droms. *Dynamic Host Configuration Protocol*. RFC 1541. [Reissue of RFC 1531 to correct errors introduced in editing; obsoleted by RFC 2131]. Bucknell University, Oct. 1993.

[190] Ralph Droms. *Dynamic Host Configuration Protocol*. RFC 2131. Bucknell University, Mar. 1997.

[191] Alfredo Andrés and David Barroso. *Yersinia: A Framework for Layer 2 Attacks*. Black Hat Europe 2005. 2005.

[192] MITRE ATT&CK. *Adversary-in-the-Middle: DHCP Spoofing*. MITRE ATT&CK Technique T1557.003. 2024.

[193] Tatu Ylönen. *The Story of Getting SSH Port 22*. SSH.com Blog. [Ylonen's account of obtaining port 22 from IANA in July 1995]. 2017.

[194] SSH Communications Security. *SSH History*. SSH.com. [Company founded December 31, 1995]. 2023.

[195] OpenBSD Project. *OpenSSH: Project History*. OpenSSH Website. [Official history: forked from SSH 1.2.12, first release with OpenBSD 2.6 in December 1999]. 1999.

[196] Debian Security Team. *DSA-1571-1 openssl – predictable random number generator*. Debian Security Advisory. May 2008.

[197] Richard Kettlewell and Kurt Roeckx. *Bug 363516: valgrind-clean the RNG*. Debian Bug Tracking System. [Primary development record for the Valgrind-related change to Debian's OpenSSL package]. Apr. 2006.

[198] NIST. *CVE-2008-0166: OpenSSL Predictable Random Number Generator*. National Vulnerability Database. [CVSS Score 7.8: OpenSSL 0.9.8c-1 through 0.9.8g-9 on Debian-based systems]. 2008.

[199] Debian Project. *SSLkeys*. Debian Wiki. [Debian remediation guidance explaining the 32,767 possible random-number streams per architecture]. 2008.

[200] GitHub. *We updated our RSA SSH host key*. GitHub Blog. Mar. 2023.

[201] Qualys Threat Research Unit. *regreSSHion: RCE in OpenSSH's server, on glibc-based Linux systems*. Qualys Security Advisory. [CVE-2024-6387: Race condition in signal handling, CVSS 8.1. Bug fixed in 2006 (CVE-2006-5051), reintroduced in OpenSSH 8.5p1 (October 2020)]. July 2024.

[202] Columbia University. *Henning G. Schulzrinne*. Columbia Engineering Faculty Profile. [Schulzrinne joined Columbia as professor in August 1996]. 2024.

[203] International Telecommunication Union. *H.323: Packet-based multimedia communications systems*. ITU-T Recommendation. [First version published November 1996 for voice/video over packet networks]. Nov. 1996.

[204] Mark Handley et al. *SIP: Session Initiation Protocol*. RFC 2543. IETF, Mar. 1999.

[205] Jonathan Rosenberg et al. *SIP: Session Initiation Protocol*. RFC 3261. IETF, June 2002.

[206] Henning Schulzrinne et al. *RTP: A Transport Protocol for Real-Time Applications*. RFC 3550. Columbia University, Packet Design, July 2003.

[207] Mark Handley, Van Jacobson, and Colin Perkins. *SDP: Session Description Protocol*. RFC 4566. UCL, PARC, University of Glasgow, July 2006.

[208] Mark Baugher et al. *The Secure Real-time Transport Protocol (SRTP)*. RFC 3711. [Provides encryption and authentication for RTP media streams]. Cisco Systems, Ericsson Research, Mar. 2004.

[209] YouMail. *Robocall Index: 2021 Full Year Report*. YouMail. [Approximately 50 billion robocalls in the United States in 2021]. 2022.

[210] U.S. Department of Justice. *California Man Sentenced In Deadly Wichita Swatting Case*. U.S. Attorney's Office, District of Kansas. [Tyler Barriss sentenced to 20 years for 51 charges including one count of making a false report resulting in death]. Mar. 2019.

[211] U.S. Department of Justice. *Ohio Gamer Sentenced In Deadly Swatting Case*. U.S. Attorney's Office, District of Kansas. [Casey Viner sentenced to 15 months for conspiracy]. Sept. 2019.

[212] Federal Bureau of Investigation. *The Crime of "Swatting": Fake 9-1-1 Calls Have Real Consequences*. FBI Stories. [Documents first federal swatting case in 2007 led by FBI Dallas]. 2008.

[213] Brian Krebs. *The World Has No Room For Cowards*. Krebs on Security. [Krebs describes being swatted on March 14, 2013]. Mar. 2013.

[214] U.S. Congress. *Truth in Caller ID Act of 2009*. Public Law 111-331. [Signed December 22, 2010, prohibits transmitting misleading caller ID information]. 2010.

[215] Jon Peterson et al. *Authenticated Identity Management in the Session Initiation Protocol (SIP)*. RFC 8224. [STIR standard for cryptographic caller identity verification]. NeuStar, Cisco, RTFM Inc., Comcast, Feb. 2018.

[216] Federal Communications Commission. *STIR/SHAKEN Caller ID Authentication*. FCC. [STIR/SHAKEN mandate effective June 30, 2021]. June 2021.

[217] Tim Berners-Lee. *Information Management: A Proposal*. CERN Internal Document. Mar. 1989.

[218] Vannevar Bush. As We May Think. *The Atlantic Monthly* **176**. (July 1945), 101–108.

[219] Theodor H. Nelson. Complex Information Processing: A File Structure for the Complex, The Changing and the Indeterminate. *Proceedings of the 20th ACM National Conference*. [Paper in which Nelson coined the term "hypertext"]. ACM, 1965, pp. 84–100.

[220] Tim Berners-Lee and Mark Fischetti. *Weaving the Web: The Original Design and Ultimate Destiny of the World Wide Web*. HarperCollins, 1999.

[221] CERN. *Web History*. CERN. [CERN history of the first browser/editor, server, and website, which were running by Christmas 1990]. 2019.

[222] Tim Berners-Lee. *WorldWideWeb: Summary*. Usenet: alt.hypertext. [First public announcement of the World Wide Web, August 6, 1991]. Aug. 1991.

[223] National Center for Supercomputing Applications. *NCSA Mosaic*. NCSA, University of Illinois. [First graphical web browser released February 1993 by Marc Andreessen and Eric Bina]. Feb. 1993.

[224] Matthew Gray. *Measuring the Growth of the Web*. MIT. [Wanderer results: 623 web sites in December 1993, 2,738 in June 1994, and 10,022 in December 1994]. 1994.

[225] Mosaic Communications Corporation. *Mosaic Communications Corporation Founded*. Mountain View, California. [Founded April 4, 1994; renamed Netscape Communications November 1994]. Apr. 1994.

[226] Lou Montulli. *The Reasoning Behind Web Cookies*. Personal Blog. [First-person account of designing web cookies at Netscape in 1994]. May 2013.

[227] Tim Berners-Lee, Roy T. Fielding, and Henrik Frystyk Nielsen. *Hypertext Transfer Protocol – HTTP/1.0*. RFC 1945. MIT/LCS, UC Irvine, W3C, May 1996.

[228] Roy T. Fielding et al. *Hypertext Transfer Protocol – HTTP/1.1*. RFC 2616. IETF, June 1999.

[229] Mike Belshe, Roberto Peon, and Martin Thomson. *Hypertext Transfer Protocol Version 2 (HTTP/2)*. RFC 7540. IETF, May 2015.

[230] Mike Bishop. *HTTP/3*. RFC 9114. IETF, June 2022.

[231] Eric Butler. *Firesheep*. ToorCon San Diego. [Firefox extension demonstrating HTTP session hijacking]. 2010.

[232] Twitter. *HTTPS now in beta*. Twitter Blog. [Twitter made HTTPS available January 2011 in response to Firesheep]. Jan. 2011.

[233] Facebook. *A Continued Commitment to Security*. Facebook Blog. [Facebook added always-on HTTPS option January 2011 in response to Firesheep]. Jan. 2011.

[234] Josh Aas. *Entering Public Beta*. Let's Encrypt Blog. [Announcement that Let's Encrypt's free certificate service was open to the public]. Dec. 2015.

[235] Google. *HTTPS encryption on the web*. Google Transparency Report. [Over 95% of Chrome traffic uses HTTPS as of 2023]. 2023.

[236] Apache Software Foundation. *CVE-2021-41773: Path Traversal and Remote Code Execution in Apache HTTP Server 2.4.49*. Apache Security Advisory. [Path traversal vulnerability allowing attackers to read files outside the document root; actively exploited in the wild]. Oct. 2021.

[237] Apache Software Foundation. *CVE-2021-42013: Path Traversal and Remote Code Execution in Apache HTTP Server 2.4.49 and 2.4.50*. Apache Security Advisory. [Incomplete fix for CVE-2021-41773; both vulnerabilities exploited by ransomware operators within days of disclosure]. Oct. 2021.

[238] Taher Elgamal. *Oral History of Taher Elgamal*. Computer History Museum. [Elgamal developed SSL at Netscape in 1994-1995]. 2015.

[239] Taher Elgamal. A Public Key Cryptosystem and a Signature Scheme Based on Discrete Logarithms. *Advances in Cryptology - CRYPTO '84*. [Original ElGamal signature scheme paper; basis for DSA]. Springer, 1985, pp. 10–18.

[240] Paul C. Kocher, Alan O. Freier, and Philip Karlton. *The SSL Protocol Version 3.0*. Netscape Communications Corporation. [SSL 3.0 specification authored by Kocher (independent consultant)

and Netscape engineers]. Nov. 1996.

[241] The Marconi Society. *Paul Kocher and Taher Elgamal: 2019 Marconi Prize Recipients*. Marconi Society. [Kocher and Elgamal jointly awarded for "development of SSL/TLS and other contributions to the security of communications"]. 2019.

[242] Tim Dierks and Christopher Allen. *The TLS Protocol Version 1.0*. RFC 2246. Certicom, Jan. 1999.

[243] Electronic Frontier Foundation. *The Clipper Chip*. EFF Archive. [EFF documentation of the Clipper Chip controversy]. 1993.

[244] Phil Zimmermann. *Why I Wrote PGP*. PGP User's Guide. [Zimmermann's original essay on creating Pretty Good Privacy]. 1991.

[245] Matt Blaze. Protocol Failure in the Escrowed Encryption Standard. *Proceedings of the 2nd ACM Conference on Computer and Communications Security*. [Blaze's paper demonstrating critical flaws in the Clipper Chip]. 1994, pp. 59–67.

[246] Electronic Frontier Foundation. *Bernstein v. United States Department of Justice*. EFF Case Archive. [Ninth Circuit ruling that source code is protected speech]. 1999.

[247] National Institute of Standards and Technology. *Recommendation for Random Number Generation Using Deterministic Random Bit Generators*. Special Publication 800-90A. [Original standard including Dual_EC_DRBG]. NIST, 2006.

[248] Dan Shumow and Niels Ferguson. On the Possibility of a Back Door in the NIST SP800-90 Dual Ec Prng. *Crypto 2007 Rump Session*. [First public presentation of potential Dual_EC_DRBG backdoor]. Aug. 2007.

[249] Joseph Menn. Exclusive: Secret contract tied NSA and security industry pioneer. *Reuters* (Dec. 2013). [Report on NSA's $10M payment to RSA Security to use Dual_EC_DRBG].

[250] Whitfield Diffie and Martin E. Hellman. New Directions in Cryptography. *IEEE Transactions on Information Theory* **22**. (Nov. 1976), 644–654.

[251] Eric Rescorla. *The Transport Layer Security (TLS) Protocol Version 1.3*. RFC 8446. Mozilla, Aug. 2018.

[252] Eric Rescorla. *TLS 1.3 Published: in Firefox Today*. Mozilla Security Blog. [Announcement of RFC 8446 publication; Rescorla was editor and primary author]. Aug. 2018.

[253] Google Chrome Team. *Chromium Blog: Evolving the Security Indicators in Chrome*. Google Chrome Blog.

[Chrome removed HTTPS lock icon in September 2023]. 2023.

[254] Google Chrome Team. *An update on attempted man-in-the-middle attacks*. Google Security Blog. [Chrome's certificate pinning detected fraudulent Google certificate; revoked DigiNotar trust]. Aug. 2011.

[255] Fox-IT. *Black Tulip: Report of the investigation into the DigiNotar Certificate Authority breach*. Tech. rep. [Official investigation report; identified 298,140 unique IP addresses contacting Google services during use of the fraudulent certificate, more than 99 percent from Iran]. Fox-IT, Aug. 2012.

[256] RTL Nieuws. *Onderzoeker DigiNotar: 'Er zijn mensen gedood om een andere mening'*. RTL News. [Dutch prosecutor Hans Hoogstraaten's statement on DigiNotar investigation]. Sept. 2011.

[257] VASCO Data Security International. *VASCO Announces Bankruptcy Filing by DigiNotar B.V.* PR Newswire. [VASCO's contemporaneous announcement that DigiNotar was declared bankrupt on September 20, 2011]. Sept. 2011.

[258] Codenomicon and Google Security. *The Heartbleed Bug*. [CVE-2014-0160: OpenSSL TLS heartbeat extension vulnerability]. 2014.

[259] MITRE Corporation. *CVE-2014-0160: OpenSSL Heartbleed Vulnerability*. CVE. [Buffer over-read vulnerability in OpenSSL's heartbeat extension]. 2014.

[260] Bruce Schneier. *Heartbleed*. Schneier on Security blog. Apr. 2014.

[261] Google. *HTTPS encryption on the web*. Google Transparency Report. [Percentage of web traffic using HTTPS; over 95% of Chrome traffic uses HTTPS as of 2024]. 2024.

[262] Let's Encrypt. *Let's Encrypt Statistics*. Let's Encrypt. [Let's Encrypt serves over 400 million active certificates as of 2024]. 2024.

[263] Ben Laurie, Eran Messeri, and Rob Stradling. *Certificate Transparency Version 2.0*. RFC 9162. [Obsoletes RFC 6962]. IETF, Dec. 2021.

[264] Google Chrome. *Chrome Certificate Transparency Policy*. Google. 2026.

[265] Phillip Hallam-Baker, Rob Stradling, and Jacob Hoffman-Andrews. *DNS Certification Authority Authorization (CAA) Resource Record*. RFC 8659. [CAA records allow domain owners to specify which CAs may

issue certificates]. IETF, Nov. 2019.

[266] Engineering and Technology History Wiki. *Vic Hayes*. ETHW. [Hayes joined NCR in 1974, approached IEEE in 1988, led 802.11 working group from 1990-2000]. 2023.

[267] IEEE. *IEEE Leadership Award: Victor Hayes*. IEEE 802. [For 10 years of leadership as chairman of IEEE 802.11 Wireless LAN Working Group]. 2000.

[268] IEEE. *IEEE Standard 802.11-1997: Wireless LAN Medium Access Control (MAC) and Physical Layer (PHY) Specifications*. IEEE Standards Association. [Original 802.11 standard with WEP, 40-bit encryption due to U.S. export restrictions]. 1997.

[269] National Research Council. *Cryptography's Role in Securing the Information Society*. [Study of U.S. encryption export policy and 40-bit key limitations]. National Academy Press, 1996.

[270] Charlie Kaufman et al. *Network Security: Private Communication in a Public World*. 3rd ed. [Section 3.8 identifies Ron Rivest as RC4's designer and describes its anonymous 1994 disclosure]. Hoboken, NJ: Pearson Education, 2022.

[271] Scott Fluhrer, Itsik Mantin, and Adi Shamir. Weaknesses in the Key Scheduling Algorithm of RC4. *Selected Areas in Cryptography: 8th Annual International Workshop, SAC 2001*. Vol. 2259. Lecture Notes in Computer Science. Toronto, Ontario, Canada: Springer, Aug. 2001, pp. 1–24.

[272] Erik Tews, Ralf-Philipp Weinmann, and Andrei Pyshkin. Breaking 104 Bit WEP in Less Than 60 Seconds. *Information Security Applications: 8th International Workshop, WISA 2007*. Vol. 4867. Lecture Notes in Computer Science. [PTW attack: 40,000 frames for 50% success, 85,000 for 95%]. Jeju Island, Korea: Springer, Aug. 2007, pp. 188–202.

[273] Wi-Fi Alliance. *Wi-Fi Protected Access*. Wi-Fi Alliance. [WPA with TKIP released in 2003 as interim security measure before 802.11i]. 2003.

[274] IEEE. *IEEE 802.11i-2004: Amendment 6: Medium Access Control (MAC) Security Enhancements*. IEEE Standards Association. [Ratified June 24, 2004; marketed as WPA2; introduced AES/CCMP]. June 2004.

[275] Joseph Pereira. How Credit-Card Data Went Out Wireless Door. *The Wall Street Journal* (May 2007). [Detailed account of TJX breach

via WEP vulnerability at Marshalls stores].

[276] U.S. Department of Justice. *International Hacker Pleads Guilty for Massive Hacks of U.S. Retail Networks*. DOJ Press Release 09-948. Sept. 2009.

[277] TJX Companies Inc. *Form 10-K: Annual Report*. U.S. Securities and Exchange Commission. [Annual report disclosing that at least 45.6 million credit and debit card numbers were affected by the intrusion]. Mar. 2007.

[278] U.S. Department of Justice. *Leader of Hacking Ring Sentenced for Massive Identity Thefts from Payment Processor and U.S. Retail Networks*. DOJ Press Release 10-282. [Albert Gonzalez sentenced to 20 years in prison by Judge Patti B. Saris on March 25, 2010]. Mar. 2010.

[279] TJX Companies, Inc. *2009 Annual Report*. Annual report. [Reports $171.5 million in cumulative pre-tax intrusion-related expense through January 30, 2010]. 2009.

[280] Mathy Vanhoef and Frank Piessens. Key Reinstallation Attacks: Forcing Nonce Reuse in WPA2. *Proceedings of the 24th ACM Conference on Computer and Communications Security (CCS)*. [Discovered by Mathy Vanhoef at KU Leuven, Belgium]. Dallas, TX, USA: ACM, 2017, pp. 1313–1328.

[281] CERT/CC. *VU#228519: Wi-Fi Protected Access II (WPA2) handshake traffic can be manipulated to induce nonce and session key reuse*. CERT Vulnerability Note. [Multiple CVEs: CVE-2017-13077 through CVE-2017-13088]. Oct. 2017.

[282] Wi-Fi Alliance. *Wi-Fi Alliance® introduces Wi-Fi CERTIFIED WPA3™ security*. Wi-Fi Alliance Press Release. [Official launch of WPA3 certification program on June 25, 2018]. Austin, TX, June 2018.

[283] Dan Harkins. *Dragonfly Key Exchange*. RFC 7664. [Defines password-authenticated key exchange used in WPA3-SAE]. IETF, Nov. 2015.

[284] Mathy Vanhoef and Eyal Ronen. Dragonblood: Analyzing the Dragonfly Handshake of WPA3 and EAP-pwd. *Proceedings of the 2019 IEEE Symposium on Security and Privacy (SP)*. [Discovered side-channel and downgrade attacks against WPA3-SAE within months of release]. San Francisco, CA: IEEE, 2019, pp. 517–533.

[285] Mathy Vanhoef. Fragment and Forge: Breaking Wi-Fi Through Frame Aggregation and Fragmentation. *Proceedings of the 30th USENIX Security Symposium*. [Design flaws in 802.11 frame aggregation and fragmentation dating to the original 1997 standard; CVE-2020-24586

through CVE-2020-26145]. USENIX Association, 2021, pp. 161–178.

[286] The Radicati Group. *Email Statistics Report, 2024-2028*. Radicati Group Market Research. [Table 1 estimates 361.6 billion worldwide emails sent or received per day in 2024, equivalent to about 4.2 million per second]. 2024.

[287] Cloudflare. *How Cloudflare analyzes 1M DNS queries per second*. Cloudflare Blog. [Cloudflare's 1.1.1.1 resolver processes approximately 1 million DNS queries per second]. May 2017.

[288] NS1. *Analysis of 7.5 Trillion DNS Queries*. CircleID. [Analysis revealing approximately 1 million DNS queries per second globally; public resolvers handle 60% of recursive DNS]. 2023.

[289] Geoff Huston. BGP in 2024. *APNIC Blog* (Jan. 2025). [Annual analysis of BGP routing table growth; IPv4 table grew by 6% (53,000 entries) in 2024].

[290] International Telecommunication Union. *ITU Facts and Figures 2024*. ITU Statistics. [Global internet usage statistics; 5.5 billion internet users (68% of world population) as of 2024]. 2024.

[291] NIST. *National Vulnerability Database Dashboard*. [Live counts distinguish CVE records awaiting or undergoing NVD enrichment from records not scheduled for enrichment]. 2026.

[292] Sam Sabin. *Exclusive: One-third of top U.S. cyber force has left since Trump took office*. Axios. [Reports roughly 1,000 departures and a workforce reduction of nearly one-third]. June 2025.

[293] MITRE Corporation. *CVE Program Contract Extension*. [11-month extension executed April 16, 2025; expires March 16, 2026]. 2025.

[294] FIRST. *FIRST Member Teams Directory*. [808 member teams in 110+ countries; 143 national CERTs globally]. 2025.

[295] Engineering and Technology History Wiki. *Stephen Deering*. ETHW. [Biography of IPv6 and IP Multicast inventor]. 2024.

[296] Frank Solensky. *Continued Internet Growth*. IETF 18 Proceedings. [First serious study predicting IPv4 address exhaustion, p. 53]. Aug. 1990.

[297] Robert Hinden. *Simple Internet Protocol Plus White Paper*. RFC 1710. [SIPP at this stage used 64-bit addresses, "well matched to the new generation of 64-bit processors"]. Sun Microsystems, Oct. 1994.

[298] Scott Bradner and Allison Mankin. *The Recommendation for the IP Next Generation Protocol*. RFC 1752. IETF, Jan. 1995.

[299] Stephen Deering and Robert Hinden. *Internet Protocol, Version 6 (IPv6) Specification*. RFC 1883. IETF, Dec. 1995.

[300] Steve Deering. *Watching the Waist of the Protocol Hourglass*. Keynote, IEEE ICNP '98, Austin, TX. [Deering's "hourglass" talk; the "Mid-Life Crisis" slide diagnoses the dual-stack IPv4/IPv6 problem]. Oct. 1998.

[301] Jim Roskind. *QUIC: Design Document and Specification Rationale*. Google, design document (rev. June 2013). [Roskind's rationale for building on UDP and encrypting the control structure to survive middleboxes]. 2012.

[302] The Chromium Projects. *Experimenting with QUIC*. Chromium Blog. June 2013.

[303] Adam Langley, Alistair Riddoch, Alyssa Wilk, et al. The QUIC Transport Protocol: Design and Internet-Scale Deployment. *Proceedings of the ACM SIGCOMM 2017 Conference*. [Reports QUIC reduced Google Search latency 8.0% (desktop) / 3.6% (mobile) and cut YouTube rebuffering 18% / 15.3%]. Aug. 2017, pp. 183–196.

[304] John Loughney. *IPv6 Node Requirements*. RFC 4294. [Made IPsec (RFC 4301) a MUST for all IPv6 nodes; later downgraded to SHOULD by RFC 6434]. Nokia, Apr. 2006.

[305] Ed Jankiewicz, John Loughney, and Thomas Narten. *IPv6 Node Requirements*. RFC 6434. IETF, Dec. 2011.

[306] Martin Thomson. *Version-Independent Properties of QUIC*. RFC 8999. [Defines the small set of QUIC invariants visible on the wire; everything else is encrypted to resist ossification]. Mozilla, May 2021.

[307] Dirk-jan Mollema. *mitm6 – Compromising IPv4 Networks via IPv6*. Fox-IT International Blog. [Rogue DHCPv6 DNS takeover chained to NTLM relay against Active Directory; notes all Windows since Vista prefer IPv6 by default]. Jan. 2018.

[308] Marc Heuse. *THC-IPv6: A Complete Toolset to Attack the Inherent Protocol Weaknesses of IPv6*. The Hacker's Choice, GitHub. [Includes flood_router26, which floods spoofed Router Advertisements against hosts that trust unauthenticated RA packets].

[309] Jim Hoagland. *The Teredo Protocol: Tunneling Past Network Security*. Black Hat USA 2007. [Security analysis of Teredo tunneling vulnerabilities]. 2007.

[310] Antonios Atlasis. *Security Impacts of Abusing IPv6 Extension Headers*.

Black Hat Abu Dhabi 2012. [Catalog of IPv6 extension header attacks affecting firewalls and IDS]. 2012.

[311] Netskope. *A QUIC Primer: How Netskope Handles the Quick UDP Internet Connections Protocol.* Netskope Community. [Security-gateway guidance to block UDP/443 so browsers fall back to inspectable TLS-over-TCP].

[312] Martin Thomson and Sean Turner. *Using TLS to Secure QUIC.* RFC 9001. [Section 9.2 warns that 0-RTT application data can be replayed by an attacker]. Mozilla, sn3rd, May 2021.

[313] Geoff Huston. *Google Hits 50% IPv6.* APNIC Blog. [Google's measured IPv6 client fraction crossed 50 percent globally in April 2026]. Apr. 2026.

[314] Kevin Mandia. *Interview on CBS Face the Nation.* CBS News. ["This was not a drive-by shooting on the information highway. This was a sniper round from somebody a mile away from your house."]. Dec. 2020.

[315] David E. Sanger. Obama Order Sped Up Wave of Cyberattacks Against Iran. *The New York Times* (June 2012). [First detailed public account of Operation Olympic Games].

[316] NOS Nieuws. 'Nederlander saboteerde atoomcomplex in Iran, Den Haag wist niets'. *NOS* (Jan. 2024). [Report on de Volkskrant's identification of Erik van Sabben].

[317] Eduard Kovacs. Dutch Engineer Used Water Pump to Get Billion-Dollar Stuxnet Malware Into Iranian Nuclear Facility: Report. *SecurityWeek* (Jan. 2024). [Updated January 16, 2024; discusses competing accounts of the delivery mechanism].

[318] SolarWinds Corporation. *An Investigative Update of the Cyberattack.* SolarWinds Blog. [SolarWinds investigative update: initial access September 4, 2019; fewer than 100 customers actively exploited]. May 2021.

[319] CrowdStrike. *SUNSPOT: An Implant in the Build Process.* CrowdStrike Blog. Jan. 2021.

[320] Mandiant. *SUNBURST Additional Technical Details.* Mandiant Threat Intelligence. Dec. 2020.

[321] SolarWinds Corporation. *Form 8-K: Report of Unscheduled Material Events.* Securities and Exchange Commission. Dec. 2020.

[322] The White House. *Fact Sheet: Imposing Costs for Harmful Foreign Activities by the Russian Government.* White House Statements and Releases. [Official US attribution of SolarWinds to SVR]. Apr. 2021.

[323] Microsoft Threat Intelligence Center. *Deep dive into the Solorigate second-stage activation: From SUNBURST to TEARDROP and Raindrop*. Microsoft Security Blog. [Technical details on SUNBURST dormancy period (12-14 days) and second-stage malware]. Jan. 2021.

[324] Kevin Mandia. *Testimony, "Weathering the Storm: The Role of Private Tech in the SolarWinds Breach and Ongoing Campaign"*. U.S. House Committee on Homeland Security / Oversight, 117th Cong. ["So this was the varsity team on offense"; "the special ops robbing the house, not some average criminal"]. Feb. 2021.

[325] Brad Smith. *Interview on CBS 60 Minutes: the SolarWinds Attack*. CBS News. [Microsoft president: "the largest and most sophisticated attack the world has ever seen"; estimated more than 1,000 engineers]. Feb. 2021.

[326] Brian Fung. *The SolarWinds Hackers Weren't Necessarily After Your Data. They Wanted Something Bigger*. CNN. [Rep. Katie Porter on the "solarwinds123" password; the company blamed an intern]. Feb. 2021.

[327] Executive Office of the President. *Executive Order 14028: Improving the Nation's Cybersecurity*. Federal Register. May 2021.

[328] MITRE Corporation. *CVE Program Funding Status*. [CISA contract expires March 16, 2026. Near-shutdown April 2025 averted with 17 hours notice]. 2025.

[329] Jen Easterly. *Statement on the Near-Lapse of MITRE's CVE Program*. LinkedIn; reported by ClearanceJobs. ["like tearing out the card catalog from every library at once"]. Apr. 2025.

[330] National Institute of Standards and Technology. *NIST Updates NVD Operations to Address Record CVE Growth*. NIST. [Backlog exceeded 27,000 unenriched records; full analysis restricted to KEV, federal, and EO 14028 critical software]. Apr. 2026.

[331] CISA. *Known Exploited Vulnerabilities Catalog Statistics 2025*. [Catalog grew 20% in 2025 while CISA workforce shrank 74%]. 2025.

[332] Matthew Gray. *Background for Matthew Gray*. MIT. [Author biography identifying the World Wide Web Wanderer as the first autonomous agent on the web and its use to track web growth since 1993]. 1993.

[333] Martijn Koster. *ALIWEB - Archie-Like Indexing for the WEB*. Nexor Ltd. [Announced November 30, 1993]. Nov. 1993.

[334] Martijn Koster. *A Standard for Robot Exclusion*. Web Robots Pages. [Original robots.txt proposal]. 1994.

[335] Digital Equipment Corporation. *AltaVista Search Engine*. DEC. Dec. 1995.

[336] Martijn Koster et al. *Robots Exclusion Protocol*. RFC 9309. IETF, Sept. 2022.

[337] Common Crawl Foundation. *Common Crawl: Open Repository of Web Crawl Data*. Common Crawl. [Nonprofit 501(c)(3) archiving the web since 2008]. 2008.

[338] OpenAI. *ChatGPT: Optimizing Language Models for Dialogue*. OpenAI Blog. [Launched November 30, 2022]. Nov. 2022.

[339] UBS. *ChatGPT May Be the Fastest Growing App in History*. UBS Research. Feb. 2023.

[340] OpenAI. *Overview of OpenAI Crawlers*. OpenAI Documentation. [Documentation for OpenAI's web crawler, announced August 7, 2023]. 2023.

[341] Google. *Google's Common Crawlers: Google-Extended*. Google Search Central. [Introduced September 28, 2023; documentation states that Google-Extended is a robots.txt product token without a separate HTTP user-agent string]. Sept. 2023.

[342] The New York Times. *The Times Sues OpenAI and Microsoft Over A.I. Use of Copyrighted Work*. The New York Times. Dec. 2023.

[343] Dhruv Mehrotra and Tim Marchman. *Perplexity Is a Bullshit Machine*. WIRED. June 2024.

[344] Robb Knight. *Perplexity AI, Robots.txt, and Other Questions*. rknight.me. June 2024.

[345] Cloudflare. *Perplexity is using stealth, undeclared crawlers*. Cloudflare Blog. Aug. 2025.

[346] Aravind Srinivas. *Perplexity CEO Interview*. Fast Company. June 2024.

[347] W3C TDMRep Community Group. *TDM Reservation Protocol (TDMRep)*. W3C Community Group Report. Feb. 2024.

[348] European Parliament and Council of the European Union. *Regulation (EU) 2024/1689 Laying Down Harmonised Rules on Artificial Intelligence*. Official Journal of the European Union. [Article 53(1)(c) requires general-purpose AI model providers to maintain a policy for compliance with Union copyright law, including rights reservations under Directive (EU) 2019/790 Article 4(3)]. June 2024.

[349] Internet Hall of Fame. *Steve Crocker*. Internet Hall of Fame inductee biography. [Biography covering Crocker's UCLA work, the Network Working Group, and the start of the RFC series]. 2012.

[350] Leonard Kleinrock. *The Day the Infant Internet Uttered its First Words*. UCLA Computer Science Department. [Kleinrock's account of October 29, 1969, 10:30pm: "lo" message sent by Charley Kline]. 2009.

[351] Fox-IT. *DigiNotar Certificate Authority Breach: Operation Black Tulip*. Interim Report. [Forensic analysis of the DigiNotar CA compromise]. 2012.

[352] Federal Bureau of Investigation. *Business Email Compromise: The $55 Billion Scam*. Internet Crime Complaint Center PSA. [BEC cost US and global organizations $55.5 billion between October 2013 and December 2023]. Sept. 2024.

[353] Linus Torvalds. *What would you like to see most in minix?* Usenet: comp.os.minix. [August 25, 1991: "I'm doing a (free) operating system (just a hobby, won't be big and professional like gnu)"]. Aug. 1991.

[354] Vint Cerf. *I Remember IANA*. RFC 2468. [Memorial RFC for Jon Postel]. MCI, Oct. 1998.

[355] Richard Pearson. Jon Postel, Pioneer of Internet Technology, Dies at 55. *The Washington Post* (Oct. 1998).

[356] Cybersecurity and Infrastructure Security Agency. *PRC State-Sponsored Actors Compromise and Maintain Persistent Access to U.S. Critical Infrastructure*. CISA Joint Cybersecurity Advisory. [Advisory on Volt Typhoon's pre-positioning in critical infrastructure]. Feb. 2024.

[357] Eric Tucker. A 9th Telecoms Firm Has Been Hit by a Massive Chinese Espionage Campaign, the White House Says. *Associated Press* (Dec. 2024). [Reports Deputy National Security Adviser Anne Neuberger's confirmation of a ninth compromised U.S. telecommunications company].

[358] Dustin Volz et al. China's 'Salt Typhoon' Hack Shows Critical U.S. Telecom Vulnerabilities. *The Wall Street Journal* (Oct. 2024). [Early investigation of Salt Typhoon's compromise of U.S. telecommunications networks and access to lawful-intercept systems].

[359] Jon Postel. *File Transfer Protocol Specification*. RFC 765. USC/Information Sciences Institute, June 1980.

[360] M. Horowitz and S. Lunt. *FTP Security Extensions*. RFC 2228. Cygnus Solutions, Bellcore, Oct. 1997.

[361] Cybersecurity and Infrastructure Security Agency. *Heightened DDoS Threat Posed by Mirai and Other Botnets*. CISA Alert TA16-288A. Oct. 2016.

[362] Eli Rosenberg and Herman Wong. *A Police Officer Fatally Shot a Man While Responding to an Emergency Call Now Called a 'Swatting' Prank*. The Washington Post. [Contemporaneous report on the December 28 killing of Andrew Finch following a hoax emergency call]. Dec. 2017.

[363] Kim Zetter. *Countdown to Zero Day: Stuxnet and the Launch of the World's First Digital Weapon*. Crown, 2014.

[364] Andy Greenberg. The Untold Story of NotPetya, the Most Devastating Cyberattack in History. *Wired* (Aug. 2018).

[365] Codecov. *Bash Uploader Security Update*. Codecov Blog. [Disclosure of CI/CD supply chain compromise]. Apr. 2021.

[366] Cybersecurity and Infrastructure Security Agency. *Kaseya VSA Supply-Chain Ransomware Attack*. CISA Alert. July 2021.

COLOPHON

This book was typeset by the author with LuaLaTeX. The text is set in IBM Plex Serif; chapter titles, labels, terminal transcripts, and every RFC and protocol name are set in IBM Plex Mono—a nod to the fixed-width terminals on which this story was first written. IBM Plex was commissioned by IBM from the type foundry Bold Monday and released as an open-source family in 2017: a fitting typeface for a book about standards built in the open.

The diagrams were drawn in Ti*k*Z. The terminal sessions, RFC excerpts, and breach boxes are custom LaTeX environments. Citations are managed with biblatex and biber. The cover art is an algorithmic network mesh rendered in Python—drawn by a program, not generated by an AI image model.

The text is set 11 point on a 6 by 9 inch trim. Its primary sources are the Requests for Comments themselves, archived at `rfc-editor.org`, read alongside the public vulnerability record—the CVE list, CISA's advisories, and the incident reports named throughout.

builttheinternet.com · 2026

www.ingramcontent.com/pod-product-compliance
Lightning Source LLC
LaVergne TN
LVHW052025200926
848481LV00005B/1588